OVER THE
BOARDS

The Ron Ellis Story

RON ELLIS
with KEVIN SHEA

foreword by Paul Henderson

Fenn Publishing Company Ltd.
Bolton, Canada

OVER THE BOARDS
A Fenn Publishing Book / October 2002

Copyright 2002 © Ron Ellis and Kevin Shea

Fenn Publishing Company Ltd.
Bolton, Ontario, Canada

Distributed in Canada by H. B. Fenn and Company Ltd.
Bolton, Ontario, Canada, L7E 1W2
Printed in Canada

National Library of Canada Cataloguing in Publication Data

Ellis, Ron 1945 –
  Over the boards: the Ron Ellis story / Ron Ellis; with Kevin Shea; foreword by
Paul Henderson.

ISBN 1-55168-231-1

1. Ellis, Ron 1945 – 2. Hockey players—Canada—Biography. Toronto Maple
  Leafs (Hockey team)—Biography.
I. Shea, Kevin, 1956 – II. Title.

GV848.5E44A3 2002   796.962'092   C2002-904157

DEDICATION

After my mother and father, who gave me life and brought me up to the best of their ability, there are three very special people who deserve this dedication and much more.

Thank you to Jan, my childhood sweetheart, for teaching me the true meaning of love and commitment and for bringing out the best in a shy, introverted guy she stills calls "Ronnie" after thirty-six years of marriage.

Thank you to Kitty (Kathleen), my daughter, our heavenly gift, who has been Daddy's special little girl and who, while growing into a wonderful young woman, helped me become the father she needed.

Thank you to R.J. (Ron Jr.), our miracle child, who has been the son that every father prays for. I continue to burst my buttons with pride because of the manner in which he lives and conducts his life.

I have been truly blessed by a loving heavenly Father.

Ron Ellis

CONTENTS

When I got the news about the big trade that would send me from Detroit to Toronto in 1968, I was not happy. In fact, I was really upset. I knew trades were part of the game, but that didn't mean I had to like them. I had come up through the Detroit Red Wings system, made my NHL debut as a Red Wing, and had some very good years in Detroit. I'm sure Ronnie couldn't have been too happy from the other side, either. He would have been a good friend of Frank Mahovlich and Pete Stemkowski. I mean, Ronnie and Stemkowski won a Memorial Cup together as linemates with the Marlboros.

But in retrospect, the trade that brought me to Toronto was the greatest thing that could have happened to me. You don't know it at the time, but things really do happen for a reason. In Toronto, my wife Eleanor and I found a city that we love and still live in today. I discovered that Toronto could be a terrific city in which to bring up my three girls. As a Maple Leaf, I got the chance to experience the single greatest moment in my professional career — with Team Canada '72 in the Summit Series against the Russians. And I discovered a Christian lifestyle that has added an element of peace to my life that I never imagined could exist.

When I arrived in Toronto, I also started a friendship that continues to this day.

The odd thing is, Ronnie and I couldn't be any more different as far as our personalities go. I've always been the optimistic guy, the confident guy. On the other hand, Ronnie worries way too much about everything. I'm the rah-rah guy in the dressing room. Ronnie sits quietly, doesn't say two words, but leads by example. I was always able to get over things in a hurry. If we had a bad game, I'd say, "Okay, we're gonna be a lot better next time." But it would weigh on Ronnie so heavily. He'd replay the game over and over in his head. We are just totally different personalities. Maybe that's what holds our friendship together so strongly. We add balance to each other. Ron backs me off a bit if I get cocky, and I pick him up a bit when he gets down on himself. We've been great for each other over the years.

Ron and I have been through so much together. We played together on the same line with the Leafs for five or six years. Together, we put up with the manipulative ownership of Harold Ballard. Eleanor and I have enjoyed some fantastic vacations with Ronnie and his wife, Jan. I'm so proud to say that Ron and I went to war for our country with Team Canada in 1972. We not only played on the same line, but on the twenty-fifth anniversary of the tournament, Team Canada was selected the Team of the Century.

After I was introduced to a new life as a Christian, I shared my new-found peace and contentment with Ron and Jan, and through our friend Mel Stevens, they too gave their lives to Jesus. I helped Ronnie through some very dark times. When he was off work, battling depression, I called Ron every day to make sure he knew I was there for him. I know that I would run through a wall for Ron Ellis, and I can tell you without hesitation that he would do the same for me.

You're lucky if you find more than two or three great friends in your life. Ron and I have one of those great friendships. Ronnie and I will remain friends until the day we die.

Ron Ellis is one of the finest individuals you'll ever meet in your life.

Paul Henderson
August 2002

INTRODUCTION

"Why don't you write a book?"

It's a question fans and friends have asked many times over the years. Well, for one thing, the timing never seemed right. And I would also wonder, "Why would people want to read a book about Ron Ellis?"

Now that I have had my fifty-seventh birthday and have become a grandfather, I realize that my career as a professional athlete, with its highs and lows, as well as my personal challenges, might make a worthwhile book — especially if it encourages and inspires others.

Looking at my hockey life in chronological order would be attractive to the hockey enthusiast and diehard Toronto Maple Leafs fan. The highlights of my career, which include a Memorial Cup championship, a Stanley Cup win, and the chance to play for Team Canada '72 and '77; and the lowlights, including slumps, injuries and early retirement, would provide interesting reading. What I am doing today and how I am doing today might also be attractive to the reader.

This being true, I also believe that my life and career could have a positive impact on many segments of the population. The hockey life is like no other career in the working world. But it does present all the normal problems and challenges that the average person has to try to overcome. Hockey players are real people with real problems. I should know, as I have had more than my share. I have overcome a physical handicap, a speech impediment, an occasionally difficult father-son relationship, business failure, severe depression and the sandwich years my wife Jan and I are presently experiencing with the loss of parents and the adjustment to becoming first-time grandparents. The sports fan often feels the professional athlete is immune to these real-life problems.

My hope is that people who have gone through — or are presently experiencing — similar problems will be encouraged to know that someone they have watched for years has worked through them and come out on the other side a stronger person. I also believe that a book on my life and career would be educational for the young minor hockey player, and his or her parents, by providing a more balanced view of what is involved in the hockey life. Yes, a professional athletic career is glamorous — there is notoriety and financial opportunity — but there are also the possible pitfalls: trips to the minor leagues, injuries, slumps and the intense scrutiny by the media. Hockey careers are also short. Having the opportunity to see both sides of the coin from my perspective may assist a family in deciding whether the sacrifices required to make it are worthwhile.

Timing is everything, and I feel the time might be right for a book by Ron Ellis. In keeping with the celebration of the Toronto Maple Leaf franchise's seventy-fifth anniversary in 2001–02, there are segments in this book that deal with the Leafs' last Stanley Cup championship, the dynasty of the '60s and the difficult years of the '70s. More importantly, there will be some discussion about what it means to be a Canadian. In September 2002, Team Canada '72, the Team of the Century, marked its thirtieth anniversary. All of Canada put life on hold on September 28, 1972, to watch my teammate Paul Henderson score the goal heard around the world. My unique perspective on this historic series might be of interest to Canadians who saw the games. This was Canada's team, and when it was over, we were proud Canadians. Even though the gold medal win at the Olympics in 2002 was spectacular, it did not match the emotional impact held by those games in 1972 — either for players or fans.

In recent years, I have been very open about my faith and about my challenge with clinical depression. Both, unfortunately, often carry a stigma, but although I am shy and private by nature, I felt that by explaining these elements of my life, someone might feel reassured that they are not alone. There are helpful messages concerning my Christianity and my treatments for depression that I am hopeful will inspire and encourage readers of *Over the Boards*.

This project would not have gotten off the ground without a

boost from Kevin Shea, who has become a friend through the writing. His belief in the concept kept me going whenever doubts surfaced.

Nor would these words have reached book form without Jordan Fenn and the fine folks at Fenn Publishing. It was important to me that this be a Canadian project, and I appreciate being part of the H.B. Fenn family.

Now to the title. *Over the Boards* is more than a hockey expression; it's a very real reflection of the feeling I have about the way life parallels sports. You can practise, you can study game plans, you can talk about what you want to accomplish, but nothing happens until you jump "over the boards." Then, it's the real deal. If we're not prepared properly, the results may be disappointing. If we stumble and fall in the process, we have to get up and try again. Whether we're playing professional sports or just living day to day, we must do the very best we can with each opportunity. What matters most in life takes place when we go *Over the Boards*.

Ron Ellis
October 2002

CHAPTER ONE

Over the Boards

The puck squirts loose outside the Detroit Red Wings' blue line. Ron Ellis, the Toronto Maple Leafs' speedy right winger, darts past defenceman Gary Bergman and corrals the stray puck. He cuts over the blue line and winds up, driving a blast from the top of the faceoff circle. Netminder Roger Crozier throws out his right hand to make the save, but the shot catches the net behind him, and the red goal light flashes a split second later. Ron Ellis has scored for the Maple Leafs!

Ron joined the Toronto Maple Leafs for a single game during the 1963–64 season: March 11, 1964, a 1–0 Leafs victory over the Montreal Canadiens. He became a regular the next season, the only rookie that year to crack a star-laden Toronto lineup. In his third full season, 1966–67, Ron Ellis was part of the last Maple Leafs team to win the Stanley Cup. He was a mainstay of the lineup from 1964–65 until the 1974–75 campaign, which yielded the best offensive output of his career: 32 goals and 29 assists for 61 points. He retired for two seasons, returned at the beginning of 1977–78, and played until January 14, 1981, when he retired from hockey for good.

The shy, modest Ellis played all of his 1,034 regular-season games in Toronto blue and white, scoring 332 regular-season goals and assisting on 308 more for a total of 640 points. Ron Ellis is amongst the Maple Leafs' leaders in several categories. His sixteen seasons rank third behind George Armstrong's twenty-one and Tim Horton's twenty. Only four Leafs — Armstrong, Horton, Borje Salming and Dave Keon — played more games for Toronto.

His 332 goals place him third behind Darryl Sittler (389) and Keon (365). Of those goals, 186 were scored before the fans at

Maple Leaf Gardens. He chalked up 6 hat tricks during his career. Ellis's 640 career points are fifth in team history, behind Sittler (916), Keon (858), Salming (768) and Armstrong (713). Ron's career assist total of 308 leaves him eighth on the Leafs all-time, with only Salming, Sittler, Keon, Armstrong, Horton, Ted Kennedy and Bob Pulford collecting more.

You may notice that every last one of the Leafs who has eclipsed Ron Ellis in terms of productivity or longevity is an Honoured Member of the Hockey Hall of Fame. That fact speaks volumes about Ron Ellis as a player. Quiet and often underappreciated (by everyone except his coaches, teammates and opponents), Ron Ellis will always be remembered for his diligence, his commitment and his pursuit of excellence. In his book *Hockey Is a Battle*, Punch Imlach — who was twice Ellis's coach on the Toronto Maple Leafs, wrote, "Ron Ellis never gave me less than a hundred percent of what was in him." That was Ron's way, game in and game out.

And yet there is so much more to Ron Ellis that is important to know. Had he not retired for two seasons at the peak of his career, suffering from the self-doubt that later was diagnosed as severe depression, Ellis's point totals would have been significantly higher. As well, one of Ellis's appointed roles was to play a strong defensive game. To keep opposing left wingers off the scoresheet — something he did so successfully — Ron had to forgo many scoring opportunities of his own. "When we played the Chicago Blackhawks, it was my role to ensure that Bobby Hull didn't score," Ron explains. "I considered those games as lost games as far as my own production went, but I also considered it an honour that the coaches would think enough of my abilities to put me up against the best left wingers in the league."

Ron Ellis was an exceptional hockey player, yet his rise to National Hockey League stardom defied all odds. When he was born with a club foot, doctors were concerned that Ron might never walk properly. After weekly visits to Toronto's Hospital for Sick Children and a nightly regimen of ankle massages, not only did Ellis learn to walk, but his skating became one of his many strong suits. Even during his last two seasons with the Maple Leafs, when he was in his mid-thirties, Ron Ellis was still the fastest player on the team. Others may have been quicker out of the blocks, but no one could outrace him the length of the rink. Self-esteem issues left Ron with a terrible stutter that haunted him for years. Depression, which wasn't diagnosed until after he had joined the business world, clouded Ron's personal and professional life, choking his confidence and forcing him to retire for two seasons at the age of 30 — prime years for an NHL hockey player. When Ron and his lovely wife Jan tried to start a family, they learned they were unable to conceive, a discovery that disappointed the couple greatly. But one adoption and one miracle gave Ron and Jan two beautiful children, Kitty and R.J., both of whom are now married and established in careers of their own.

The transition from hockey to business was a difficult one for Ron, one which saw stops and starts that would make a Punch Imlach practice seem like a Sunday skate at the community arena. His depression grew so severe that on three occasions, Ellis was hospitalized. Strong family support, a knowledgeable medical staff and an understanding employer brought Ron Ellis back to the surface. Now happily settled, Ron Ellis is the Director of Public Affairs and Assistant to the President at the Hockey Hall of Fame.

An athlete's life appears perfect from the outside, but no one knows what goes on behind closed doors. There are no test runs in life, just as there is no turning back once you've jumped "over the boards."

CHAPTER TWO

Lindsay

The town of Lindsay sits on the banks of the Scugog River in the beautiful Kawartha Lakes region of central Ontario. The river, part of the Trent-Severn Waterway, one of the province's major recreational waterways, forms a link between Lake Ontario and the Kawarthas. At the heart of town sit the ruins of an old mill that, at one time, breathed life into the community. William Purdy and his family built the original grist and lumber mills in 1827, and in doing so, formed the nucleus of the burgeoning community. In 1833, a townsite next to the Purdy family's property was surveyed. A member of the survey party died, and he was buried at the site. His surname was Lindsay, and a sign was erected in his honour. Several years later, the sign may have been mistakenly interpreted as the name given to the new townsite.

Lindsay is a historic and beautiful town, which was the birthplace of Joe Primeau, the centre on the Toronto Maple Leafs' legendary Kid Line. It is also the birthplace of Ron Ellis.

Helen and Randy Ellis were married here in 1944, and on January 8, 1945, their first child, Ronald John Edward Ellis, was born. Randy, who was in the Royal Canadian Air Force, recalls the happy day he became a father. "I was stationed in Kingston at that time — I was an instructor. During the last month of Helen's pregnancy, she went back to Lindsay to be with her family. When I got the call and was told I had a son, I was so happy! I took my leave and hurried back to Lindsay right away to see Helen and my new baby boy.

"On the second day at the hospital, the doctor told us that our baby had been born with a club foot. Helen and I were in shock. We were an athletic family and to find out that our baby boy would need treatments was traumatic. His little left ankle turned in quite severely."

A club foot is a birth defect where one of the feet is twisted in such a way that it cannot be returned to what would be considered a normal position. A person with a club foot appears to walk on his or her ankle. Treatment is generally started soon after birth. Surgical treatment can involve the lengthening of the tendon in the heel. Non-surgical methods involve extensive therapy and manipulation of the foot to a normal position. Sometimes, the foot is placed in a cast, or special shoes are prescribed to hold the foot in its proper place.

"The doctor started treatments when Ron was one month old," continues Randy. "He had to go to Sick Kids Hospital in Toronto. The reasoning was that the younger the child is, the softer the bones are, so it was better to start early to work on the foot. The doctor came up with a brace. It secured the left leg to the right and used a metal splint taped to Ron's legs. His mother took him to Sick Kids on the train from Lindsay to Toronto once a week. It was quite a chore. Lindsay is about 130 kilometres from Toronto, so by bus there and back, it's an all-day excursion."

With each trip, the doctor cranked the brace to turn the ankle bone inward ever so slightly more. "It was my job to massage Ron's ankle every day for about half an hour. Each day, I'd add a little more pressure. It hurt him, and for a while, he associated Dad with pain." By the age of six months, Ron had kicked off his splints, and by eleven months, he was walking. To help strengthen his ankle, he was fitted with a special shoe.

In time, Randy came up with a way for young Ron to mix fun with therapy. "Wagons were very popular at the time," he recalls. "To push a wagon, you put one leg in and pump with the other one. I got an idea that I thought would help strengthen Ron's ankle. I put a board in the right side of the wagon so it forced Ron to use his weaker left leg to pump. By forcing him to use that leg, it would strengthen the ankle over a period of time. Ron used to put the dog in it and take him for a ride. He'd get quite upset if the dog jumped out and ran off!" Randy laughs.

"The ankle got turned, but Ron never had full motion in his ankle. He probably didn't regain more than 70 percent of the mobility," Randy observes. "I don't think the teams he played for ever knew. Ron developed his own skating style. He knew he couldn't use the ankle as a crutch. I'm probably the only one who could tell that Ron didn't have complete mobility. If he turned sharply in one direction, even as a pro, he would lose an edge on his left skate and sometimes fall."

The irony, of course, is that one of Ron Ellis's most notable traits was his exceptional skating ability. Press clippings from throughout his career comment on his "lightning speed," and describe him as a "crewcut speedster" and a "rocketing right winger." Even during his final NHL season with the Maple Leafs, at the age of 35, Ellis was the swiftest skater on a young, fast team.

"I did have to compensate for a loss of flexibility in my left ankle," admits Ron. "Remember that skating drill we used to do called 'shoot the duck?' I could only do this drill on my right skate, as my left ankle could not flex far enough forward to allow me to get in the 'down' position. The coaches didn't notice that I performed the drill on one side only."

With time, Ron developed a skating style that gave him good speed moving in a straight forward direction. Driving to the net with power from the right wing did not present a problem. However, there was a definite lack of power going to the net from the left wing. "Over the years of playing pro, I often thought that playing left wing but being a right-hand shot could have been a big advantage for me if my ankle had been more mobile," shrugs Ron.

* * *

On June 27, 2002, the annual Lindsay Hall of Fame Golf Tournament was held at the Wolf Run Golf Club, located southwest of town. Built in 1991 to take full advantage of the natural landscape, the course is extraordinarily beautiful. The tournament is both a fundraiser and a celebration of those men and women being honoured with induction into the Lindsay and District Hall of Fame.

Three generations of Ellises are on hand, much to the delight of those in the crowd. Ron Ellis is here, of course, as are his father Randy and his son, R.J. Rounding out the foursome is Randy's wife, Florence — Ron's stepmother. Randy and Ron Ellis are the only father-and-son combination to have been inducted into the Lindsay Hall of Fame. Ron was selected in 1994, his Dad six years later.

The atmosphere is warm and light-hearted, full of the inside jokes poked amongst friends. The tent buzzes all evening, as everyone catches up on each others' lives. Those in attendance run the gamut from strapping young men in their twenties, like R.J., to athletic seniors like Randy. Another former NHLer is present: Dave Gardner, who played in the 1970s for the Montreal Canadiens, the Cleveland Barons and a handful of teams in between, and who now has a cottage near Lindsay. The group is predominantly male, but there are a number of women in attendance, too; their banter is every bit as jovial and sports-related as the men's.

Randy Ellis is a delightful gentleman who looks much younger than his 79 years. His appearance at the golf tournament has caused quite a stir. He is well known and liked by those in attendance, and it has been a few years since his last appearance. Every few minutes, Randy is stopped by another acquaintance who wants to say hello, share a story or ask after the Ellis family.

Randy was born in Brampton, Ontario, in 1923, but his family moved to Lindsay when he was quite young. "I played hockey in Lindsay as a boy, although one year the arena burned down and was not rebuilt for three years." In 1940, he played for a team in nearby Fenelon Falls that barnstormed the area. "We played good, strong senior teams and industrial teams, with the winning team taking home the gate." Led by the 17-year-old Randy Ellis, the team went undefeated.

During the summer of 1941, he was reading the *Globe and Mail* and noticed that the Toronto Marlboros were holding tryouts. He packed his skates and took the bus to Toronto to try his luck. The odds were stacked against his making the junior club, but Randy managed to impress coach Eddie Powers, who had guided the NHL's Toronto St. Patricks during the 1924–25 and 1925–26 seasons. "But then I got a call from home — my older brother John was very ill and in the hospital." Not knowing what to do, Ellis took the bus back to Lindsay. Soon afterward, his brother died of kidney failure at the age of 28.

"Two weeks later, I returned to the Marlboros and was welcomed back," Randy continues. "I practised with the team for two weeks, then got my chance to play when Gaye Stewart was moved up to the Marlboros' senior team. I was in the right place at the right time. I went from being a walk-on at training camp to right wing on the first line." Randy scored 7 goals and 2 assists in the thirteen games he played. George Mara, who went on to become one of the directors of Maple Leaf Gardens between 1959 and 1970, was the leading scorer on the Marlboros that year. Other teammates included Doug Adam, Don Webster and Red Garrett, all of whom went on to NHL careers. Garrett was killed in action during World War II.

"We didn't get paid, and I was living in a rented room in Toronto, so I got a job at Eaton's in the factory to pay for my room and board," mentions Randy. The Marlboros finished fourth in the Big 7, as the Ontario Hockey Association's Junior A league was called in 1941–42. They won 12, lost 10 and tied 2. The Brantford Lions led the league during the regular season, but it was the Oshawa Generals, under interim coach Charlie Conacher, who went on to challenge for the Memorial Cup.

The following season, the OHA split into two divisions. The Marlboros skated to an 8–12–1 record to finish second behind the Oshawa Generals in the three-team East Division. The third team, the Toronto Young Rangers, withdrew before the season ended, although it did return the next year. Again, Oshawa went to the Memorial Cup finals, its fifth appearance in six years.

"Years later, I ran into Charlie Conacher in the lobby of Maple Leaf Gardens. He asked me why I had chosen to play for the Marlies in '41, and why I hadn't played for the Generals. He told me a story I hadn't heard before: Oshawa had sent a scout up to Lindsay to get me to sign with the Generals, but the scout talked to the manager of the Lindsay Arena, who told him my parents wouldn't let me leave home. Of course, he made up that story — he really wanted to keep me in town to play hockey in Lindsay that season. I tried out for the Marlies and never even knew that Oshawa was interested in me," he says with a smile.

Randy joined the air force before his second season with the Marlies. He was stationed in Toronto, making it possible for him to continue playing for the junior team.

In January 1943, after Eddie Powers had a heart attack and died, Harold Ballard took over the coaching reins. "Ballard was very fair and a real jovial guy," Randy recalls. "The players loved him. The press used to call him 'Smiles.' He never once laced me down." The two became quite friendly. Because of his air force responsibilities, Randy Ellis was unable to practise with the

Marlboros, but Ballard would pick him up in time for games. The redheaded Ellis played in nineteen games, scoring 10 goals and 8 assists for 18 points.

"My sister Anna introduced me to a girl from town named Helen Brown. She went to high school with us, but was a grade below me. I never knew her before our introduction." Helen Bernice Brown was a girl from a Lindsay farming family who, like her future husband, was a fair athlete, one who excelled at softball.

"My mother, she was quite the lady," Ron says, pausing for a moment. "Mom was a very hard worker. In fact, both my mother and my Dad had a wonderful work ethic and sacrificed a lot for their children. Not many women could have done the kind of work my Mom did, day in and day out, at Sand Lake, our resort. She did the work of ten people. But my mother always found time for the family as she dished out her unconditional love. Her love was the glue that held a large family together, no question."

During the war, Randy was still able to play some hockey. He played for Kingston RCAF in 1944–45, with Peterborough's Senior B team in '45–46, and with the Lindsay Intermediates in '46–47. Then, with 2-year-old Ron in tow, Randy and Helen moved to Scotland so that Randy could play with the Dunfermline Vikings of the Scottish Hockey League. "The league was all Canadian players at the time," Randy remembers. "In fact, the teams were put together in Toronto at the Ravina Gardens." Ravina Gardens, now long gone, was located not far from High Park in Toronto's west end. In 1947–48, the speedy centre led the league in goals and points, breaking scoring records by accumulating 91 goals and 67 assists for 158 points in sixty-three games.

The next season was equally eventful. Randy was the Vikings' playing coach, and in sixty games he scored 67 goals and 85 assists for 152 points. He also scored the winning goal in a Scottish National Team victory over the gold medal–winning Canadian Olympic squad. His exploits came to the attention of Charlie Conacher, who by now was coaching the Chicago Blackhawks. Randy was invited to the Hawks' 1948 training camp in North Bay, Ontario. Chicago had a formidable team that featured Hall of Famers Doug and Max Bentley, Bill Mosienko and Conacher's brother Roy.

The prospect of an NHL career convinced Randy Ellis to move his young family back to North America. At training camp, Wally

Kilrea, a former NHLer himself, saw Randy play and asked that he be assigned to the team he was coaching, Chicago's Eastern Hockey League affiliate in Grand Rapids, Michigan. "We were playing against the Boston Olympics one night, and I hurt my knee." Ellis winces as he relates the tale. "I was leading the league in scoring at that point, too. I only missed a few games — you didn't want to take time off because someone might come along and fill your spot."

Ellis scored 21 goals and 28 assists, helping the Rockets to a 26–21–14 record, good for third place. Randy was also called up to the Kansas City Mohawks of the United States Hockey League, where he was held pointless in three games.

In 1950–51, Ellis played for the EHL's Johnstown Jets. Again, it was Wally Kilrea, by now the Jets' coach, who sent for him. The team finished first overall, with Randy scoring 14 goals and 22 assists in forty-six games. Randy had hoped to join the Chicago Blackhawks one day, but the knee injury stood in his way. "My knee was never the same after hurting it during that season in Grand Rapids. I played on it, but I knew I had no future in hockey. So I rejoined the Air Force and stayed with them for the next nineteen years."

Randy's air force career kept the Ellis family on the move, first to Centralia, in southwestern Ontario, then North Bay, Toronto and Ottawa. Four more children followed Ron: Roger, born in 1951; Robin, in 1953; Rosemary, in 1955; and Randy Jr., who came along in 1960.

"Roger was a very good hockey player as a youngster," Ron recalls. His team, the Toronto Torrids, played in the world-renowned PeeWee Tournament in Quebec City, winning it all. "Roger had ability, but he came down with rheumatic fever and had to miss a couple of key years. Still, he played a season of Junior B hockey in St. Thomas. Of the three boys, Roger had the most desire to play pro. When he was off sick, he took up the guitar and became quite good. It helped fill the void that hockey left for him. He organized a group called the Northern Lights and they went around and played a lot of the lodges. Roger went on to Humber College, in Etobicoke, Ontario, and got his papers in mechanical engineering. He played hockey at Humber, too, and was one of the key players on a tour they took to Switzerland. After he graduated, my old friend Doug Moore hired Roger to work at

Maple Leaf Gardens. He worked at the Air Canada Centre, too. Now, he lives up in Barrie and works at the hospital there.

"Robin and Rosemary were both very athletic," mentions Ron. "Whatever they tried, they did very well. Both of them took up figure skating and did very well within their zone. In fact, Rosemary judged skating all over Ontario for many years. "Robin's a really hard worker," Ron states. "She went to Canadore College in North Bay and is now a cardiology technologist at the hospital in Collingwood. She lives nearby in Wasaga Beach.

"Rosemary lives in Port Sydney, not far from Dad and Florence in Huntsville. After attending Georgian College in Barrie, she became a computer analyst for the Department of Tourism and Environment.

"Randy Jr. was just a year old when I left home. He was born prematurely and was pretty tiny, but he ended up being the biggest of the three Ellis boys. Randy was a really good hockey player. He excelled right through minor hockey and played alongside Tom McCarthy, Charlie Huddy and Rick Lanz on the 1977–78 Oshawa Generals in the OHL." After a year, Randy Jr. decided he wanted to play college hockey in the United States, but the fact he had played major junior hockey rendered him ineligible. He spent a season with a Junior B team in Newmarket and then, having regained his NCAA eligibility, he enrolled at Northeastern University in Boston. His coach was Fern Flaman, an Honoured Member of the Hockey Hall of Fame. "Randy Jr. met his wife there and now lives in the States, working for Lucent Technologies," Ron says.

Ron remembers how he spent his summers for many years. "Mom and Dad bought a fishing camp in Muskoka in 1948 and turned it into a tourist resort that became a longtime family business. It was located just north of Huntsville on Sand Lake, and was called Sandhurst Vacationland." When they bought it, Sandhurst consisted of no more than three log cottages, but over the years, more cottages were added, as was a restaurant.

"All the kids pitched in to help Mom and Dad run the resort in the summer. Before I went away to play hockey, it was my job to take the kids away at dinnertime. I would've been 12, and Roger was 5, Robin 4 and Rosemary 3. I had to take them down to the beach so Mom could get dinner ready. Dad was still in the Air Force — he'd take his month's leave in June so he could open

Sandhurst, but Mom and I pretty much ran the resort while he was away.

"I always looked forward to getting up to Sandhurst in the summer. That was a very enjoyable time for me because that's when I'd see my brothers and sisters," Ron says with a grin.

"After I turned pro, I bought some property next to my parents and we formed a company and became partners. It was a good investment for me. I bought about fifty acres of land for $16,000. With the combined properties, we had a quarter-mile of beautiful beachfront. You couldn't buy that land today for $500,000. We continued to enlarge the operation. My side of the property became the tent-and-trailer facility.

"When Mom and Dad were getting a little bit older, we had to make some decisions as to the family's future at the resort. The other brothers and sisters were married and off working on their own things. I knew that running the resort was not what I wanted to do with the rest of my life. I'm sure Mom and Dad would have liked for me to take over the lodge someday, but I knew it wasn't right for Jan and me, and it wasn't where I wanted to bring up my children. Mom and Dad decided they wanted to do some different things, so we sold Sandhurst in 1979."

The new owners operated the resort for two or three years before running into some difficulties, so the Ellises reacquired it and built it back up. "We got it back on its feet over the course of two summers, then we sold it again, for good, in 1982."

In April 1993, Helen Ellis died of breast cancer. "My Mom was a strong-willed person, full of love and compassion, but she was from the old school." Ron takes a moment before continuing. "She just refused to go for a second opinion, mainly because she didn't want to hurt the doctor's feelings. That's just the way she was. But it cost her. She went on a holiday, and by the time she came back, the cancer had progressed to such an extent that it was the beginning of the end. Mom did not like to go to doctors. She'd do anything not to go to a doctor, but that philosophy was part of her demise. The last part of Mom's life was not very pleasant.

"It was a shame, because Mom and Dad had finally retired. They'd sold the resort, bought a Winnebago and started to travel. They were really enjoying life. They were very hard workers. They deserved to have this time just to go where they wanted when they wanted. When Mom got ill, that all came to an end." The 69-year-old mother of five had just celebrated her forty-ninth wedding anniversary and was living in Huntsville when she passed away.

Randy Sr., meanwhile, had been working on behalf of the Canadian Oldtimers' Hockey Association, serving a term as president. "But his real love was organizing oldtimers' tournaments all over North America and, at times, in Europe," Ron recalls. "He and my mom went to a lot of tournaments together." Randy Ellis continues to play oldtimers' hockey to this day.

Randy picks up the story there, and there is a fair measure of pride in his voice. "The original Central Ontario team was made up almost entirely of guys who played in Scotland after the war. For at least twelve years, that team attended the Snoopy Tournament down in California. I think we won the gold medal ten times and silver the other two times." Snoopy's Senior World Hockey Tournament was conceived by the late Charles M. Schulz, the creator of the "Peanuts" comic strip, who was a huge hockey fan and an avid player. The tournament takes place at the arena he built and owned in Santa Rosa, California. "I'm the last original member of that team," says Ellis, who at 79 is still a high-scoring centre, and who at one time was flanked by wingers who were 82 and 85 years of age. "I was recruited to join the Western Seniors team based in Coquitlam, B.C.," Randy announces. "We just came back from the Snoopy Tournament (in July 2002) and we won it all again." In 1986, Randy Ellis was inducted as a builder into the Canadian Adult Recreational Hockey Association's Hall of Fame for his contributions to oldtimers' hockey.

* * *

Seated at the table at the Lindsay Hall of Fame Golf Tournament alongside Randy, Ron and R. J. Ellis is a charming woman with a warm smile. When tournament organizer Ron Jewell announces the winner of the women's award for longest drive, the recipient lets out a shriek of delight — it turns out to be none other than Florence Ellis, Randy's wife and Ron's stepmother.

Florence met Randy at the Snoopy Tournament in July 1993. "I was a widow," explains Florence. "In fact, my husband died about the same time as Randy's wife, Helen. My husband and I never had children. I had been a tomboy growing up. I used to be a pretty good tennis player, too. A lot of my friends were Canadian, mostly from B.C., so I knew about hockey and, in fact, was a Leafs fan.

"I met Randy at the tournament and we hit it off," smiles Florence. Before long, the two were making plans for a life together. "When I said 'I do,' it was the best thing that could have happened to me," Florence beams. They were married in June 1994. "I never miss one of Randy's games," Florence says proudly. Around her neck she wears a tasteful gold medallion of a hockey player, indicative of her new sport of choice.

"I wouldn't go to a tournament without her," admits Randy.

Ron hugs Florence, and says sincerely, "My Mom held our family together through the years, but we are very pleased that Dad has found a companion. Florence is the best thing that could have happened to my dad at this point in his life." Florence holds Ron a little tighter for a few moments, wiping away the tear that is welling up in the corner of her eye.

CHAPTER THREE

Minor Hockey

In the fall of 1953, Randy Ellis registered his eldest son, Ron, to play hockey. The family was living in North Bay, Ontario at the time, and 8-year-old Ron would play for the Ferris peewee team. Ron got off to a later start in the sport than most boys, but the other boys hadn't had a club foot to deal with. Now that it had been rectified to a satisfactory degree, Ron quickly made up for lost time. He came by his talent honestly, as Randy had been a terrific hockey player. But Ron was also born with something else — a full measure of desire to excel.

A year later, the Ellises moved to the Toronto area, and Ron played with Malton of the Toronto Township Hockey League, based out of the Dixie Arena in what is now Mississauga. An exceptional player, Ron was selected to his league's all-star team, which won the Ontario Little NHL Junior A title. The All-Star Atoms swept the three-game round robin, defeating Georgetown, 7–1, and St. Catharines, 4–0 — with Ellis recording hat tricks in each game — to warm up for a 7–0 drubbing of Parry Sound. Ron scored 1 goal in that game, giving him 7 for the tournament and the Pat Patterson Trophy as the tournament's most valuable player.

By 1956, the Ellis family had moved on to the nation's capital, and Ron was playing in Ottawa's Cradle Hockey League. One of his teammates on the Woodroffe team was Mike Walton, who would also be Ron's teammate with the Maple Leafs between 1965 and 1971. Walton and Ellis were two of the better players in the Cradle league over the next two seasons.

In 1957–58, Ron played for Merivale and finished the season as the minor bantam scoring champion, collecting 15 goals in eleven games — including 5 in one contest. Ron Ellis and Mike Walton were both named to the league's all-star team, which played a two-game series against the Montreal district champions, the Loyolas. One game was played in each city, and after winning in Ottawa, Ellis, Walton and their teammates played in the Montreal Forum, where they won 4–2. Mike Walton scored a hat trick for Ottawa, while Ron scored the other goal — and assisted on all 3 of Walton's.

Montreal Canadiens star Jean Beliveau was on hand to congratulate the Cradle league all-stars, while the Habs' Hall of Fame defenceman Doug Harvey appeared at a banquet afterwards, presenting the tournament MVP award to Ron Ellis. In a speech, Harvey told the boys, "In order to reach the NHL, you must keep in mind two things. Learn to skate and listen to your coaches."

Ron attended W. E. Gowling Public School for grades 7 and 8. The school, located on Carling Avenue at Merivale Road, was built in 1947 in the middle of a post-war housing development. While there, Ron encountered a teacher who would play an integral role in his life. "Ross Andrew really had an impact on my life. He taught phys. ed. and music. I played every sport going and excelled. However, what I remember most about Mr. Andrew was his interest in me as a person, in addition to what I could do on the field.

"That meant a lot to a shy kid," Ron admits. "It had an effect that lasts to this day."

Ross Andrew remembers when he first heard about Ron Ellis. "I had been told by one of my teaching colleagues at another school that this incredibly talented young hockey player was going to be coming to us because he was moving into the area. The year before, the first indoor hockey league was developed in Ottawa. It was called the Cradle league. I didn't pay much attention to what was going on with it at that point, but obviously, Ron was some hotshot player. It didn't take very long in phys. ed. class to realize that this young man was multi-talented in athletics."

Andrew's physical education curriculum consisted of touch football in the fall, hockey in the winter, track and field and softball in the spring, "And then, with one week of training, we could put together an all-star team for competition between schools." In Grade 7, Ron was on all of the all-star teams, and in the three team sports, Gowling's teams were city champions. "We had a lot of very good athletes and had quite a bit of success," Andrew says.

"Ron was always a blocky kid," he recalls. "He was never very tall, although he wasn't short. He wasn't stumpy. Everything fit, but he had wider shoulders than the average adolescent, and a thicker body. A lot of it was from doing a lot of athletics.

"Ron was a halfback in football and he lined up at centre as a hockey player. "He was the only right-hand shot I had on the whole team," Andrew remembers. He was also a pitcher on the school's softball team. "Ron was very good at all of them. He was incredibly easy to coach as a youngster — partly because he was so focused and so intense about anything he did, whether it was math or music class. At that time, I was teaching music and physical education, which is an odd combination. But even in music class, which is supposed to be relaxing and kind of fun, Ron was always focused on getting the job done. I was stuck teaching music because they needed some tough guy at the school to keep the hoods in line. And I did. The boys and I had an agreement — you don't cut up in my music class and I won't step on your fingers when you're doing push-ups. I never had to do this with Ron."

By the end of seventh grade, Ron Ellis was known to everyone at school, and he was elected Head Boy. "Ron was very mature," Ross Andrew recalls. "He was captain of all the all-star teams. Unfortunately, that was a year when we didn't have very much to go with him. But he gave it his best shot every time. In the hockey championship, the opposing team put three men on him, because there wasn't any point in worrying about anybody else. It was hard for him to get out of his own end, but he did score a goal, although it was in a losing cause.

"I can remember Ron, dressed in a brown suit and tie, speaking at Gowling's graduation dinner in the spring. It was especially impressive because Ron had a speech impediment. He used to stammer quite a bit. I hated to call on him in class unless I was sure he was certain of the answer and could give it without being embarrassed."

"I don't really know why I stuttered," Ron says. "Now that I can look back on it, I guess it must have been a result of self-esteem issues, like my depression turned out to be. I don't know why, but I always second-guessed myself. Always. Even as a Leaf, every training camp I worried that I was going to get cut. I was always shy in school, and maybe the fact that my Dad was in the Air Force and we moved around a lot contributed to my shyness and lack of self-esteem.

"My stutter was bad. As a junior, later on with the Marlboros, I was especially sensitive about it, because I was starting to do some interviews." But, he concluded, speaking would be the only way to get over his impediment, and so he never turned down a request for a radio, TV or newspaper interview. "I also made public appearances and learned to play the guitar and sing. The stutter eventually subsided, but, even now, there are times when I'll stutter if I'm nervous or shy."

"The only time Ronnie didn't stutter was when he was with me," his wife Jan points out. "The only time. I guess he was comfortable and confident when we were together."

"When I was with Jan, I felt very comfortable. Jan always amazed me how she could carry on a conversation with anyone she met, whether it be a salesperson or the CEO of a large corporation. When she and I were together, we would talk and laugh for hours and there would be no stammering. This was one of the reasons I fell in love with this special girl," admits Ron.

Ron recalls a painful story from early in his pro career. "I met a fan at the Air Canada Centre during the 2001-2002 season. We had a nice chat, then he brought up a time I was interviewed on TV in my first year with the Leafs. He remembered that Yvan Cournoyer was on with me, and how sorry he felt for Yvan as he had such a terrible time speaking. The fan was right about the interview, but he had the wrong guy. It was Ron Ellis who couldn't say his own name. I felt humiliated at the time, compounded by the fact that my family and friends would be impacted as well. When I was under pressure or nervous, it seemed as if every muscle in my body tensed up.

"Wendy Sittler, who I adored, gave me a lovely compliment a few years before she left us," smiles Ron. "With her big heart, Wendy once again had been reaching out to someone she knew who had a speech impediment. She called me one day and asked for the name of the doctor I had visited and the type of therapy that had helped me with my stutter. I had to tell her that there was no doctor or special therapy involved. Wendy simply said, 'Ron, that's wonderful. It must have been difficult, but you did it!'"

* * *

One day in seventh grade, Ron talked to Ross Andrew about his club foot. "I showed him some exercises on the steps in the gym that he could use to strengthen his ankle," Andrew recalls. "Ron was very private about a lot of things, but I think it's a lot easier for a male phys. ed. teacher in an elementary school to get close to kids than anybody else. I was taken into confidence by a lot of young people. Ron took a while, but he did help me to understand what I could do to help him.

One of Andrew's anecdotes centres on Ron's highly developed sense of responsibility. "That year, we put on a city-wide physical education show organized by the coordinator of phys. ed. programs. It was taken around to seven or eight schools around the city, with a finale at one of the senior high schools. Ron was one of the group of boys and girls my partner and I chose to participate in the show, but we were also asked to provide the stage crew for this mobile show. I asked Ron to organize the stage crew as part of his responsibilities. He was captaining the group of performers, but he was also captain of the stage crew. It took a load off my back, because I was doing a lot of other things at the same time. He was so good about it and so good at it. Ron was very well organized.

"One of the things he did on stage during our stage show in the spring of 1959 was bounce a pair of balls, one on either side of his body, and keep them arrhythmic — not in rhythm — which is very difficult for most kids to do. He could do all kinds of things like that. To some boys, bouncing a ball all by itself is a problem, but keeping two of them out of rhythm is quite fascinating.

"Ron's life was quite structured because it had to be. He was playing sports at school, as well as hockey in the city-wide program at the Ottawa Auditorium, and he had an agreement with his parents about studying. There was a component in each day in which he did his studying. Ron was very up to speed on everything. He wasn't the greatest student in the world, but he was a good worker and well thought of by anybody who taught him.

"His peers may not have been close to him, but they respected him. He was friendly, but he pushed people away a lot. I don't mean that in a pejorative sense — he just liked his privacy.

"On one or two occasions, Ron's father Randy would show up at our outdoor hockey practice. We did all of our sports out of doors in those days. Randy had played pro hockey. I remember him primarily for what *didn't* happen one day. We were on the ice — Ron would have been in Grade 7 — and I was trying to show him how to draw the puck back on his opposite side on a faceoff. As a right-hand shot, he was fine at pulling the puck back behind him to the right, but he was having trouble getting the puck back on the left side. I said, 'This is what I think will work. Try it.'

"Ron looked up, over my shoulder, and I realized that that was where Randy was standing. All I heard Randy say was, 'Listen to what Mr. Andrew is saying.' It was the nicest compliment I ever had from a parent in that kind of context. Randy probably had forgotten more about hockey than I ever knew!"

In his rookie year with the Leafs, Ron was able to set aside a pair of tickets for Andrew and his eldest son, who would have been 11 or 12 at the time. After the game, Ron met with his mentor, and presented him with a stick autographed by the whole team. "Whose hockey stick was it? It wasn't Ron's. It was Eddie Shack's. Peter, my son, still has the stick. His eyeballs were rotating at that point. It was typical of Ron's attitude towards himself."

That year, Ron's parents had moved back to Ottawa. Somehow, Ross Andrew, who was now a principal, found out and asked him if he'd come and present some sports awards at his school. "So he did, and he was just great with the kids," recalls Andrew.

"It was sort of a mutual admiration society," concedes Ron. "I really thanked Mr. Andrew and gave him a lot of credit for the input he had in my life."

"I haven't seen Ron in a direct sense for many years," says Andrew. "I've seen him interviewed on TV and I've heard him interviewed on the radio, and of course, I used to watch him playing with the Leafs. I did try to catch up with him once when he still owned his sporting goods store in Brampton. But the time that I chose to go into the store to see if he was around was when he was wrestling with the demon depression.

"According to the staff person, Ron wasn't in the store very often in those days. I just left it at that. I didn't realize that Ron suffered from depression until I heard him interviewed by Shelagh Rogers on CBC Radio.

"Of all the kids that I've taught, Ron is one of the three or four remarkably outstanding youngsters," Andrew concludes. "Not because of what he did afterwards, but because of what he was at the time. You knew each of the students was going to do something with their lives, and they did. Ron Ellis was a remarkable young man."

* * *

Any doubts that Ron Ellis was a star in the Ottawa area were erased during the 1958–59 hockey season. Ron was the captain of his bantam team in the Cradle league, the Westgate Flyers, who won the league championship. Ron finished second in scoring and was named the league's most valuable player. When the trophies were handed out at that year's league banquet, an impressive array of NHL stars was in attendance, led by Maurice "Rocket" Richard and King Clancy. So, too, were four winners of the NHL's rookie-of-the-year honours: Kilby MacDonald, of the 1939–40 New York Rangers; Larry Regan, who won the Calder Trophy in 1957 as a Boston Bruin; Frank Mahovlich of the Toronto Maple Leafs, who won the Calder in 1958; and the most recent recipient, Ralph Backstrom of the Montreal Canadiens.

In 1959–60, Ellis advanced to the midget ranks, playing for Leitrim, and the team won the Citizen Shield championship. Ron also participated in the fifth annual Cradle league all-star game. Early in the season, he caught the eye of Bob Davidson, a former captain of the Toronto Maple Leafs who was now the team's director of scouting and one of the finest judges of young talent in National Hockey League history.

Just before Christmas, Ron's father received a letter on Toronto Maple Leafs stationery.

Dec. 15, 1959

Dear Mr. Ellis,

I have had good reports from Brian Lynch
regarding your son Ron and, from all accounts,
he is a good hockey player.
    We have a number of boys from the Ottawa district playing hockey in Toronto such as Brian
Smith, Andre Champagne, Terry Clancy and Bill
Smith from Hull and they are all doing well.
    If Ron was interested in playing hockey in

Toronto next year I would like very much to talk this over with you when I come up to Ottawa around February 1st, 1960.

I would appreciate hearing from you and if you have any questions I will be very pleased to answer them.

Yours very truly,
Bob Davidson

In those six-team days before the advent of the amateur draft, NHL clubs relied on a network of sponsored junior and minor-pro teams to ensure a steady supply of talent. Scouts would fan out across Canada and comb American hockey hotbeds to recruit the best players from local youth organizations. Once signed, they became the property of the parent team until they were traded, sold or dropped. The rights to many players were obtained when they were 14 or 15 years old. These youngsters would play their way onto the NHL teams' Junior B, Junior A and minor-pro affiliates, develop their skills, try to rise through the ranks, and someday play a role on the NHL teams. Many were called — few were chosen.

"Bob Davidson talked to my Dad at the arena the next time he came to town," Ron explains. "It wasn't long afterwards that Punch Imlach and King Clancy came to our house. After being introduced to Punch and King, I remember being sent upstairs for a while. Imlach and Clancy wanted me to play in the Leaf organization. It would mean leaving home the next year and moving to Toronto. My parents knew that was part of the process, and were assured by Punch and King that I would be placed in a good home. That fall, I would be playing for the Weston Dukes."

At 15, Ron Ellis became a member of the Toronto Maple Leaf family. In fact, he was following in his father's footsteps, since Randy had played for the Leaf-sponsored Toronto Marlboros between 1941 and 1943. "If I was going to play junior hockey, it was important to me to try to become a Marlie like my father," Ron admits.

In 1960–61, Ron moved to Toronto to play for the Weston Dukes, the Marlies' Junior B affiliate, which played in a league that included the St. Michael's Buzzers, Brampton 7-Ups, Dixie Beehives, Newmarket Redmen, Unionville Jets and Whitby

Hillcrests. The competition was a step up from the midget hockey he had been used to.

He almost didn't make the team.

"When I went to camp, the Dukes could only keep three imports on the team, and there were four of us trying to earn a spot. That final spot on the team came down to a choice between me and a boy from Quebec," Ron says. "I started to relax during the last couple of days of scrimmages and my play improved, so the coach decided to keep me. It looked like a good decision after I went on to lead the team in scoring." The coach of the Dukes, Alex Davidson, had played in the Leaf system and was the brother of Leaf scout Bob Davidson. Over the years he would take his share of ribbing as the guy who almost sent Ron Ellis home.

"Since I was the last import selected, we decided to keep any information about my club foot private. We didn't want anyone's assessment of my talent to be altered by my physical challenge."

The Toronto press picked up on Ron's abilities right away. George Gross of the *Toronto Telegram* wrote: "A team player from the word go, Ron seems destined to go places in the hockey whirl. We hope so because he plays the game the way it should be played … all out and no false starts." Ellis led the Dukes in scoring with 18 goals and 17 assists for 35 points in twenty-seven games, good for ninth in the league. He also saw action with the Marlboros Junior A club, playing in three games and recording two goals and an assist. His first game was a 3–3 tie against the Peterborough Petes.

"My first game with the Marlboros was my first game at Maple Leaf Gardens," Ron reminisces. "There was a defenceman with Peterborough who was just a giant. He would have been 19 or 20 and just huge, and I remember thinking, 'What the heck am I doing out here?' I remember that vividly.

"To go from the Dukes to the Marlboros was quite an adjustment. Going from the Weston Arena, which holds fifteen hundred people, to the Gardens, with fifteen *thousand* seats — that was a big jump. But the thing that really impressed me was how much bigger everyone was in Junior A. Not so much the Marlies, because we had a pretty good-sized B team in Weston that year, but the clubs we played against. I was still 165 pounds and 15 years old and I was playing against men!" recalls Ellis with a laugh.

The scoresheet would suggest Ron was quick to get over his

butterflies in that Peterborough game, as he scored a goal and helped set up another.

Brian Conacher, who joined the Marlboros in 1958–59, remembers the young kid called up from Weston. "Ronnie was just good. He wasn't flashy — he wasn't a hotshot. He wasn't a guy who picked up the puck and skated from one end to the other. He was just a very, very good, solid hockey player. He wasn't a big player. He wasn't an aggressive, rough player. He was just a good hockey player."

The *Toronto Star* was more enthusiastic: "One of the big factors in the upsurge of the [Marlboros] is the outstanding centre ice performance of Ron Ellis, 15-year-old import from Ottawa. Ellis has to rate as one of the best kids to wear a Marlie uniform in some time."

CHAPTER FOUR

Junior

When Ron Ellis signed with the Toronto Maple Leafs organization in 1960, he was taking his first step along what many would have expected to be a lengthy journey towards the NHL.

In those days, the plan was for a young player to make his way from Junior B hockey to one of Toronto's two Junior A franchises: the Marlboros and the St. Michael's College Majors. Those who made the grade at this level would be sent to one of the Leafs' minor-pro affiliates for additional seasoning. While today's NHL teams have a single "farm team" in the American Hockey League — and some don't even have one all to themselves — the Toronto Maple Leafs of the mid-1960s had *three*: the Rochester Americans of the AHL, the Tulsa Oilers of the Central league and the Victoria Maple Leafs of the Western league.

A look at the parent club's roster in 1960–61 attests to the job Bob Davidson and his scouts had done in locating talent. Like a creek feeding a river, the Marlies and Majors had supplied the Maple Leafs with an astounding number of players: George Armstrong, Bob Baun, Carl Brewer, Dick Duff, Billy Harris, Tim Horton, Dave Keon, Frank Mahovlich, Bob Nevin, Bob Pulford, Ron Stewart and backup goalies Cesare Maniago and Gerry McNamara.

Any youngster who signed his name to a Maple Leafs option form would have been aware he was following in some distinguished footsteps. But becoming a member of the Leaf family had its pitfalls. The outpouring of talent from the farm system during the late '50s had left few roster spots to be filled. A young defenceman would be hard pressed to steal a job from Horton, Brewer, Baun or Allan Stanley. A centre, like Ron Ellis, would have to wait in line behind Keon, Pulford, Harris, and Red Kelly. It was often said that there was enough surplus talent on the Toronto Maple Leafs' top minor-league team in Rochester that the club could have been parachuted intact into the NHL and beaten out the lowly Boston Bruins and New York Rangers for a playoff berth.

Nor was there much turnover. The team that won Stanley Cup titles in 1962, '63 and '64 remained virtually intact.

But the major obstacle young players confronted was that Maple Leafs coach and general manager Punch Imlach favoured veterans. Most of the homegrown stars named above had made the team before Imlach arrived in Toronto in 1958. When he needed to augment the lineup with role players, he sought out those with lengthy minor-league track records.

All of which makes Ron Ellis's ascent through the ranks that much more remarkable. "I played three years of Junior A hockey and still had a year of eligibility left when I turned pro," he points out. Only Carl Brewer could make a similar claim.

Ron arrived with the Marlboros just as the Maple Leafs were making a significant change in their approach towards the junior clubs they sponsored. At the root of the change was the Maple Leafs' "other" junior club, the Majors, who were operated by St. Michael's College School, a highly regarded Roman Catholic high school established by the Basilian Fathers in 1852. The Majors were founded in 1906, and began their affiliation with the Toronto Maple Leafs shortly after Conn Smythe bought and renamed the Toronto St. Patricks franchise in 1927.

Jim Gregory, a former St. Mike's player who served as general manager of the Maple Leafs between 1969 and 1979, picks up the story. "Father David Bauer was one of my coaches — he and I hit it off really well. He took over the St. Mike's hockey operation in 1958 or '59 and I assisted him. One thing led to another, and in 1959 he got me an interview with Stafford Smythe and I was hired to coach St. Mike's."

The Majors won the Memorial Cup — the junior hockey championship of Canada — in 1961. But the handwriting was on the wall for the storied team. The school's administrators had been dissatisfied for some time with the length of the season and the amount of travel the Ontario Hockey Association schedule demanded. "For a while, we had an interlocking schedule with the junior league in Quebec," Gregory points out. In a letter to Conn

Smythe, Father Bauer explained that the school's concerns included "growing professionalism, [the] long schedule and rough play which so often results in unfavourable publicity — difficult for the educational institution to handle gracefully." Finally, in 1961, St. Mike's advised the Maple Leafs that it was no longer interested in being involved with Junior A hockey.

"We had a meeting with [Stafford] Smythe and [Bob] Davidson, who were in charge of the amateur program for the Maple Leafs in those days," Gregory recalls. "We formed the Toronto Metro Junior A League. The players would not have to travel. They played all their games in Toronto."

For the league's first season, the Marlies and Majors were joined by the Whitby Mohawks, Brampton 7-Ups and Unionville Seaforths. Outside of the two Toronto clubs, there was only a handful of players who went on to professional careers. Chief among these were Bill Collins of Whitby, who went on to play ten NHL seasons, and Wayne Carleton, who spent part of the year with Unionville. "The Leafs couldn't get me to play with the Marlies," says Carleton. "I started the season with Unionville, then Toronto traded for me to get me to the Marlies." Carleton developed into a "can't-miss" prospect for the Maple Leafs, and after five NHL seasons, he made his mark as a high-scoring winger in the World Hockey Association. Unionville was also home to Barry Watson, the son of Hall of Fame Leaf Harry Watson. Ken Broderick was the goaltender for the Brampton 7-Ups. He went on to play for the Canadian National Team at the 1964 and 1968 Olympics, and later saw duty in both the NHL and WHA.

The local media were unafraid of calling the Metro Junior A league what it certainly appeared to be. "The league is regarded in some quarters as merely a practice loop for St. Mike's and the Marlies," said one newspaper account at the time. Brian Conacher, who played his last season with the Marlboros in 1961–62, admits, "Even as a young player, our perception was that it didn't have quite the panache that being a member of the [OHA] did." Rod Seiling is quick to point out, however, just how good the two primary teams truly were: "St. Mike's and the Marlies were very competitive. We were as competitive and as strong as we would have been if we had been playing in the [OHA]. The Leafs didn't adjust their scouting formula during the Metro Junior A league's run."

The Marlies were coached by the Leafs' former goaltending great Turk Broda, who played thirteen sensational seasons and helped the team to Stanley Cup titles in 1942, 1947 through '49, and 1951. "Turk started coaching the Marlboros during the '54–55 season after he retired from the Leafs," Ron recalls. "He was fun-loving, a great motivator.

"One thing I remember is that he had cataracts and couldn't see the clock. He had to keep asking the players how much time was left.

"I was really fond of him. It was a treat to know him. He'd throw in the odd story here and there about his days as a Leaf, and we all found them fascinating. He was a great coach for a junior team; he had a natural way of connecting with young men."

Ron's teammates on the Marlboros that season included Dave Dryden in goal, and Arnie Brown on defence. Dryden went on to play in both the NHL and WHA, while Brown was part of the 1964 blockbuster trade with the New York Rangers that brought Andy Bathgate to Toronto. The captain of the Marlboros was Gary Jarrett, who played in five NHL seasons and four WHA campaigns.

Ron's introduction to full-time Junior A competition had its cost; in his first game of the '61–62 season, he took five stitches to the nose. It was a minor setback in a fine rookie season during which Ron scored 17 goals and 12 assists in thirty-three games.

* * *

By the following season, St. Michael's had abandoned its Junior A program altogether. "I moved the team from St. Mike's," Jim Gregory recounts. "The school had tried the Metro league for one year and didn't like it, so they dropped out. I took over the team and the program and moved everything to another school. We looked for a program that would give parents a chance to make sure their kids were able to go to school. We considered two or three schools, including St. Jerome's College in Kitchener, and ended up at Neil McNeil."

The Neil McNeil Maroons, based in Toronto's Beaches neighbourhood, were joined by the Marlboros and Brampton, as well as Knob Hill Farms (the former Unionville Seaforths), the Whitby Dunlops (who had been called the Mohawks the year before) and the Oshawa Generals. Replacing Ken Broderick in Brampton was

Andy Brown who, as a member of the Pittsburgh Penguins, would become the last NHL goaltender to play without a mask in 1973–74. He then continued to play in the WHA, still maskless, until 1976–77. His goalkeeping partner was Lyle Carter, who played a handful of games for the California Golden Seals in 1971–72. Bob Kilger, who is a member of Parliament from the Cornwall, Ontario, area — as well as the father of NHL veteran Chad Kilger — starred with Knob Hill Farms.

Jim Gregory recalls that the Oshawa entry added a new dimension to the league. "When the league was originally discussed, it was going to be made up completely of players who were brought there by the Toronto Maple Leaf organization. Wren Blair, who was working with the Boston Bruins, approached us about putting in a team sponsored by Boston." The move would spare the Leafs the trouble of filling twenty roster positions, while improving the level of competition. A 14-year-old Bobby Orr was a key component of the Oshawa Generals, as were Wayne Cashman and Ron Buchanan. Cashman played in more than 1,000 NHL games during his fifteen years as a tough yet productive winger for Boston. Buchanan played just three games for Boston, spending most of his time in the Bruins' organization playing for their Central league affiliate in Oklahoma City. He later played four seasons in the WHA.

One of the stars of the '62–63 Marlboros was Brit Selby. "Ron and I were both quiet and disciplined," remembers Selby. Peter Stemkowski was added to the team partway through the season, and recalls that his style contrasted with that of Selby and Ellis. "Ronnie lived in Toronto and basically stayed at home. We really didn't socialize much in Toronto. A lot of the socializing was done when we went on the road. Brit Selby was the same — after games, they had their friends and their family because they were from Toronto. Actually, a lot of the guys were from Toronto. They went their way and I was this kid from Western Canada who stayed in a boarding house and I went in the other direction. We never really got together. I think I probably met Ronnie and Brit's parents after a game."

Stemkowski laughs when he thinks about coach Broda. "Turk was from Brandon, Manitoba, and I was an import from Winnipeg. Being a fellow Manitoban, Turk took me under his wing a bit.

"The very first day I joined the Marlies, there's Ron Ellis and a guy named Duncan MacDonald. They were a couple of real speedy guys on the team and top prospects. The first day I stepped onto the ice, Turk introduced me as 'Pete Stemkowski, a kid from the West who's gonna be with our team this year.' Then he says, 'Duncan, you and Pete get on the goal line and go twice around. Let's see what this kid has.'

"I had to race him around the rink a couple of times. He beat me, but I think I made it a pretty good race."

Despite wrenching his back and breaking his left thumb in a home game against Brampton, Ron Ellis had another very good season in 1962–63, scoring 21 times and adding 22 assists for 43 points. When the league's all-star teams were announced, Ron was chosen as the second team's centre. The first team consisted of Gary Dineen (Neil McNeil), Mike Corbett (Neil McNeil) and Duncan MacDonald (Marlboros) at forward, Jim McKendry (Neil McNeil) and Frank Ridley (Marlboros) on defence, and Dave Kelly (Knob Hill Farms) in goal. Joining Ron on the second team were forwards Terry Vail (Oshawa) and Grant Moore (Marlboros), defencemen Rod Seiling (Neil McNeil) and Bobby Orr (Oshawa), and Gary Smith (Neil McNeil) in net.

At mid-season, Father David Bauer — who had left St. Mike's to form and train the 1964 Canadian Olympic hockey team on the campus of the University of British Columbia — brought the nucleus of his National Team east to join the Toronto Metro Junior A All-Stars in a game against a touring Russian team. From UBC, Father Bauer brought Ken Broderick, Dave Chambers, Barry MacKenzie and Terry O'Malley. Broderick, having played with both the Toronto Marlboros and Brampton 7-Ups, knew most of his All-Star teammates. Chambers had attended St. Mike's, and would one day coach the Canadian National Team and the Quebec Nordiques. The Metro league was represented by Marlboros Ron Ellis and Grant Moore, as well as Gary Smith, Rod Seiling and Gary Dineen of Neil McNeil. The game was played at Maple Leaf Gardens. "The Russians came over in their tattered uniforms and spanked us 6–0," admits Ron. "No contest." It certainly wouldn't be Ron Ellis's last brush with international competition.

* * *

In their OHA heyday, the Toronto Marlboros and St. Mike's Majors would pack Maple Leaf Gardens for their weekend doubleheaders. But fans weren't flocking to see the Metro Junior A league's games — Brampton, Whitby, Neil McNeil and Knob Hill Farms were all having financial problems.

Stafford Smythe of the Maple Leafs went back to the OHA with a proposal that the league readmit the Marlboros, as well as a second team to be placed in London, which would be stocked with the best players from Neil McNeil, Knob Hill Farms and Brampton. The Oshawa Generals, who had been absent from the OHA for six years, also asked for permission to rejoin the circuit. The league accepted the Marlies and Generals, but rejected the idea of a London team.

"One morning last fall," wrote Milt Dunnell in the *Toronto Star*, "Smythe called to say the high priests of junior hockey in Ontario had decreed that Maple Leaf Gardens would be allowed to enter only one club in the league that actually is nothing more than a farm system for the NHL clubs. Smythe considered this a snub. Well, what did he expect? A few years earlier, Smythe had picked up his pucks and walked out of the league — taking the Marlboros and St. Mike's with him. His avowed purpose was to operate more economically and to develop more hockey players by having more teams. He organized the Metro League, which was pretty much a Gardens house circuit."

Stafford Smythe, the president of Maple Leaf Gardens, was aghast. "They're forcing us to squeeze all our talent into one team," he protested. "How stupid can they get? We'll have the strongest junior club in Canada. Nothing in this league will touch us.

"We'll win the Memorial Cup, too. That's not a prediction — that's a statement of fact."

Hap Emms, the general manager of both the Generals and the Niagara Falls Flyers, just shook his head. "If I had a chance to pick the best players from four clubs, I think I might come up with a winner, too." Both executives would find their words prophetic.

"At training camp for the Marlboros, we combined the best players from Neil McNeil and the Marlboros and put them into the Ontario Hockey Association Junior A league," Jim Gregory remembers. "That was just an awesome team." Gregory took over as coach, after having been with Neil McNeil in the same capacity.

He brought Andre Champagne, Gary Dineen, Jim McKenny, Gerry Meehan, Rod Seiling, Gary Smith and Mike Walton — Ron's old Ottawa teammate — with him.

Ron Ellis was one of those who kept his job with the Marlboros team in 1963–64. "Jim Gregory did a wonderful job coaching us that season," he says. "He didn't let us rest on our laurels. He instilled in us a desire to always improve. It would have been easy for us to get a little cocky.

"Jimmy did a wonderful job when you look at that team and realize how many talented players went on to NHL careers. We had a powerhouse." The Marlies skated to a 40–9–7 record in league play and, true to Staff Smythe's prediction — er, statement of fact — they won the Memorial Cup.

"When I first came to Toronto, I became aware of Ron by repu-tation first," says Seiling. "I saw him out on the ice and obviously could see that he was going to be a great hockey player. We played against each other for a while, then played together as teammates. We've been teammates off and on for the rest of our lives and we've been friends all through that time."

As Pete Stemkowski mentioned, a junior team differs from an NHL squad in that many of the players are still living at home, and fraternization is therefore restricted to games and practices. "I didn't live in Toronto during the year the Marlboros won the Memorial Cup," Seiling recalls. "I played all the games, but didn't practise a whole lot. I was enrolled at what was then Waterloo Lutheran University — now Wilfrid Laurier University. The arrangement was that I'd play all the games, but I lived at home in Elmira during the week and in Toronto on the weekends. We played so many games I never found it a problem at all."

The Marlboros took off fast and stayed ahead of the pack all season. Coach Jim Gregory reassured fans, stating, "Complacency and overconfidence have beaten many a good club, but I'm sure it won't happen to us." As part of his game plan, Gregory switched Ron, a centre throughout his career to that point, to right wing, putting together a line of Ellis, Peter Stemkowski at centre and Wayne Carleton at left wing.

"At the time, you're kind of young and naïve, but when you look back, Carleton and Ellis were two of the biggest prospects that the Toronto Maple Leafs had," says a modest Stemkowski, who had also been earmarked for professional success. "I loved playing with Ronnie Ellis. He had great speed. You had to marvel at his legs. I had never played with or against anybody who had that kind of outside speed. As the centre ice man, I just held onto the puck, let him get a stride on the defenceman, then wing it over there. He had tremendous talent."

Ron adapted well to his new position, finishing third on the team in scoring with a club-high 46 goals to go with 38 assists for 84 points. He was ninth in the OHA in points and fourth in goals. Stemkowski led the Marlboros with 103 points, followed by Mike Walton with 92. Hap Emms had to admit, "That boy Ellis is in a class by himself — a fine hockey player."

"We had a wonderful club," smiles Ron. "We had size, we had skill, we had toughness. It was a dream to play on a team like that. Each of us on our line scored over 40 goals." Stemkowski and Wayne Carleton each scored 42 goals that season. "That's a pretty good line when you can all score 40 goals."

"We were three different types of players size-wise, but our line just gelled," Carleton says. "Ronnie was just a great hockey player who could really skate. Stemmer was a hard-nosed guy from Winnipeg, and I was big and strong. Our junior team was bigger than the biggest NHL team, averaging ten pounds more. It was a good collection of characters and great players. There have certainly been some great lines in junior, and some exceptionally good teams. Our team in '63-64 was called one of the best junior teams ever." The Marlboros scored a phenomenal 336 goals in fifty-six games — an average of 6 per game. The second-best output in the league was the 289 scored by the second-place Montreal Junior Canadiens.

Although Gregory made sure his charges focused on the business at hand, a few of the boys found time for a little bit of fun. Stemkowski remembers the nightlife in Toronto in the early 1960s. "Gary Smith and I used to sneak over to Le Coq D'Or. Rompin' Ronnie Hawkins used to play there. I didn't have proof of age, but I used to go have a beer or two. The college kids used to hang out there. There was a little topless bar on Yonge Street; we used to sneak in there — the bouncers all knew who we were. We'd slide in, sit in the corner and have a beer or two. Nothing that a 19- or 20-year-old doesn't do today."

Stemkowski recalls that although he didn't often get together socially with his Toronto-based teammates, "as a team, we were very, very close. Winning is fun, and we had a lot of fun the year we won the Memorial Cup."

"I had watched Ron Ellis play for a long time," recalls Jim Gregory, who scouted for the Maple Leafs when he wasn't coaching at St. Mike's. "He was a terrific player and terrific young man." That assessment is consistent with Gregory's words in an October 1964 article in *Hockey Pictorial* magazine: "'He's one of the finest boys I have ever had anything to do with. He has never given me any problems whatsoever; always did exactly as he was told and never had a word of complaint. I could never have enough praise for him. I firmly believe he is headed for a great future in the NHL and fully expect to see him in a Leaf uniform this season."

"If you asked the players, some of them would tell you I was a tyrant while others thought I was a father figure," explains Gregory today. These days he is the NHL's senior vice president of hockey operations. "I tried to treat them all the same ... I certainly thought I had a lot of time for everybody, but Ronnie was a special person to me because he was a sponge, wanting to learn. He asked questions and I tried to give him the best answers I could.

"He was very easy to have as a player in junior hockey. I can't remember him ever once being a problem. You can't say that about many players. He just did what he was supposed to do."

"I give Jim Gregory credit for my success that season," says Ellis with a note of appreciation. "He was the one who suggested I move to the right wing."

Gregory explains that decision. "When we watched Ronnie, he used to take the puck and carry it. He was a terrific skater and puck handler. We had a lot of players at centre ice, and we didn't have a lot of wingers. But that wasn't my total motivation — we put other centremen on the wing as well. But the way he played, I just thought Ron would play better as a winger. I talked to him and he was amenable to the idea. He was the second team all-star right winger behind Yvan Cournoyer that year."

"Moving to the right wing was my big break," Ron confirms. "Of course, you needed to have talent and a desire to make it to the NHL, but timing and a good break are usually important in every player's road to becoming a pro.

"As this was my first year at right wing, I was schooled in the way the Toronto Maple Leafs wanted their wingers to play," Ron points out. "A Maple Leaf winger was supposed to patrol his side and not move into the centre-ice area. We had responsibilities in both ends of the rink that made it mandatory that we not leave our designated zones.

"Over the years, I have been criticized for being a mechanical player," he concedes. "I think there is some truth to this observation. However, I am comfortable with the style, and it kept me in the league for a long time."

Oddly enough, although the club ran away with the OHA title in 1963–64, no Marlies were selected to the first all-star team. The forwards were Yvan Cournoyer (Montreal), league scoring leader Andre Boudrias (Montreal) and Dennis Hull (St. Catharines); Bobby Orr (Oshawa) and Doug Jarrett (St. Catharines) anchored the blue line while Chuck Goddard of the Peterborough Petes was selected as goalie. Toronto *was* well represented on the second team, however; in addition to Ellis, winger Wayne Carleton and defenceman Rod Seiling earned berths. Fleshing out the side were Ron Schock of the Niagara Falls Flyers, Bob Jamieson of the Petes and Bernie Parent, a Flyer as well, in goal.

* * *

While starring with the Marlboros, Ron was attending Downsview Collegiate Institute. One of his schoolmates, Marty King, recalls the reaction Ron elicited in the hallways. "Like the Big M parting the Rangers' defence, it didn't take long for the knowledge that a young Marlie star, and possible future Leaf, was in our midst to spread through Downsview. However, Ron was elusive — on and off the ice. His proclivity towards shyness and his desire to avoid notoriety at all cost, combined with a very heavy academic workload and his hockey obligations, left him little or no time for 'hanging out.' I caught glimpses of him in the halls and on the athletic field, where he excelled at jumping events and where his piston-like thighs would have carried him for infinite rushing yardage had the Leaf organization given him the okay to indulge in high school football.

"Some of my friends and I decided we had better check out this future Leaf. Having never seen Ron play, I wondered how he could possibly make a championship squad that had the likes of George Armstrong, Ron Stewart, Bob Nevin and Andy Bathgate on the right side. Then I saw him play.

"About a dozen of us from Downsview took in a Saturday Junior A matinee at Maple Leaf Gardens to see a match against the Niagara Falls Flyers. Two things about this game stick out in my mind. One, Wayne Carleton wound up for a slapshot from just inside the red line and fired the puck into the wire mesh covering the clock at the south end of the building. A hush fell over the Gardens as people admired what 'Swoop' had done. The other thing I remember was that Ron Ellis could flat out fly. There below me was a teenaged 'fire hydrant,' skating as if he should be wearing the *rouge, blanc et bleu* of the hated Habs. I thought to myself, 'Some speed on the right side where George Armstrong, Bob Nevin and Ron Stewart play would be great.'

Obviously, Punch Imlach was having similar thoughts.

King recalls Ron Ellis in the classroom. "We were in Mr. Fors's Grade 13 geography class together. I was making googoo eyes at the girls, who paid as much attention to me as opposing goalies did to Brent Imlach. I couldn't see the blackboard because I was sitting behind Ron, who has no neck, and all I could see were massive shoulders that seemed to grow out of his ears. If I sat up really straight I could see, because I'm 6' 3" and Ron's about 5' 10". Ron once said to me, 'Marty, if I had your size, I'd be in the NHL right now.' Wow! He blew me away! 'Mom! Dad! Ron Ellis wants to be a big boy like me! Thanks for the genes, folks!'

"Up until then, I had felt like a big, awkward lummox, but now I was Moose Vasko, Jean Beliveau and the Big M all rolled up into one. All of a sudden, I felt better about myself. Ron has a way of doing that for people."

The 1964 Downsview yearbook shows a handsome Ellis sporting a crew cut, a pleasant smile tracing his lips. He is dressed immaculately in a sport coat, white shirt and tie. But most telling is the caption below the photo: "Ron has been the Boys' Sports Representative for two years at Downsview and has participated in all sports. He will attend a college in the U.S. on a hockey scholarship. We know he will probably become the best defenceman on the Maple Leafs, even though Ron usually complains, 'I just wasn't on, that's all.' If Ron isn't at home doing his homework, then you are sure to find him hiding in Maple Leaf Gardens."

* * *

Most observers predicted that the star-studded Marlboros were a shoo-in for the Memorial Cup title. First they would have to navigate successfully through the OHA playoffs.

In the first round, the Marlboros met fourth-place Niagara Falls, who had finished the season with 60 points — 27 fewer than Toronto. "We swept the Niagara Falls Flyers," remembers Ron. "Then we beat the Montreal Junior Canadiens to win our league. They had Yvan Cournoyer, Andre Boudrias, Serge Savard and Rogie Vachon."

Having won the OHA title, the Marlies' next foe would be the North Bay Trappers of the Northern Ontario Hockey League. "We shellacked them, and finally, we beat the Nôtre-Dame-de-Grace Monarchs in the Eastern final. They played in the Montreal Metro Junior Hockey League."

Bill Plager, the youngest of the three Plager brothers to play in the NHL, had been added to the Monarchs lineup for their Memorial Cup drive. He had earned the spot after a fine season with the Lachine Maroons. "I played with Bill in St. Louis years later," mentions Brit Selby, as he recalls the only playoff game the Marlboros lost in 1964. "We lost a game to Nôtre-Dame-de-Grace, who just happened to be coached by Scotty Bowman. Scotty's team played an extreme trap. That word didn't become popular until the past couple of years, but that system took us by surprise and we lost the game in Montreal."

There was another reason for the loss, remembers Ellis: "When we went up to Montreal for the first game in that series, it was right at exam time and a number of us were in Grade 13 and were writing our major exams. We didn't take a full squad up for the first game and they beat us 7–2. But we came back to beat them four straight."

In those days, the Memorial Cup was staged in the hometown of the Eastern and Western champions on an alternating basis. In 1963, the finals had been held in Edmonton, so this year was the east's turn. The Edmonton Oil Kings, the defending Cup champions, defeated the Estevan Bruins for the Western title and the right to face the Toronto Marlboros. It was Edmonton's fifth consecutive trip to the national finals, while eight years had passed since the Marlies' last appearance.

"We played all of the games at Maple Leaf Gardens," Ron recalls. "Glen Sather was the captain of the Oil Kings. They picked up Fran Huck from the Regina Pats and Larry Mickey from Moose Jaw." Huck had led the Saskatchewan Junior Hockey League in scoring in 1963–64, firing 86 goals and 67 assists for 153 points in sixty-two games. Mickey would be Ron's teammate on the Maple Leafs in 1968–69.

In the first game, Ellis scored 2 goals to pace the Marlboros to a 5–2 win. Game two saw the Marlies eke out a 3–2 victory. Toronto won the third game 5–2, then completed the sweep of the best-of-seven series with a 7–2 victory. The Memorial Cup belonged to the Toronto Marlboros for the first time since 1956.

Maple Leaf Gardens was an exciting place to be during the spring of 1964. The Marlboros' Memorial Cup victory on May 11, 1964, came only sixteen days after the Toronto Maple Leafs defeated the Detroit Red Wings to capture their third consecutive Stanley Cup title on April 25, 1964.

"This is the greatest team we've assembled since the St. Mike's team of 1934," Stafford Smythe proclaimed. Gardens Vice President Harold Ballard bettered his partner: "It's the best junior team ever."

CHAPTER FIVE

First Game

"As I reflect back, Punch Imlach took advantage of the situation," says Ron Ellis when he thinks about signing his first National Hockey League contract.

"My father was a pilot in the air force, flying the Hercules aircraft out of CFB Downsview at the time. He was on a world tour and was away for a month. This was about halfway through my final season with the Marlboros, and Punch called me into his office. Punch likely knew my Dad was away when he called me in and put the pressure on me to sign with the Leafs. I was pretty naïve. My goodness, I was only 18 years old!

"I have a lot of respect for Punch. He could be very aggressive and very persuasive. I remember Punch's desk looming about four feet above me — he had me sitting in a chair that was so low that I had to stretch my legs straight out to be able to sit down. And he said, 'This is the story. I want you to sign here. This is what you're getting. This is the same as everybody else gets.'

"I should have said, 'I appreciate this offer, but I need some time and I want to wait until my Dad gets home.' But I didn't do that. I felt pretty bad. I know I disappointed Dad big time. I know he wanted to enjoy that moment with me. I did talk to Mom a little bit about it, but the pressure was being applied and I must admit, I was also excited about signing a contract with the Toronto Maple Leafs.

"Punch presented the situation in such a way that I felt that if I didn't sign then and there, I wouldn't get another opportunity. The word around was that I was investigating college scholarships. It was almost as if Punch was saying, 'If you don't sign now, you might as well go to school.' So what do you do?

"I have a feeling that Harold Ballard made certain the contract was fair — Harold really respected my Dad, whom he had coached in his Marlie days."

Ron had known the day would come when he would sit across a desk from Punch Imlach and be asked to sign an NHL contract. He wanted to be prepared for that eventuality, and hoped the deal he signed would take his priorities, as well as those of the hockey club, into account. "My Dad and I had talked about NHL contracts often, and I also discussed them with my teammates. My main concern was that I wanted to guarantee that I got a fair chance to show the Leafs what I could do, as well as prove to myself that I could play in 'The Show.' There was a clause that said I couldn't be sent down to a minor-league team like the Rochester Americans in my first year. My thinking at the time was that if I couldn't make it in the NHL, I wasn't going to waste my time in the minors. I wanted to give the big league a real shot and see if I belonged. I still had school in the back of my mind."

Ron signed a two-year contract which took effect with the 1964–65 season (the Leafs were anxious for him to sign before the end of the '63–64 schedule in case they decided to call him up for a tryout). Including a signing bonus, the deal was worth about $25,000. "The word was that Yvan Cournoyer of the Canadiens and Dennis Hull of the Chicago Blackhawks all signed for about the same amount. The three of us young guys all turned pro that year, and none of us had very much control over our careers. Player agents were not on the scene at that time. The owners were strong and there was little negotiation, especially for a first-year player. It was almost as if the owners said, 'This is it. Take it or leave it.'

"I wasn't concerned about bonuses," Ron continues. "I just wanted a chance to see if I could play. I figured everything else would just fall into place. Imlach had a bonus in the contract that stated if Ellis scores 30 goals, he gets $1,000. No one on the Leafs other than Frank Mahovlich had scored 30 goals in ten years!

"If I had been smart, the bonus would have been for 10 goals, because 30 as a rookie was not realistic. But my main concern was that the contract provided enough money so that if I didn't stick with the Leafs, I could finance my own education. That was my mindset for the first two years. Jan and I were going steady and we were serious about getting married. I told her, 'Honey, I need these two years before we can get married because I might be going back to school,' and she went along with it."

For Ron Ellis, signing a contract with the Toronto Maple Leafs was a much bigger step than most could imagine. It took a special sort of player to make the six-team NHL; Ron was very aware of that, and he wanted to be certain he was that type of player. But he also knew that by playing in even a single professional hockey game he would forfeit his chance at winning an athletic scholarship south of the border. The NCAA did not look kindly upon pro trials. It was a dilemma for a bright young man who had all the talent he would need to play pro hockey, but who also had the necessary aptitude to pursue a more cerebral occupation.

"You're Ron Ellis and you've got a problem," the *Telegram* commented. "You think perhaps you'd like to be a civil engineer, but your Mom and Dad don't particularly want that. Neither do your two younger brothers and your two younger sisters. And your girlfriend goes along with them." So, for that matter, did Punch Imlach and Jim Gregory, the latter of whom had called Ellis the finest right wing prospect he'd seen since George Armstrong. "It's a tough choice you have," the *Tely*'s man smirked. "One which three million other kids wish they had!"

The two schools on which Ron had set his sights, Michigan Tech and Cornell University, were both highly regarded colleges with fine hockey programs. And players were beginning to demonstrate that a degree and an NHL career did not have to be mutually exclusive: Tony Esposito, who would graduate from Michigan Tech in 1967, and Ken Dryden, a member of Cornell's Class of '69, both went on to outstanding pro careers that culminated in their induction into the Hockey Hall of Fame. "I got a call from Lou Angotti, who had been in the Maple Leaf organization [with St. Mike's] in the late 1950s," recalls Ron. "Lou had gone to Michigan Tech and been an all-star there. He put in a good word for me. After he got his degree, he went on to a fine NHL career. I played against him for years."

Ron was torn, but after much careful consideration — with input from Bob Davidson and his father — he decided to give pro hockey a try. But he remained cautious, committing for only two years. "If I can't make it by then," he said at the time, "I'll assess the situation again. If I fail to make the grade, I think I'm smart enough to return to my schoolbooks and get an engineering degree."

41

* * *

On March 11, 1964, Ron Ellis played his first game in the National Hockey League. "I was very nervous — I have to say I was scared. I had trouble sleeping the night before. So anyway, the big day comes. I didn't have the morning skate; I just went down to the game that night. I didn't tell a soul except for Jan and my parents. None of my friends at school even knew.

"It was a Wednesday-night game at home against the Montreal Canadiens. Unbelievable! I drove down to the Gardens and walked into the room. The guys were great! The reason they made me feel so comfortable was the Marlie connection — there was that bond between the Marlies and the Leafs. A number of the guys in the room had played for the Marlies. They tried to get me settled down a little bit, but I don't think I said one word the whole night I was there. I was just in awe!

"I didn't know whether I was going to play or just sit on the bench," admits Ron. "I didn't know what was going to happen. Then Punch walked in and said, 'Starting lineup: Kelly, Mahovlich and Ellis.' Gulp! So I not only played, I started the game!

"I played a regular shift. Frank got the only goal of the game and we won 1–0. I didn't get an assist, but I was on the ice for the goal. What a game! Most of the night I was lined up against John Ferguson. I think he took at least one, maybe two penalties against me.

"It was just a dream night. Just to be in that room, to pull on the Toronto Maple Leaf sweater. Simply a wonderful, wonderful night.

"A lot of it's a blur to me," admits Ron. "Certain things stick out — starting the game, Ferguson taking a couple of penalties. He didn't goon me; I got away from him, so he had to trip me. I remember one other thing: Jacques Laperriere was on the point, and the draw came back to him. It was my job as the right winger to go out to cover the left defence. He took the shot and I just kept coming and I ran right over him. And I remember him saying, 'Effin' rookie,' as he lay there on the ice!"

Ellis smiles as he continues to reach for memories. "It went well. I remember it being much faster than junior hockey. I played well and our line was effective and I think I got some chances to show my skills. It was a dream — to win the game 1–0 against Montreal. That was a barnburner of a game!"

The next day's *Globe and Mail* reported, "Ron Ellis, 19-year-old Marlboro scoring star, made few mistakes and certainly did not look out of place. Canadiens took two penalties for fouling him. On one, Beliveau grabbed him as he was breaking through for a shot." "The Maple Leafs may not need Andy Bathgate after all," wrote Jim Proudfoot in the *Toronto Star*. In the *Telegram*, George Gross stated: "Ron Ellis, the 19-year-old Marlboro junior right winger, stepped into the pro whirl Wednesday night for the Leafs and didn't look a bit out of place in Toronto's 1–0 win over the Canadiens. He didn't score, didn't have a shot on the net, but he patrolled his wing like a veteran and played every shift with his more renowned linemates, Mahovlich and Kelly."

Ron didn't keep any souvenirs from that first game. "We didn't think about that back then," he says. "The stick was probably just one of my sticks from the Marlies. I can't even remember what number I wore, although I've since been told that I wore Number 8. I wore 8 with the Marlies, so that's why I might have been given that sweater to wear."

Former Leafs trainer Bob Haggert explains further. "In the 1960s, the sweater numbers only went up to the twenties. I would assign one of the available numbers to the rookies who came up to the Leafs. Rookies never opened their mouth. I said, 'Here's where you sit, here's what you're wearing and here's the number you're wearing.'

"But I had a policy that when players joined the Leafs, I gave them brand new equipment. And if you got traded from another team to Toronto, you immediately got brand new equipment. That was one of our ways of saying, 'Welcome — we're a first-class organization.'"

"Punch just wanted to bring me up for the one game to give me that little shot," Ellis surmises. "I'm not even sure why — somebody may have been hurt — but it was just a dream come true.

"And the next day," chuckles the amiable star, "I was back in school!"

Marty King, Ellis's longtime friend, has his own recollections. "I recall Ron's first game as a Leaf so well because I never saw it! Can you believe that I opted to attend the grand opening of Yorkdale Shopping Centre over watching a Wednesday-night Leaf home game? My friend Harv had season tickets and invited me to attend the game, but for some insane reason, I chose Yorkdale instead. In my own defence, Punch Imlach had a habit of sneaking juniors into the lineup for their debut without any fanfare at all, and to this day, I claim that I didn't know Ron was going to play that night."

"I was in Grade 13 at Downsview Collegiate when I got called up for that game with the Leafs," laughs Ellis. "I wanted to make sure I kept up my marks in case I was going to take a scholarship. I had an English teacher named Miss Kirby. She was a lovely lady and a veteran teacher. I didn't know what she thought of me — I had to really work hard in that class. I was good at the maths and sciences, but English gave me trouble. I just kept plugging away. Her class was the last class of the day, and I went in and sat down. 'Well, class,' she said, 'may I have everyone's attention? I think everyone should congratulate Mr. Ellis on his game last night!' My jaw hit the floor. We had a different rapport after that.

"School was very important to me. No one ever had to tell me to do my homework. If I reflect back, maybe doing well in school was my way of proving I was okay. I had a terrible stutter growing up. Perhaps it was my way of saying, 'Maybe I can't talk very well, but I can get great marks.' But it was also part of my personality to try to do well in whatever I did. I had first class honours all the way through school until Grade 13. That was the first time I didn't get first class honours, but that was also my last year of junior and the year we won the Memorial Cup. I was taking nine credits — and they were all tough courses — while trying to play hockey with the Marlies at the same time. They were all maths and sciences, plus an English. But I still passed with no problem.

"I was one of the few guys who would take my books on the bus when we were playing on the road. When you're taking that many courses, there was no other time to do the work. I did it on the bus. I didn't study on the way to the games — I was too busy trying to get my head around the game. But on the way home, I would sit at the front of the bus, away from the postgame conversations, and I'd hit my books. It's something that I had to do," Ron says emphatically. "It was very important to me."

"Ronnie and I still went to school while we were playing junior, which was an anachronism at the time," observes teammate Brian Conacher. "Ronnie was bright. He had a good mind and a good respect for education. He was conscientious about his schooling. I was a bit of an anachronism, too; I went on to university after I graduated from high school, and I think that was a bit of a bond between Ronnie and I. We became friends around the Leafs and have remained friends ever since."

"I was also trying to keep my options open," Ron says of his dedication to his studies. "I guess I realized there was a possibility I would play professional hockey, but if it didn't happen, I didn't want all my eggs in one basket. I was hoping I could fall back on a scholarship if I didn't make the Leafs. I was interested in Cornell and Michigan Tech, although I never got to the point where I went down and had a look around the campuses.

"I had been quite interested in engineering because I was good in maths, but if it came right down to it, I probably would have ended up being a phys. ed. teacher, like my Grade 7 and 8 teacher, Ross Andrew. I thought maybe I could encourage young people and put positive strokes in their lives."

CHAPTER SIX

Rookie Season

To become a member of the Toronto Maple Leafs was as high an honour as there was for an aspiring hockey player in the 1960s. But with that distinction came a strict code of conduct to be adhered to.

Bob Haggert, the team's longtime trainer, recalls the "business-first" atmosphere around Maple Leaf Gardens in those days. "You went to work every day. You wore a suit. You shaved before you went to work. The guys who scraped the ice between periods wore a cardigan and a shirt and tie. The guy who drove the Zamboni wore a suit. The floors in the corridor of the Gardens were washed every day.

"And rookies just knew their place. There was a pecking order. You came from the junior team, or the odd guy came from the American Hockey League, and you had to fit into that lineup. We got guys in trades, but every one of the trades Imlach made was for established players — Imlach didn't trade for kids. It made it tough for the young guys on the Marlboros. You had to earn your way onto the team.

"Ron was very quiet when he came up, but he was always quiet," recalls Haggert. "Most rookies were seen and not heard."

"I used to sit beside Red Kelly in the dressing room," Ron laughs. "That was a pretty quiet corner!"

"Ronnie just slotted in as a rookie," Haggert continues. "Stemkowski and Conacher and those guys didn't come into the dressing room yelling and hollering. I guess Mike Walton did — he was pretty good at making noise. But in a dressing room with Mahovlich, Keon, Kelly, Horton, Stanley, Bower and Sawchuk — those were some pretty prominent players. No rookie was going to step in and tell *those* fellows how to play the game. Imlach wouldn't let it happen, either."

Peter Stemkowski confirms the "silence is golden" rule that applied to young players. "Back then, when you broke into the National Hockey League, you didn't say anything. For the first season, if I got a 'Good morning' out of Dave Keon or Bob Pulford or one of those guys, that was a big deal. I showed up, said 'Good morning,' put my gear on, played, showered, got dressed and left. Back then, you had to prove yourself. 'You prove to us that you can play at this level, then we will accept you.' It was incredible pressure, but at the time, you didn't realize it."

Keon, one of the stars of the Leafs at the time, agrees. "When Ronnie came up in '64–65, we had just won three Stanley Cups in a row. It was fairly difficult, but Ronnie was a great player. He was given the opportunity and he made the best of it. It was a different time then. You came out of the farm system, and ownership had so much more sway over what could happen to players, it made it difficult to make the club.

"Punch had a hard time dealing with younger players — he obviously didn't feel comfortable putting them into situations — so he would much rather trade for older players. It was one of the reasons that the franchise deteriorated a little bit. We had good young players in our farm system but ended up trading them all away."

Ron's contract ensured that he would stay with the big club and not be demoted to the minors during his first season. And it was an opportune time for him to crack the Toronto lineup. Bob Nevin had been traded to New York in February 1964, leaving a void to be filled at right wing. As a result, Ron was the only rookie to play the whole year for the Leafs in 1964–65.

Stemkowski, who had been Ron's linemate with the Marlies, was another rookie hopeful. He made it into thirty-six NHL games that season despite being assigned to the minor leagues at first. "After we won that Memorial Cup, a whole bunch of us from the Marlies turned pro," he recalls. "We went to Peterborough for training camp. We knew that not too many of us, if anybody, was going to crack the Leaf lineup. They were winning Cups and had the old-school guys — there weren't going to be any young kids cracking that lineup! Towards the end of training camp, they started assigning players. A whole handful of the guys were going to the Tulsa Oilers of the Central Hockey League, but I was assigned to Rochester." Even though he was ticketed for Toronto's farm club, "I was a little bit miffed. I wanted to be with my friends. Why would I want to be in Rochester? I played with Nick Harbaruk and Andre Champagne and all those guys the year before and I was familiar with them.

"I asked Punch, 'Why do I have to go to Rochester? I want to go to Tulsa.' He said, 'No, I want you close to Toronto in case I need you quick.' So I went to Rochester. I wasn't too crazy about it, but I had to go."

"The Marlies had a pretty big following because fans knew they were watching potential future Leafs," Ron says. "The local papers ran the odd story about the team, so I guess there was some knowledge that I was coming. But not just me — Stemkowski got press and so did Wayne Carleton — they had big hopes for him."

"Punch wanted discipline. Unfortunately, I didn't fit that mould," Carleton says. "I was just a country boy. He didn't tolerate people who had differing opinions from his. That cost me a Stanley Cup in '67. Imlach and I certainly didn't get along. But Ronnie went and did his thing. He was up and down that wing like he was on train tracks. Punch liked Ronnie.

"There were many guys who didn't get along with Punch," Carleton continues. "It was his way or the highway. But that's sports. When you're playing for somebody you like and believe in, it gives you confidence. But it was hard to respect Punch. I mean, he had good players anxious to get a shot and he played Brent Imlach — those kinds of things." Brent, Punch's son, played two games with the Leafs in 1965–66 and one game in '66–67, before playing five years of Canadian university hockey. "But Ronnie fit. He was very loyal. Ronnie was a very nice guy. He's still a very nice guy. I liked to carouse a little bit, but Ronnie was straighter. In fact, I roomed with Ronnie before I was traded to Boston [in December 1969]. I think the Leafs wanted to keep me on the straight and narrow!"

Ellis recalls his first Leafs roommate, the veteran Andy Bathgate. "Andy was, and still is, a class act. He was also a very knowledgeable hockey man. He had a great shot. He tried to give me lessons on how to hold the stick. Andy had his own theory on how to hold your stick and how to shoot. He's an excellent golfer, and the technique involves holding the stick the same way you'd hold a golf club in your fingers while swinging. He tried to show me how this would help me, but I couldn't do it. No one could do it like he could. I certainly listened and I tried, but it was something that he had grown up with."

Bathgate had played in the NHL for more than a decade, but he was relatively new to the Toronto Maple Leafs. During the 1963–64 season, Punch Imlach had declared that he would need one more goal scorer if the Leafs were to win a third consecutive Stanley Cup. On February 22, 1964, he got his wish. The New York Rangers traded Bathgate and Don McKenney to Toronto for Dick Duff, Bob Nevin, Rod Seiling, Arnie Brown and Bill Collins. Bathgate was easily the key to the deal, as he had finished second in scoring to Gordie Howe in 1962–63 and won the Hart Trophy as most valuable player in 1959.

"I was surprised by the trade to Toronto, but very pleased. I was very disappointed in New York," admits Bathgate. "We would develop good young players, then we'd deal them off before they had a chance to help the team. Muzz Patrick was the coach, and he was a heavy drinker. We had our battles. I was the captain of the Rangers and not afraid to speak out, and Patrick thought I was too big for my britches. I knew I had been on the trading block for two years, so I told Patrick I'd like to get on a Stanley Cup contender.

"During my eleven years in New York, we never once practised on Madison Square Garden ice under realistic game conditions. They wouldn't turn the lights up, so we had to keep our shots low. The ice was so poor there, too; it was always being covered over for basketball or boxing. Hockey was treated as just an added attraction to fill empty dates at Madison Square Garden. The conditions were certainly not conducive to winning hockey. It was just so discouraging year after year.

"In 1959, I got a telegram from Frank Selke in Montreal congratulating me on winning the Hart Trophy and being named to the All-Star Team. I didn't even hear from my own team!"

Rod Seiling had mixed emotions about being sent the other way. "I signed with Toronto because I wanted to be a Maple Leaf. That was a dream of mine, growing up. But on the other hand, it was an opportunity to go right into the NHL. The players joked that New York and the Bruins used to play for the Patrick Cup because we had Muzz, while [his brother] Lynn Patrick was

Boston's general manager. Between the Rangers and the Bruins, the team that finished fifth won the Patrick Cup. The other four teams played for the Stanley Cup." The two teams were often engaged in this futility stakes race: in 1964–65, the Rangers would miss the playoffs for the sixth time in seven seasons, while it was the sixth time in a row that the Bruins failed to qualify for post-season play. "The worst part about being traded to New York was hearing about it on the radio," Seiling concludes. "The Leafs never bothered to call. However, that was hockey in those days."

The trade ended up benefiting both teams. Bathgate was one of the keys to the Leafs' winning their third straight Cup title, while the injection of new talent helped ease the Rangers back into playoff contention. In 1966–67, the New York Rangers would finish fourth and make the playoffs for the first time in five years.

"Ronnie was taking university courses, so he was pretty quiet and often studying," recalls Bathgate. "Neither one of us were drinkers, so we'd just go back to the room when we were on the road. I used to get a lot of phone calls, though, and Ron used to laugh and say he wasn't my roommate, he was my secretary, answering the phone all the time for me.

"Ronnie Ellis had dynamic speed up the wing, but I never felt he used it properly. Ronnie got lots of opportunities, but he didn't have that softness in his hands to finish. There's a real knack to it, but I wanted him to cut across the front of the goal, then hang the puck in the top of the net. At one point, we were both injured and out of the lineup — I had a broken thumb and Ron was out with a concussion — so we'd go out and work on it. Ron tried and tried, but just wasn't getting it. After a while, it just becomes instinct, but you have to work hard to get it there. Ronnie never did get that move down. I think it could have changed his whole career. Instead of scoring 20 goals a season, I think he could have scored 35 or 40.

"You played each team fourteen times a season in the '60s, so the goalies knew all your moves. Ron needed a change of pace. If he had been taught in junior, he could have been an outstanding hockey player. Ron had power, he had strength and he was a great skater. He just didn't have the confidence to be a top goal scorer. Years later, we were both playing oldtimer hockey, and he made that move and scored. Then he skated over to me and said, 'How's that for soft hands?' We both had a good laugh."

A spot in the lineup wasn't the only thing Ron Ellis inherited from Bob Nevin. "Bobby Nevin got traded to New York and that meant Number 11 was available," Ron says.

"I didn't have much say in the matter. Punch said, 'Ellis, you're wearing 11. It's my lucky number. You'll have a good year.' So I wore 11, no problem. You didn't say 'no' to Mr. Imlach in those days, that's for sure."

"Punch was right off the wall when it came to superstitions," Bob Haggert says. "He actively believed in them all. His two favourite numbers were 7 and 11. Seven, of course, was Horton's, but he began to assign 11 to key rookies. It was Punch's way of saying, 'I like you and good luck.'"

NHL players used to be equally faithful to their game day routine, Ron admits. "You'd go down for your skate at ten or ten-thirty. But in those days, we didn't put our equipment on, we just went out in our shirt and tie and our skates. The guys went out on the ice just to make sure their skates were sharpened properly and that the stick was the one we wanted to use that night, and then we went off. Today, most teams have a full workout on game day.

"After the skate, we'd have a team meeting. Then I'd go back home and have a pre-game meal. Mrs. White, whom I boarded with in my first season, did a great job of preparing the meal. It was always steak and a baked potato — the regular diet of all players at that time. Then you'd lie down for a couple of hours. The games in the '60s began at eight, so I'd be back at the Gardens for six.

"When we were on the road, the team went together to a restaurant or a bar after the game. George's Spaghetti House, at Dundas and Sherbourne, became the popular place in Toronto, mostly because of Bobby Baun's connection with the place. George's looked after the boys. It was a place to go after practice where we wouldn't be bothered. We could sit, be comfortable, be alone, listen to a little jazz and have a little lunch together. Baun, Carl Brewer and Bob Pulford got to like the spot, so that's where we went. George's was the hot place in Toronto when I turned pro."

"The team stuck together on the road during the six-team era. We were family. I remember Timmy Horton, whom I loved dearly. We were on a road trip and we arrived the night before the game. I remember Tim said, 'Come with me, rook. I'm gonna teach you how to drink beer tonight!' So I just said, 'Okay, Tim,' and I sat beside him and he watched over me. He wasn't a heavy drinker. He just wanted me to feel comfortable.

"It was during these times when the guys would start sharing information," Ellis reveals. "I miss Tim. I was one of the last people to see him alive on the night he died in 1974. Tim was playing for Buffalo at the time and he used to park in the Leafs' parking lot when he came to Toronto. After the game, Jan and I walked back to the lot with him. We were devastated when we heard the news on the radio the next morning that Tim had died in a car crash."

Ron's thoughts turn to another team leader. "George Armstrong likes to come across as a fun-loving, carefree guy, but really, he was very observant. He would know when it was the right time to go to a player and say, 'Hey, we're going on the road tomorrow. I think you and I should have a bite to eat.' He'd talk to you and get you laughing. He invited me to join him for dinner a few times that first season. I can still remember listening to the Chief's stories and feeling the pressure ease, and nine times out of ten, the next night you'd score a goal. He just knew when it was the right time to sit with somebody to help get them going. He had a great knack and that's what made him a valuable captain."

Dickie Moore joined the Toronto Maple Leafs in 1964–65 after a one-year retirement. He had played twelve seasons with Montreal, where he was an integral part of the Canadiens dynasty that won five consecutive Stanley Cup championships. In 1957–58 and 1958–59 he led the NHL in scoring, setting a league record in the latter season with 96 points.

"We were on a train trip somewhere, and that was the night the boys decided they were going to initiate me. I was badly outnumbered; Horton, Allan Stanley, Pulford and Marcel Pronovost held me down while Dickie Moore took out a razor. He did a heck of a job shaving off all my body hair — the whole shebang! I knew that that wasn't a good time to be fighting. Today, they make the rookies pay for a huge team dinner, but back when I was a rookie, we didn't make enough money!

"A few years ago, I was being interviewed by Valerie Pringle on *Canada AM* and they had Dickie Moore on the line. Unfortunately for me, the story of my initiation became public. Dickie said, 'Remember the train ride, Ron?' Valerie started digging and the story came out. We had fun with it during the interview. It wasn't a hazing. It was just 'zip-zip' and 'Don't move, Ron.' It made me feel part of the team."

* * *

It didn't take long before Ron felt part of a team on the ice. "I remember my first goal vividly," he says. "We had started the season on the road that year and we beat Detroit 5–3. The next game was at the Gardens: October 17, 1964. We were playing the Boston Bruins — Eddie Johnston was in net. Bobby Baun made a good play to get the puck out of our end. I picked it up, and Frank Mahovlich and I had a two-on-one. I got to the top of the circle, took a slapshot from my favourite spot and scored. Carl Brewer went to the net to retrieve the puck for me."

Playing on a line with Mahovlich and Bathgate, Ellis scored twice in a 5–1 Hallowe'en night victory over Chicago. The press started to compare the Leafs' new right winger to stars of the past — including Charlie Conacher. "I knew Charlie Conacher was a great Leaf, but I never got to see him play," Ellis says. "You'd hear about the Kid Line, so I knew a little about Charlie Conacher. My dad watched all those early Leaf stars play, so we talked about them quite often. It was an honour to be compared to Conacher, but let's face it, there is only one Charlie Conacher.

"I got off to a real good start. Two weeks into the season, I was tied with Bobby Hull for the goal-scoring lead with 5 goals. Then I had to go back to Downsview Collegiate for commencement ceremonies! The lieutenant-governor of Ontario, William Earle Rowe, started handing out the diplomas. When it was my turn, he goes into this speech about how fortunate everyone was to have Ron Ellis in their school. I thought, 'What is going on here?' He'd made a point of singling me out and I just wanted to crawl under the table. All I was doing was coming back to get my diploma. I was so embarrassed. All my friends were saying, 'Oh, Ron, you're blushing!' I was so shy and conservative and this kind of attention was all new to me."

High school pal Marty King graduated that same November night. "I will never forget that evening. In fact, it's arguably my most vivid recollection of Ron Ellis. We were all being commenced one at a time on the stage in the auditorium. The lieutenant-governor was handing us our diplomas to polite applause. However, when Ron's turn came to be honoured, the proceedings took a twist. The lieutenant-governor was an enormous Leaf fan and began to explain to all of us that Mr. Ellis was not only leading all rookie scorers at that moment, but that he had more goals than Bobby Hull, to which the auditorium erupted into a standing ovation.

"My young friend's face turned red — the colour of the most expensive seats at Maple Leaf Gardens at that time. Ron really didn't like being in the spotlight! To this day, I like to remind Ron that his complexion lit up not only the auditorium that evening, but probably all of Downsview, including the runways on the air force base where he lived. Talk about humble!"

Ron continues to reminisce about the 1964–65 season. "Christmas night, we were playing Chicago. I got knocked out cold at centre ice. We were killing a penalty, the puck got into my feet, and as I looked down to kick it up to my stick, and Al MacNeil of the Blackhawks caught me on the jaw with his shoulder. I went down like a ton of bricks. Red Kelly thought I was dead — he really did! He was ready to give me the last rites. I was out cold for ten minutes and didn't move a muscle during that time. They brought the stretcher out and I was taken off the ice.

"Now, here is an example of how the game has changed. Haggy — Bob Haggert — woke me up with smelling salts and asked, 'Are you okay?' I said, 'Oh yeah, I'm okay.' In those days, all they had in the training room was a heating pad and an ice bag, not like the ultramodern equipment you see in the locker rooms today. If Haggy had doubts about my condition, they were overridden by my desire to get back on the ice. I went back to the bench and played a regular shift to finish the game under Haggy's watchful eye. We tied the Hawks 3–3.

"The next night, Boxing Day, we played Chicago again, except this time in Chicago. The game was played at a fast pace and I got through it without taking a hard hit." Chicago defeated the Leafs 5–3 that evening.

On January 1, Boston shut out the Leafs 3–0. But Toronto lost more than a game that day. "I had a collision with Leo Boivin," begins Ellis. "It wasn't a vicious hit — I saw him coming out to the blue line to take me out and I prepared myself for the hit, but that impact, mostly because of the prior hit from MacNeil, did the damage. A concussion is caused when the brain moves against the skull, and after the collision with Boivin, I couldn't stop myself from going down. The Leaf doctors took time to examine me and they realized that the first hit had been a lot more serious than they originally thought. They concluded I had a serious concussion. I missed the next ten games."

Stepping in to replace the injured rookie was Ron's former Marlboro teammate, Brit Selby. "Punch and I were having some trouble with contracts, but we settled the contract before I played," Selby says. "I happened to play against Detroit, New York and Chicago early in the new year, and I was fortunate enough to get a couple of goals in those three games."

Ron remembers preparing to return to the Leaf lineup. "The Leaf doctors wouldn't let me come back unless I agreed to wear a helmet for a while. They said, 'Ron, you can't take a chance. You must have hit your head on the ice when MacNeil hit you.' It was the first time I had ever played with a helmet, and I wore it for the rest of that season.

"I wanted to get that helmet off as quickly as I could. I didn't grow up wearing a helmet, so it wasn't a normal piece of my equipment. All of a sudden, you're at the pro level and you're putting on a helmet for the first time. The problem is, in an NHL arena, the temperature at ice level could be 65 or 70 degrees Fahrenheit and you sweat profusely. I had real trouble keeping the sweat out of my eyes. That's why so many of the players had a difficult time adjusting to helmets when they became mandatory.

"When they made the rule in Junior A hockey that guys had to wear a helmet, it just became natural that they would continue to wear them in the pros. But for us, it was very, very tough to adjust. The only other players on the Leafs who wore helmets were Red Kelly and Billy Harris. The next season, I thought I was fine, so I got rid of mine."

During Ellis's absence, Andy Bathgate broke his thumb and Dickie Moore continued to struggle with bad knees. Punch Imlach shuffled his players with the panache of a casino blackjack dealer. Tim Horton was moved up to right wing, where he played extremely well on a line with Dave Keon and Eddie Shack. After Ron returned to the Toronto lineup on January 17, Don McKenney and then Billy Harris were sent down to Rochester.

In the final game of the season, on March 28, the Maple Leafs blanked Detroit 4–0. Johnny Bower earned the shutout, which gave the Toronto tandem of Bower and Terry Sawchuk the lowest goals-against average in the NHL and entitled the veterans to share the Vezina Trophy. The Maple Leafs finished the season with a record of 30–26–14, putting them in fourth place, 2 points behind the Chicago Blackhawks. Detroit and Montreal came one-two in the standings.

Ron Ellis scored 23 goals in his rookie season, tying Frank Mahovlich for the team lead. "The one thing I'll always remember took place in the dressing room after I scored my twentieth goal. I was taking off my gear, and all of the guys came around and shook my hand. Twenty goals was a real plateau then. I'll always cherish that moment. That was a special time." Dave Keon was the only other Leaf to break the 20-goal barrier that year. Ron's 39 points in 62 games put him fifth on the defensively-minded squad.

After one road trip that winter, Imperial Oil selected several Leaf players to film a commercial for Esso gasoline that would air during the Stanley Cup playoff telecasts. Keon, Pulford, Baun and the rookie, Ron Ellis, were picked up at Toronto International Airport and flown by helicopter to Heart Lake, north of Brampton. Ron forces a smile at the memory. "It was freezing that day, and the helicopter was having trouble flying because of high winds. That was some scary ride!" The commercial showed the players, wearing their full equipment and uniforms, skating on the frozen surface of the lake towards some automobiles.

The Leafs faced Montreal in the 1965 semifinals. The Canadiens took the first two games, 3–2 and 3–1. Ron Ellis scored Toronto's only goal of game two. The third game saw the Leafs win 3–2 on Dave Keon's goal at 4:17 of overtime. Toronto also won the fourth game, 4–2, as Ron contributed the third-period goal that tied the game. Then Montreal took game five by a 3–1 score and finished off the Leafs with a 4–3 overtime win in game six. Ron also scored a goal in the first period of that last game. "I was able to make a contribution to the team, but Montreal beat us four games to two," Ron remembers. "In the sixth game, Claude Provost scored late in the first overtime period [16:33] to knock us out." The Canadiens went on to defeat the Chicago Blackhawks to win the Stanley Cup.

"That was the beginning of the demise of the Toronto Maple Leafs dynasty," Ron observes. "Guys were starting to retire." Carl Brewer would retire prior to the next season over a contract dispute. Andy Bathgate, Billy Harris and prospect Gary Jarrett were traded to the Red Wings. Ron Stewart was shipped to Boston. Don McKenney was claimed on waivers by Detroit and Dickie Moore retired for a second time. The face of the Toronto Maple Leafs would be radically different in 1965–66.

Ellis has another regret about the 1964–65 season. "As I look back now, it would have been nice to have my name on the Calder Trophy as rookie of the year," he says with a smile. "At the time, though, I didn't give it a lot of thought. I was just happy to be in the NHL. I was selected as the Associated Press rookie of the year, but that wasn't the same as getting the Calder Trophy." The league chose instead to honour Roger Crozier, the goaltender who had made a big splash with the first-place Detroit Red Wings. "He played fifteen games the year before, but he was still eligible for the award in '64–65," Ellis points out. In '64–65, Crozier played in all seventy games for Detroit and led the league with 40 wins and 6 shutouts. "That was just bad timing for me. Roger Crozier deserved it. He had an outstanding year."

"You can talk about timing," he says. "It can be a major factor in a successful career. That was an occasion when the timing was not right for me. There haven't been many times that a guy led his team in goals and didn't win the rookie-of-the-year award.

"This is not a case of sour grapes by any means, but it just shows you about the importance of timing. The next season, Brit Selby, who's a longtime friend of mine, won the Calder Trophy. Brit and I had played together with the Marlboros and then again, of course, with the Leafs. But in 1965–66, Brit was playing left wing for Toronto and won the Calder Trophy with 14 goals and 27 points. The runner-up was a big defenceman out of Detroit, Bert Marshall. Brit deserved to win the Calder that year. That just shows you the way the game goes."

* * *

The Toronto Maple Leafs in those days had an arrangement with Imperial Oil whereby they provided a few players to go on promotional tours of Canada. "They happened to select me to go out to Newfoundland," remembers Ron fondly. "We made a few stops and I really enjoyed it. Newfoundlanders were warm and friendly. The folks at Imperial Oil took good care of me. We visited a lot of the Esso stations where they were running a promotion called 'Put a Tiger in Your Tank.' I got to meet a lot of people, and was pleased to learn that most were Leaf fans."

To celebrate the success of their native son, the town of Lindsay proclaimed June 19, 1965, to be Ron Ellis Day. The organizers included former Leaf Gus Bodnar, who lived in Lindsay at the time. Bodnar, who would also play for the Chicago Blackhawks and Boston Bruins, won the Calder Trophy as a Leaf in 1944. In 1967, he coached the Toronto Marlboros to a Memorial Cup championship.

"Gus spearheaded the celebration," Ron recalls fondly. "Being my hometown and the home of my mom and dad, it was something that was quite enjoyable. They held a banquet, which was attended by a good number of people, including family and friends. I had a chance to say how proud I was to have been born in Lindsay, and that Lindsay would always be my hometown.

"The organizers had planned a parade for the next day, but they weren't too sure about the weather, so it was cancelled, but then they decided to go through with it after all. It ended up being a pretty small parade because of the confusion as to whether it was going ahead or not. My relatives ran from one corner to the next, waving as I drove along in the back of a convertible.

"It was still an enjoyable time and a real honour. The banquet was fantastic and everybody tried their best to help me celebrate my first year with the Leafs."

Ron was born in Lindsay, but lived there only a few years. Like most military families, the Ellises picked up stakes every few years. "We lived in so many places when I was growing up — Ottawa, Toronto, North Bay, Centralia. But I consider Lindsay my hometown, probably because we always went back there for Thanksgiving and Christmas to visit the relatives. Even after all these years, I still feel that Lindsay is my hometown."

CHAPTER SEVEN

Second Season

During the off-season, Ron Ellis spent time at his family's resort, Sandhurst Vacationland. "I would train there for the upcoming season, mostly by running and using some light weights. I wasn't into the heavy weights at the time, although I did get into them later.

"In the '60s, very few guys would touch weights — Timmy Horton was the exception. We didn't even have a weight machine in the dressing room. There wasn't one anywhere. Now, when you see the full workout facilities at the Air Canada Centre, it's mind-boggling."

In mid-July of 1965, Ron felt strong and displayed no negative indications from the previous season's concussion. "I was really looking forward to coming back strong after a successful first year. I was sprinting along the beach one day, and I stepped in a hole, wrenching my knee. I figured I'd done some damage, but I wasn't sure to what extent. Jan was up there with my family and me at the time, so I said to her, 'I think I'll drive down to Toronto, just to get the knee checked, for some peace of mind.' So I drove down, expecting that I only needed to give the knee a rest and it'd be fine.

"The next day, I was in the hospital having an operation to remove cartilage! Today, they go in with a very small incision and you're back on your skates in about three weeks. In 1965, it was a fairly major ordeal. They'd make two large incisions on either side of the knee. As a result, it took a lot longer to recover."

It looked as if Ron would be on the sidelines as the 1965–66 season began.

"I recall that Karl Elieff, the Leafs' physiotherapist, was

astounded at how strong my knees were. During my recuperation, I was doing leg exercises that involved lifting all 150 pounds of Karl Elieff while sitting on the foot of my bad leg. Karl remarked that he had never seen anyone do that, not even Tim Horton. I went to Peterborough, where training camp was held that year, but didn't work out with the team. I skated by myself. That was kind of tough. But I did get myself back in shape in time to play the first game. Whether that was a good idea or not, I'm not too sure. I didn't play any of the pre-season games and certainly wasn't in game shape."

During training camp, Punch approached Ron one day and said, "Ellis, you had a good year wearing Number 11. I want Brit Selby to have 11 this year."

"Yes sir, Mr. Imlach!" was Ron's reply. "What else is available?"

"He rhymed off three or four numbers and he mentioned 8. 'Eight? I wore that with the Marlies when we won the Memorial Cup.' That's why I took Number 8."

After having worn Number 11 as a rookie, Ron was surprised at the change. "Number 11 was Punch's favourite number," recalls Brit Selby. "Punch's method was very militaristic," Selby says. "What he said, everyone had to go along with." Imlach's superstition would pay off again; Selby scored 14 goals and 13 assists for 27 points playing left wing for Toronto and was awarded the Calder Trophy as the NHL's best rookie. "It was a pleasant bonus at the end of the year," Selby mentions. "In fact, the Maple Leafs didn't even contact me to tell me I had won it. A newspaper writer by the name of Red Burnett contacted me."

Number 8, however, got off to a very slow start. "Not being in game shape and trying to pick up where I left off in the playoffs took its toll," Ron frowns. "By Christmas, I only had 5 goals. I had a good second half, and I ended up with 19." This time around, there would be no handshakes to celebrate a twentieth goal. "In the last game of the season, in Detroit, I hit the goal post twice. I just couldn't hit that 20-goal plateau in my second year.

"It would have been nice, because I hold the Leaf record for consecutive 20-goal seasons — I had ten in a row. But if I could have scored that twentieth goal in '65–66, it would have been twelve straight seasons with 20 or more goals. But that's the way it goes. It was a half-decent year and I avoided the so-called sophomore jinx."

In 1965–66, left winger Paul Henderson of the Detroit Red Wings was firmly established as a goal scorer in his own right, scoring twenty-two times. "I hated guys like Ronnie Ellis," Henderson says. "First and foremost, he thought defensively — he would hardly ever gamble. Guys who thought offensively gambled and took chances. But Ronnie always had to be 50 percent sure that he could get the puck, or else he would peel off and come back and check you. He was the worst guy to play against. I hated playing against him!"

The Leafs finished the season in third place with a 34–25–11 record for 79 points, 11 behind Montreal and 3 behind the Blackhawks. Frank Mahovlich and Bob Pulford tied for the club scoring lead with 56 points each. The Big M scored 32 goals to lead the Leafs in that category.

The Maple Leafs again faced the Canadiens in the semifinals, but were no match for the class of the league. Montreal swept the Leafs in four games, and went on to beat the Detroit Red Wings for the Stanley Cup.

CHAPTER EIGHT

Stanley Cup

The Toronto Maple Leafs didn't make many changes for the 1966–67 season. Perhaps Punch Imlach didn't feel the team needed to alter its chemistry to any great extent. Brian Conacher, who had played a single game with the Maple Leafs in 1961–62, and two more in 1965–66, was one of only two rookies to see any appreciable amount of ice time for Toronto in '66–67. Mike Walton, who played six games for the Leafs the year before, was the other.

As hockey players are wont to do, the Leafs of the 1960s were tagged with nicknames that had something to do with their background or some other attribute. For example, because of his captaincy and his Native heritage, George Armstrong was called "Chief." Leonard Kelly was, of course, "Red" because of his hair colour. Bobby Baun was "Boomer," Allan Stanley was "Sam," Terry Sawchuk was "Ukey" and Frank Mahovlich "The Big M." During the 1966–67 season, Ron Ellis became known as "Chuvalo."

Ron explains: "Eddie Shack was very close to Irving Ungerman, a fight promoter in Toronto. Irv worked with George Chuvalo, and he thought I looked a lot like George. When he was in his prime, we had some facial features that were similar. When Irv mentioned the resemblance, Shackie picked up on it and started calling me 'Chuvalo.'

"I thought it was because I could take a good punch," Ron laughs, "but it was more the resemblance. And of course, once these things start in the dressing room, other guys pick up on it. So I was 'Chuvalo.' Then it got shortened to 'Chevy.' And I still get called that today. When I get calls today, it's not 'Hi, Ron,' it's 'Hey, Chevy, how ya doin'?' Lanny McDonald put another twist on it a number of years later when he started calling me 'Chevy Truck.' I think what Lanny was getting at was that I was hard to knock off my feet, at least in his opinion."

On December 10, 1966, Ron scored his first NHL hat trick, helping defeat the Blackhawks 5–3. After a 3–1 loss to the Montreal Canadiens on January 25, 1967, Punch Imlach called Ron Ellis "the best right wing in the league." But the team's fortunes were not as bright. When Imlach made that comment, Toronto was in the midst of a losing skid that would eventually stretch to ten games. Finally, on February 11, Toronto broke the streak by tying Chicago 4–4, and won the next night, 2–1, over Boston. On February 18, Punch Imlach was hospitalized with chest pains and was replaced by the Leafs' assistant general manager, King Clancy. In the ten games Clancy coached, Toronto won seven, tied two and lost only once. During that stretch, on March 4, 1967, goaltender Terry Sawchuk recorded his 100th career shutout with a 3–0 pasting of the Chicago Blackhawks. On March 12, Punch Imlach returned to the Leafs for an afternoon game against the Hawks. Toronto lost, 5–0.

"The first time I met Ron was a four-day trip to New York early in 1967," recalls Alan Eagleson, who was a player agent for a few of the Leafs, including Bob Pulford, at that time. "I was invited by Stafford Smythe to fly down with the team on their charter. On a Monday night, we went to Mama Leone's. Stafford got up and made a speech. 'We're not doing that great, but we're hanging in there. But let's get at it and see if we can't win another Stanley Cup.' During the course of that evening, Ronnie was sitting there with Pully [Bob Pulford] and Baun. I sat and talked with him that night. Of course, they went on to win the Cup that year."

Toronto finished the season in third place, with 32 wins, 27 losses and 11 ties for 75 points. Remembers Ron, "It wasn't an outstanding year. It was one of those up-and-down kind of years." The Chicago Blackhawks finished first, and would meet the Leafs in the semifinals.

Bob Haggert, the Maple Leafs' trainer between 1955 and 1968, comments: "In 1966–67, it looked like we weren't going to make the playoffs. We were going through a transition period. We still had some of the big stars from when the Leafs won three Cups in a row, but now we had a whole bunch of kids like Pappin, Stemkowski, Conacher and Ellis. We were switching from one good series of teams to another. Then in February of that year, everything just came together. We got spectacular goaltending between Bower and Sawchuk. The veterans had been there before and understood it, which helped the kids. And the kids were all busting their asses to keep their jobs. It was critical for them to do well. All the pieces fell into place."

One of those "kids," Ron Ellis, was in his third NHL season. He led the team in goals with 22. "Twenty-two goals was the top number of goals for the Stanley Cup–winning team," Ron says. "Can you believe that? It's an indication of how the game has changed." Ellis also contributed 23 assists for 45 total points, tying him with Bob Pulford for third on the team behind Dave Keon (52) and Frank Mahovlich (46).

"Chicago was the class of the league that year," Ron admits. "Everybody had them pegged as favourites. We were the underdogs in both playoff series, no question.

"But we seemed to hit the playoffs with some momentum. There were some changes made towards the end of the year that really clicked. A line of Stemkowski, Pappin and Pulford was put together late in the season. They hadn't played together all year, but they really were our top line through the playoffs. They scored a lot of key goals for us. The rest of us just held our own."

Brian Conacher was another Leaf who got the opportunity to play a larger role during the playoffs. "In the semifinals, George Armstrong was hurt, so I played right wing with Frank Mahovlich and Davey Keon," Conacher recalls. "Normally, my role was as a utility forward who could be dropped in here and there." Conacher scored 2 goals, including the winner, in the last game of the semifinals against Chicago.

Chicago won the first game, 5–2, but Toronto came with a 3–1 win in Chicago. The series shifted to Toronto for game three, and Ron Ellis opened the scoring in the first period. Toronto went up two games to one with a 3–1 win. Chicago evened the series with a 4–3 victory in game four. Back in Chicago, Imlach replaced Bower with Sawchuk after the first period, and the change seemed to spark the team. Toronto won game five 4–2 to reclaim the series lead. Then, back in Toronto, Brian Conacher had his 2-goal game to lead the Leafs to a 3–1 win. Toronto had shocked the NHL by eliminating Chicago in six games.

Ron remembers how the team had a revelation. "Getting by

Chicago made us all believe that maybe we had a chance to win it all. When you knock off the first-place team, that's big! That was when it started to sink in that we could win the Stanley Cup. We only had to win one more round."

Running parallel to the Leafs-Hawks series, Montreal ousted the New York Rangers in four straight to earn the right to defend their Stanley Cup title.

"That year, I was playing on a line with Red Kelly and Larry Jeffrey," Ellis continues. "Jeff got hurt and they moved Brian Conacher up on our line during the finals. He slid right in there and did a great job."

Conacher remembers that Stanley Cup spring: "My rare chance to play with Ronnie came in the finals against the Canadiens in 1967. Red Kelly was a seasoned veteran and a very shrewd centreman, and Ronnie and I were two disciplined wingers. Ronnie was a more prolific scorer than I was by a light-year, but I was the checking forward. It was a good combination." Conacher finished the playoffs with 3 goals and 2 assists for 5 points, and added 21 minutes in penalties — second on the Leafs to Tim Horton. Ironically, it was the gentlemanly Jean Beliveau of the Canadiens who led all playoff performers in penalty minutes that spring with 26.

"Another guy I thought who had an outstanding playoff was Mike Walton," Ron points out. "Mike was playing the point on the power play. He could be very effective. And of course, Dave Keon was great and went on to win the Conn Smythe Trophy. The other key to the whole '67 win was our two goaltenders. They were just outstanding. Both Bower and Sawchuk played hurt in the playoffs. Just unbelievable efforts on their parts. They were the key."

The finals opened in Montreal on April 20, 1967. Terry Sawchuk started the game in goal for Toronto, but after allowing 4 goals in two periods, Imlach replaced him with Johnny Bower. Nonetheless, the Canadiens won decisively, 6–2. Henri Richard recorded a hat trick, Yvan Cournoyer scored twice and captain Jean Beliveau added a single for Montreal, while Jim Pappin and Larry Hillman responded for Toronto.

In game two, still in Montreal, Johnny Bower played the game of his life, slamming the door on the Canadiens, 3–0. Toronto goals came from Peter Stemkowski, Tim Horton and Mike Walton. "At the time, whenever you could beat Montreal in

Montreal, you had to be doing something right," offers Ron. "Once we won at the Forum, we found our confidence."

The third game, in Toronto, went to overtime, with the hosts prevailing 3–2. Beliveau and John Ferguson scored for Montreal, while Stemkowski and Pappin responded for Toronto to send the game into extra time. At 8:26 of the second overtime period, Bob Pulford scored to win the game. Rogie Vachon stopped 62 shots in the thrilling contest, while Johnny Bower handled 54.

Toronto was up two games to one going into the fourth game in Toronto. But Johnny Bower was injured during the pre-game warmup and Terry Sawchuk was forced to start the game. Beliveau and Ralph Backstrom scored twice each, while Richard and Jimmy Roberts added a goal apiece to thump Toronto 6–2. Walton and Horton scored for the Leafs.

Game five saw the series return to Montreal. Bower was unable to play, so Sawchuk started in goal once again. Utility forward Leon Rochefort opened the scoring for Montreal in the first, but that was to be Montreal's only goal. Toronto responded with goals by Pappin, Conacher, Dave Keon and Marcel Pronovost to win 4–1. Gump Worsley relieved Vachon in the third period.

Ron remembers how badly the Leafs wanted to finish off the series in Toronto. "We had to win at home. We didn't want to go back to Montreal. Could anyone win three games in Montreal? We *had* to win it at home." Game six took place at Maple Leaf Gardens on May 2. Gump Worsley started for Montreal, and Terry Sawchuk for Toronto, and both were sensational.

"I was so happy to be there; to be part of it," beams Ron. "It was so exciting to think that if we won this game, we won the Stanley Cup and a boyhood dream would be fulfilled!

"It was a solid first period. Both teams played hard, but there was no scoring, which made things a little more tense. In the second period, I was fortunate enough to score the first goal of the game." Ron Ellis opened the scoring at 6:25 of the period. Jacques Laperriere of Montreal had fired a slapshot, but Allan Stanley got a leg in front of it and the puck bounced to Red Kelly. Suddenly, Kelly and Ron Ellis had a two-on-one. "Red took the puck down the ice," describes Ellis, visualizing the play as if it were being replayed on a television screen. "Until he hit the blue line, I paced myself. I was making sure I didn't go offside. When Red crossed the line, I broke hard for the net so I could force the defenceman to make a quick decision. Red was such a smart player — he knew to wait until I was in position before firing. That way, he might score, or if Worsley made the save, he knew I might get the rebound. And that's what happened: the puck came right to my stick after Red's shot. I saw a lot of net and I threw the puck upstairs."

The playmaker, Red Kelly, describes the goal from a different vantage point. "I saw Ronnie breaking out with me at our blue line. The puck came out to the middle. The Montreal defence-man hesitated, then started to back up. I got the puck and saw Ronnie coming down on my left side. I tried to pull the defence-man over so I could get the puck to Ronnie, but he stayed between us. I had to shoot. Worsley made the save, but couldn't control the puck and Ronnie barged in and scored on the rebound."

The photograph of the goal can be found on the cover of this book. "That ended up being a big goal for us," says Ellis. "It gave us our start and got the fans behind us. I thought we controlled the game from that point on. And then our goaltending just became phenomenal. The team realized they were a period and a half away from the Cup. Everybody just reached down and played their hearts out."

Jim Pappin followed Ellis's goal with one of his own later in the second period. Former Leaf Dick Duff closed the gap with a goal in the third. Then, in the last desperate minute, Canadiens coach Toe Blake pulled his goaltender.

With just over a minute to play, Toronto is leading Montreal 2–1. The Canadiens are trying to force a face-off in the Leafs' zone, and with that whistle, they'll get it. Toe Blake has called Worsley over to the bench, so the Canadiens will have an extra attacker for this all-important faceoff to the left of Terry Sawchuk. Fifty-five seconds left in regulation time. Oh, my — Punch Imlach has defenceman Allan Stanley taking the faceoff against Beliveau! The puck is dropped. Stanley ties up his man in the faceoff circle and Kelly swoops in to grab the puck. He dishes it off to Pulford at the Leaf blue line. Pulford cuts across the ice and produces a perfect backhand over to Armstrong, who's skating up the right

wing. The captain fires from outside the blue line —
scores! Armstrong, into an open net! The Leafs are up
3–1 and the Canadiens won't come back in this one!

The Toronto Maple Leafs had won the Stanley Cup!

Ron Ellis's memories are as bright as his smile. "They brought the Stanley Cup out on a table, and we weren't even allowed to lift it off the table — only our captain could touch it. Things were so different then. The Cup was presented to George Armstrong, our captain, and then George waved us all in for a team photo around the Cup. We weren't allowed to parade around the ice with it. When I see the Stanley Cup winners do that today, I say, 'Boy, that would have been wonderful!' I also would have loved to have taken the Cup home to Lindsay for a day, the way they do now. The celebrations were a little more reserved then. And it was Toronto's fourth Cup in seven years, so a lot of the guys had won it before. But for me, it was certainly a highlight of my life.

"At the time, I didn't allow myself to really experience that moment the way I should have. My personality, my makeup, had me already worrying about making the team the next year. That's where my mind was. I didn't allow myself to really let go and enjoy the moment. Oh, sure, I was happy — absolutely. But there was a little bit of reservation there; I was holding back. Maybe I didn't think I deserved it. I just don't know. I was very conservative, very laid back, very introspective. I just didn't allow myself to enjoy the moment. As the years went by, I would ask myself, 'Why didn't I?' But that sort of mindset dominated my early life. I'm not that way anymore. My battle with depression has forced me to address these personality traits and, I'm happy to say, I am much better in this area today."

"I was so concerned about getting ready for the next year, and just trying to make the team again. That was my mindset. Silly or maybe ridiculous, but that's where I was at."

"There was a great deal of turmoil during the year," recalls David Keon. "We played well, then we didn't play very well. But in the playoffs, for one month, we played very, very well. We had some injuries, but everybody contributed. We were the best team for a month. That's really what it boiled down to." Keon, who contributed 3 goals and 5 assists to the Leafs' attack, was awarded the Conn Smythe Trophy as the most valuable player during the 1967 playoffs. But as integral as his offence was to the championship, it was Keon's relentless skating and defensive play that earned him the honour.

"We went to Stafford Smythe's house for a party the next night," remembers Ellis. "It was fantastic, just to be with your teammates and experience such an accomplishment. There were some other events over the next few days — a parade and some other things. But instead of taking the week and really enjoying all aspects of the win, right after the parade, I turned to Jan and said, 'Honey, I'm sorry, but we have to go up to the resort and get to work.' So we didn't stay with the rest of the team and celebrate. We did the party at Stafford's and the parade — those were wonderful things — but the guys wanted to do a few more things. I said, 'No, we gotta go.' My wife wasn't very happy about it.

"Without a doubt, it was a little obsessive-compulsive of me. The Stanley Cup victory only happened once for me, and I should have taken the time to really enjoy the moment with my wife and my teammates. I should have called my Dad and said politely, 'You're not going to see me for a week.' But I didn't. I knew my Dad and Mom were up at the resort and they were working their butts off. I left the Stanley Cup celebration to cut grass amongst the blackflies."

"Winning the Stanley Cup was the second biggest achievement of my professional life. It comes behind Team Canada in 1972. Wearing the red maple leaf holds a slightly higher spot for me, only because of the emotions that we went through. But winning the Stanley Cup was certainly number one, no question, at the time. It was the Canadian boy's dream — first of all, to play in the National Hockey League and then to win the Stanley Cup."

CHAPTER NINE

Expansion

When the Toronto Maple Leafs won the Stanley Cup in the spring of 1967, it marked the closing of a chapter in National Hockey League history. For twenty-five seasons, the league had been made up of the same six clubs, none of which lay west of Chicago. In February 1966, the governors of the six teams voted to expand the league's ranks to twelve, effective in 1967–68. For the first time since 1926 — when New York, Chicago and Detroit joined — brand new teams would compete in the NHL.

Naturally, the new clubs — the Los Angeles Kings, Minnesota North Stars, Oakland Seals, Philadelphia Flyers, Pittsburgh Penguins and St. Louis Blues — would need players. To help them stock their rosters, the league organized a draft whereby each of the six established teams reserved, or "protected," one goaltender and eleven skaters; the rest were put into a pool from which the expansion teams could pick and choose. Each time an "Original Six" team lost a player to the draft, it was entitled to add one of its unprotected players to the "protected" list. Each expansion team would draft a total of twenty players.

"Everybody knew expansion was on the horizon," states Ron Ellis. "A lot of our players knew that they weren't going to be protected. I think the guys had it in their mind that, after the '66–67 season, there were going to be a lot of changes."

On the other hand, Dave Keon says, "I guess you could say we were oblivious to the upcoming draft. We realized the younger players were likely going to be protected because they were the team's future and would probably be staying with the Leafs."

"Some players were quite happy with the advent of expansion," continues Ron. "For some, it was an opportunity to extend their careers. For others, it offered the chance to play full time. A number of guys got a chance to play an additional four or five years because of expansion. But you knew that a lot of guys you'd played with, or some of the fellows in the farm system, might end up with new teams. Without question, it changed the game forever."

On June 6, 1967, the expansion draft was held in Montreal, after each of the six new teams surrendered their $2 million cheques for the right to enter the league. Toronto was hard hit, losing players from the current roster as well as promising youngsters from the minors. The Los Angeles Kings selected Terry Sawchuk, plus farmhands Ed Joyal, Bill Flett, Lowell MacDonald and Mike Corrigan. Red Kelly retired to become the Kings' first coach. The Oakland Seals took Bob Baun, Kent Douglas, Aut Erickson — who had played with Toronto in the playoffs the previous spring — and prospects Terry Clancy, Gary Smith and Mike Laughton. Gerry Ehman would be traded to the Seals in October. Brit Selby and Don Blackburn were chosen by the Philadelphia Flyers, while Larry Jeffrey was a selection of the Pittsburgh Penguins. The St. Louis Blues plucked Al Arbour, John Brenneman, Larry Keenan, Darryl Edestrand, Fred Hucul and Gary Veneruzzo from the Leaf farm system. Minnesota was the only team that did not claim a player from the Toronto organization, although at Christmas, Toronto sent Milan Marcetta, who had played just three games with the Leafs — all of them in the '67 Stanley Cup playoffs — and J.P. Parise to the North Stars. In addition, the Leafs loaned veteran Bronco Horvath to the Stars as an emergency replacement after Bill Masterton died on January 15, 1968, as a result of a head injury suffered in an on-ice accident.

"Come training camp that fall, it was a different team," says Ellis with a sigh. "Bobby Baun had been having a feud with Punch Imlach, so it was no surprise that he wasn't protected. Baun didn't play much in the finals the year before. And you could only protect one goalie, so we knew either Bower or Sawchuk would be gone. And Eddie Shack was traded to Boston two weeks after the Stanley Cup celebration."

"I wasn't part of that '66–67 team," Brit Selby recalls. "After six games with Toronto, I was sent to Vancouver in the Western Hockey League. The following spring, the expansion draft took place and I was picked up by Philadelphia. I had been thinking about it all year because I hadn't been playing. I had a broken leg, so I was very fortunate to be picked up by Philadelphia. It was an opportunity to get out of the Leaf organization and to experience a new city with new players."

"It's sad to see your friends go, whether through expansion or a trade," says Ron with a note of resignation. "I don't like change, but you have to accept it. Sometimes your best friend gets traded."

Ellis remembers being at the centre of trade rumours. "For a few years early in my career, I had a no-trade clause. Later, there was a constant rumour in Boston that I was going to be traded for Kenny Hodge. Every time I went into Boston, the fans would be yelling, 'We don't want you, Ellis!' There must have been some validity to the rumour because of the reaction of the Bruins' fans, but it never happened, I'm happy to say. That was about the only time I ever heard my name in trade talks, but I'm sure it happened behind closed doors."

A trade that shocked many fans was made on March 3, 1968, when Toronto sent Frank Mahovlich, Peter Stemkowski, Garry Unger and the rights to Carl Brewer to the Red Wings, receiving Paul Henderson, Norm Ullman and Floyd Smith in return.

"At the time, I was sorry to see Frank go. I had a lot of respect for him," Ron states. "And I thought Garry Unger was going to be a superstar one day. It was sad to see a young guy with that kind of potential leave. But in retrospect, it was probably a real break for me. The following year, I ended up on a line with Norm Ullman and Paul Henderson. I have to say, playing with those two guys was a very enjoyable period of my career. We were a line for the better part of six years, and we were able to be productive when the Leafs were going through some very tough times."

Peter Stemkowski was stunned when he got the news of the trade. "I heard about it the day before it was announced. Somebody had a pipeline to the telephone operator at Maple Leaf Gardens. Jim Pappin, my roommate and linemate, called me and said, 'Hey, you've been traded.' I said, 'Yeah, yeah. Who you kiddin'?' He said, 'I overheard somebody calling from the Gardens. You're going to be traded.'

"I was pretty shook up. First of all, we won the Stanley Cup the year before. When I went back to Winnipeg that summer, I had neighbourhood kids knocking on my door telling me how proud they were. You had that national exposure when you played in Toronto. Every Saturday, whether you lived in British Columbia or

Nova Scotia, you watched the Toronto Maple Leafs on *Hockey Night in Canada*. I enjoyed that kind of exposure.

"Now I was going to Detroit with Frank Mahovlich and Garry Unger. Detroit? What the hell did I know about Detroit? I was faltering, the team was having some problems and I think Punch just wanted to shake things up. But it turned out okay. I got a chance to play with Gordie Howe."

Norm Ullman recalls that he had heard rumblings about a trade for two or three weeks. "My name had been mentioned in the papers, and my wife and I had talked about what would happen if the trade took place. I had been with the Detroit organization my entire career. I started with the Edmonton Oil Kings in junior, and they were a Detroit-sponsored team. I thought I would finish my career in Detroit. I had played there for thirteen years. But the team wasn't doing well — both Toronto and Detroit were floundering — so they had to do something.

"A trade affects the family more than it affects the player. The kids were in school and had friends they didn't want to leave. They had roots in Detroit, and now they had to start all over. Hockey's pretty much the same whether you're playing in Detroit or Toronto, but the change is tougher on the rest of the family. It really affected my son."

"It was tough," recalls Paul Henderson. "I was devastated. I knew both teams were in trouble. Detroit was in trouble on defence. We lost Doug Barkley to an eye injury, Marcel Pronovost had already been traded to Toronto and Bill Gadsby retired. Those were the three mainstays back there, and the prospects in the minors didn't look good. And if you looked at Toronto, they were a team in transition.

"But you put your best foot forward. Players don't have any say in where they play. In hindsight, at the time, it was not good — I was devastated when I was traded. But in reality, it was the best thing that ever happened to me. Normie and I got to play with Ronnie in Toronto. We were a lot more offensively minded than he was. It's not that Ronnie couldn't score — he had a great shot — but he thought about defence first. That was just because of our personalities.

"There's no question that's why the line fit together so well," Henderson says. "You knew you could always count on Ronnie. The fact of the matter is, that influences you, too. Ronnie made me a better defensive player, because I became very aware that I had a responsibility. For a few years there, I think Ronnie and Normie and I were as good a line as there was in the league."

Ullman agrees. "Ronnie was a tremendous player. He was a dependable player. He was a great skater, who went up and down his wing. He had good speed. Paul Henderson had a lot of speed, too. We worked together well."

"Playing with Norm and Paul kept my interest up as well as my desire to keep playing," Ron says. "It was a tough time to be playing in Toronto. We weren't making the playoffs. But our line was productive. That was the line I played with the longest during my career. Some people called us the HUE Line. Over the period we were together, the line was balanced and productive and we enjoyed some good times together on and off the ice. That kept us going and made it more enjoyable during the dark days."

The record book contains the proof of the line's success as well as its balance. During the six years that the line played together, Ellis scored 152 goals and 299 points, Henderson collected 157 goals and 307 points and Ullman added 152 goals and 419 points.

"The three of us were close socially, too," says Ellis. "Paul and I more so, because we were a little closer in age. We're all very good friends still today. I've got all the time in the world for Normie Ullman. His wife Bibs has been a tremendous support for my wife, Jan. Even today, they talk. And Eleanor, Paul's wife, is a lifelong friend of Jan's too."

"Our wives hit it off," admits Paul Henderson. "Then we started going on holidays together. After a couple of years, Brian Glennie and Ronnie and I became very tight. It was just one of those friendships. We got close right off the bat and we stayed close over the years."

A newspaper profile of the crewcutted, 22-year-old Ron Ellis provides some early insight into Ron's sense of self-doubt. "Ellis has found it frustrating not being able to achieve the goals he has set for himself in hockey. 'My views of the game have certainly changed since I broke in at 19. I felt I was on top of the world and the cheers were great. But things have changed. I worry continually. I feel the pressure, something that I shouldn't at my age. What's going to happen when I get older? I'm the type who takes everything to heart. I keep it inside me." Ron was already thinking about his future after hockey, and wisely so. He talked about his family's camp, Sandhurst, near Huntsville, Ontario. "I'd like to devote more time to the camp and eventually teach school. Ten years in the NHL is enough."

As Paul Henderson indicated, it was a difficult season for both the Maple Leafs and the Red Wings. The league had been split into two divisions, East and West, with the "Original Six" in the East and the expansion clubs in the West. In 1967–68, both Toronto and Detroit failed to qualify for the East Division, even though the Maple Leafs' 76 points were more than any team in the West managed to rack up.

Ron Ellis managed to post solid numbers despite playing with a cracked left wrist that required him to wear a brace. The injury made him a less accurate shooter during the last quarter of the season. Still, he ended up with 28 goals and 48 points, both of which were career highs. In the latter category he was third-best among those who'd played the full season with the Leafs. When his Detroit and Toronto stats were combined, Norm Ullman ended up with 72 points, putting him seventh in the NHL.

The individual success did not completely ease Ron's bitter sense of disappointment at finishing out of the playoffs. "There was a definite lack of foresight on management's part," he says. "Our farm system was very strong at the time, but we got hit hard by expansion — we lost a lot of key guys from the farm system." The farm system itself had been gutted in 1966–67, as the Maple Leafs sold their American Hockey League team, the Rochester Americans, and their Western Hockey League affiliate, the Victoria Maple Leafs. "Leaf management made a decision in '67 that won us a Cup," says Ellis, "but we went with a veteran team, and within a year or two, a number of those players retired. We had a lot of holes to fill, but no farm hands were available. Management certainly knew that we were going to have six to eight guys retire, and they certainly had to be aware our farm system was going to be hit the hardest. I give Montreal credit — they were hit hard, too, but they made deals that allowed them to survive. I don't think the Leafs' management gave it much thought — a little arrogance, perhaps. We ended up more like an expansion team than the expansion teams were. That's how sad it was."

"It was the end of the run," says Bob Haggert sadly. "Players got older, players got traded, players had gone to expansion. In my opinion, it was the end of the glory years for the Toronto Maple Leafs."

CHAPTER TEN

Number 6

On December 12, 1933, the playing career of Irvine "Ace" Bailey came to an abrupt end.

The backdrop for one of hockey's darkest moments took place in Boston during a game between the Toronto Maple Leafs and the Bruins. In the second period, the Bruins were about to enjoy a two-man advantage against the Leafs, and coach Art Ross sent out Eddie Shore, their star defenceman, as part of the power-play unit. Similarly, the Leafs sent out their expert penalty killer, Ace Bailey, along with King Clancy and Red Horner.

Ace Bailey was born in Bracebridge, Ontario, on July 3, 1903, and played junior hockey in Toronto and senior hockey in Peterborough before joining the Toronto St. Pats in 1926–27. During that season, the team was sold to a syndicate led by Conn Smythe and renamed the Maple Leafs. The rookie finished sixth in the NHL in scoring with 15 goals and 13 assists for 28 points. Two seasons later, in 1928–29, Bailey won the NHL scoring title with 32 points, of which 22 were goals. The next season, forward passing was introduced to the NHL and scoring exploded. Bailey's offensive output grew to 43 points, yet he did not finish among the NHL's top ten. With the rise of Toronto's Kid Line of Charlie Conacher, Harvey "Busher" Jackson and Joe Primeau, Ace's role on the team changed. He would now be a defensive specialist, and his point production slipped accordingly.

In a 1985 *Toronto Star* article, Bailey described the action on his final shift. "Red Horner bodychecked Shore into the boards, picked up the puck and headed toward the Boston goal. Shore was in behind the blue line and was offside. On the way out, he took my feet from under me. I wasn't watching and when I fell, my head hit the ice and I went into convulsions." Longtime Leafs fan

Tom Gaston, who later befriended the retired Bailey, described the play this way: "The game was down in Boston and in the second period, Eddie Shore carried the puck up the ice. King Clancy knocked him down and Shore thought a tripping penalty should have been called. He was livid! King picked up the puck and started a rush into the Bruins' zone. Ace Bailey dropped back to cover the defence position for Clancy. When Shore picked himself up and started to skate back into Boston's end, he came up behind Ace and sent him flying. Nobody seems to know whether Shore thought Bailey was Clancy and was trying to get revenge for the hit, or whether Shore was seeing red and hit anybody in a Leafs uniform. Ace's head hit the ice with incredible force, and he just lay there on his back with his legs twitching. It wasn't the hit that hurt Ace — it was the way he fell that did the damage. He never saw Shore coming at him."

In the 1930s, the concept of wearing a helmet to play hockey was almost entirely foreign. Players would occasionally don a helmet after suffering a concussion, but would discard it as soon as the headaches subsided. One of the earlier helmet-wearing NHL players was Jack Crawford, a career Boston Bruin and former teammate of Shore's whose career began in 1937–38. But his helmet use was not to protect his head; he wore one to disguise his baldness after a skin disorder robbed him of his hair.

As soon as Ace Bailey hit the ice, pandemonium ensued. Horner knocked Shore unconscious with a punch to the jaw while teammates tended to Bailey. A drunken Bruins fan accused Bailey of faking his injury and was punched in the mouth by Conn Smythe, the owner of the Maple Leafs. The fan pressed charges, so the Boston police locked Smythe up for the night. Smythe later paid the spectator's dental bills.

Bailey was awake when he was taken to the team's dressing room, where he was examined by the Bruins' team doctor. When Bailey fell unconscious, Dr. Kelley called for an ambulance, suspecting that the Leaf had fractured his skull. While they waited for the ambulance, Eddie Shore, with a newly stitched cut on his scalp, made his way to the room where Bailey lay and apologized.

The Leafs were badly shaken, but they had a game two days later in Montreal, so they had to leave Bailey and Smythe behind.

When the details of Bailey's injury reached the Bruins management, Conn Smythe was released from jail. Smythe, who had been told that his star forward was at death's door, instructed Toronto's assistant general manager, Frank Selke, to make plans to bring Bailey's body back to Toronto.

Meanwhile, at Boston's Audubon Hospital, two neurosurgeons happened to be visiting and they attended to Bailey. One, Dr. Donald Munro, performed two high-risk operations over the course of a week, drilling holes into Bailey's badly fractured skull to relieve the pressure. The doctors didn't hold out much hope for survival, and on two occasions, Ace Bailey was administered last rites.

Bailey's father set out for Boston by train, bent on killing Eddie Shore. He armed himself with a handgun. When Smythe found out, he called Selke once again. Selke contacted a friend who was a Boston policeman, who found Ace's father in the bar of the Leafs' hotel and was able to disarm him. The senior Bailey was put on a train back to Canada. His gun was returned by mail two weeks later.

When Ace's prognosis had improved sufficiently, he was allowed to return to Toronto to complete his recovery. He arrived at Union Station on January 18.

Ace Bailey never again played in the NHL.

Shore was suspended until January 28, during which time he missed sixteen games. Red Horner, the Toronto defenceman was suspended for six games.

The Bruins set aside almost $8,000 in gate receipts from a game between Boston and the Montreal Maroons and sent the money to Bailey. On January 24, the league's board of governors voted to organize a charity game, to be played in Toronto, whose proceeds would also go to Ace Bailey. The game would feature the Toronto Maple Leafs playing a group of players selected by an NHL executive committee.

The game was held on Valentine's Day, 1934, and among the team that took the ice to face the Leafs were eighteen men who would eventually be chosen as Honoured Members of the Hockey Hall of Fame. Among those selected to participate in what was arguably the first-ever NHL All-Star Game was Eddie Shore.

Tom Gaston remembers the game. "There was a table at centre ice with sweaters on it, and Ace Bailey was there, wearing glasses and a knee-length brown overcoat. He presented each one of the all-stars with a white sweater with 'NHL' running diagonally across the front. The players were introduced by Foster Hewitt in numerical order, so Eddie Shore, wearing his usual Number 2, was the second player to come forward to receive his sweater from Ace. They looked at each other and clasped hands sincerely. That's what the crowd was waiting for, and they went wild! To this day, I think that was the loudest I ever heard a Toronto hockey crowd. It was incredible! As for Ace, he never held a grudge against Shore."

After Bailey had handed out all the all-stars' sweaters, Conn Smythe walked out onto the ice. A hush fell over the Gardens as he handed Ace Bailey his Leafs sweater with the familiar Number 6. "No other player on a Maple Leaf hockey team will ever wear Number 6," he pledged. The crowd erupted once again in a heartfelt show of support for Bailey.

Bailey's Number 6 was the first uniform number to be retired in the NHL. A year later, Boston would retire Lionel Hitchman's Number 3 after his ten-year career as a Bruin came to an end.

Bailey forgave Shore immediately and the two spoke often over the years. "I hold no grudge," Bailey said later. "I see Eddie often when he comes up to Toronto for the games. It was just one of those things that happens."

"Forgiving is one of the hardest things we do as people," Ron Ellis observes, "but it was never hard for Ace. In the years we knew each other, we never even spoke of the incident."

In 1935, Conn Smythe got Bailey a job as coach of the University of Toronto's senior team. Smythe himself had coached the team between 1922 and 1927, before Lester Pearson, the future prime minister of Canada, took over the reins. The team wasn't much when Ace took them over. The University of Toronto Varsity Grads were part of the International Intercollegiate League made up of teams from Harvard, Princeton, Yale, Dartmouth, McGill, the University of Montreal and Queen's. The annual winner of this league won the David Pearson Thompson Trophy. A university publication called *Torontonensis* noted, "Five years of hard work and sacrifice on the part of Ace Bailey has been finally rewarded and the handsome Thompson Trophy comes to Toronto." The team won each of its twenty games that season. With the outbreak of war in Europe, intercollegiate competition ended with the 1939–40 season.

Bailey went on to a successful business career, but he never retired from hockey. For forty-seven years he served as an off-ice official at Maple Leaf Gardens, beginning as a timekeeper in 1937, and he never missed a game. Then, in 1984, Bailey received a letter from the Gardens, informing him his services were no longer required. The letter was signed by Harold Ballard.

It was as a Gardens penalty timekeeper that Bailey spied an industrious winger named Ron Ellis in the mid-1960s.

"Ace Bailey had been watching me — he was there every game. I knew who he was, of course, but there had never been an opportunity to meet with him and talk. We might have said 'hi' in passing, but that was it." Still, Ellis had made an impression on Bailey, and in 1968 the former star would pay Ron the highest of compliments. "For some reason that still amazes me, Ace made a decision to take his Number 6 out of retirement. He went to Harold Ballard and requested that I be allowed to wear his retired sweater number.

"Harold had been pretty fond of my dad, so he might have been very happy to hear that. Harold said, 'Fine.' One day, Ace Bailey stopped me in the hallway at Maple Leaf Gardens and asked me if I would wear his number. He told me it would mean a lot to him if I did.

"This came completely out of left field — I was flabbergasted. It was the greatest honour of my career and I will always be grateful to Ace Bailey."

A press conference was held in the Hot Stove Lounge, adjacent to Maple Leaf Gardens. On hand was Ace's teammate, Joe Primeau. King Clancy, the Leafs' assistant general manager and a teammate of Bailey's, was the master of ceremonies. "Ace Bailey was one of the greatest I ever played with," Clancy remarked, before calling Ron Ellis "one of the greatest kids I ever had anything to do with." Then Bailey handed Ron a Maple Leafs sweater with the reactivated Number 6 sewn onto the back and sleeves. "This is a big occasion for the Bailey family," Ace said shyly. "Ronnie, the very best to you."

"I promise to play with the same style you played," replied Ron.

"In those days, it was an honour to wear certain numbers," says Bob Haggert. "Not now. Number 9 was famous in Toronto as Teeder Kennedy's number. It didn't get issued for a long time after his retirement." Leafs management finally bestowed the number on Dick Duff, whom they felt might become the heir to Kennedy's legacy.

"For Leaf management to give Ace Bailey's Number 6 to Ron Ellis was a monumental event in the team's history," says Haggert. "I worked with Conn Smythe, Hap Day, Harold Ballard and Stafford Smythe, and never once during my years with the Leafs did anyone ever say, 'I wonder what we'll do with 5 or 6.' Those numbers were gone — gone forever. So when it was decided to give Number 6 to Ronnie, it was based on the fact he was a good hockey player, but more importantly, the fact he was a sensational human being. Ace Bailey liked Ron for the person he was, and therefore was honoured to have his number reactivated. It's part of folklore now, but it was a very big deal at the time. The feeling was, of all the people Ace Bailey and Leaf management could think of, who was best suited to wear Number 6? The only name that came up was Ron Ellis."

"Ace and I used to appear at the odd card show together. I really enjoyed it," remembers Ron. "We became close friends. When I was invited to the Team Canada '72 training camp, I told Ace, 'If I make the team, I'm hoping I can wear Number 6 in your honour.' I made the team and got to wear Number 6."

The Maple Leafs planned to honour both Ace Bailey and Bill Barilko by officially retiring their sweater numbers in a pre-game ceremony on April 1, 1992. But a players' strike shut down the league for ten days beginning on March 30. Ace Bailey was admitted to hospital on April 1 after suffering a stroke, and he died on April 7, at the age of 88. He never got to see his sweater raised to the rafters.

A memorial service to celebrate the life of Irvine "Ace" Bailey was held at St. James–Bond United Church in Toronto on May 1, 1992. Fittingly, one of those who spoke at the service was Ron Ellis.

On October 17, 1992, Ace Bailey's Number 6, alongside Bill Barilko's Number 5, was hoisted to the rafters of Maple Leaf Gardens, retired once and for all. Ron Ellis was on the ice with Ace's daughter Joyce during the emotional ceremony.

* * *

The 1968–69 season started off wonderfully for the Leafs' new Number 6. Imlach called Ron Ellis "my best player" and predicted that he would be an NHL All-Star that season. He also stated that

Ron was being groomed to take over as captain of the Maple Leafs when George Armstrong retired. Ron scored a goal in the first game of the season, a 2–1 victory over the Wings in Detroit. But then, he fell into an extended slump. "There's been pressure on me and I've felt it," Ron said at the time. "A lot of people perhaps have been expecting me to be a star and all that jazz. It would be great, but right now, all I'm interested in is getting out of this [slump]. I'm trying not to worry about the slump, but when you're a person who worries, it doesn't matter how many people tell you not to worry — you do anyway."

After starting the season with Norm Ullman as his centre, Ron was moved to a line with Dave Keon and Murray Oliver. "I thought we had a pretty good line," says Keon. Although mired in a mini-slump at the time, Ellis scored his 100th career goal on Christmas night in Chicago.

On January 18, 1969, a Jim Dorey slapshot from the blue line caught Ron in the head and almost tore his ear off. The Leafs physician, Dr. Tait McPhedran, used more than twenty stitches to close a long vertical tear on Ron's ear. Ron missed the next afternoon's game in Boston under orders from the team doctors, who feared a concussion. Coincidentally, in that 5–3 loss to the Bruins, Leafs goaltender Bruce Gamble had to leave the ice after taking a slapshot to the forehead. He was replaced by Johnny Bower, who wore a mask in an NHL game for the first time in his career.

Toronto's next contest was in St. Louis. According to a report in the *Globe and Mail,* Ron was seriously contemplating retirement around that time, but those thoughts must have been erased when Ellis returned to action after his injury and scored 2 goals, including the game winner, against the Blues. "I wasn't puck-shy after the injury. In fact, the reverse was true. I was looser than I had been for several games." Ron wore a helmet, which was specially designed to protect his ear, in the game. "Helmets are awkward and too hot," Ron insisted at the time. "The perspiration runs down my forehead into my eyes and is a nuisance." Still, he conceded, "I guess we should all wear them. It would cut down on injuries." Bruce Gamble also returned to action in that game, and was cut for three stitches over his left eye. Tim Horton, meanwhile, took a six-stitch cut to the head from a high stick.

In early February, Ron was hit in the ear again, in a game against Oakland, and his wound reopened.

After a one-year absence, the Leafs were back in the playoffs in 1969, after accumulating 85 points and finishing in fourth place in the NHL's East Division. Ron finished the season with 25 goals and 21 assists for 46 points. But Toronto was no match for the powerful Boston Bruins, who won the best-of-seven quarterfinal series in four straight games. In game one, the Bruins demolished the Leafs 10–0 in Boston. The next night, Boston spanked Toronto again, this time by a 7–0 margin. "It was embarrassing," says a subdued Ron Ellis. "It was my lowest moment as a Leaf. I think Davey Keon and I felt it the most. I know when we came back to Toronto, we were able to make it closer, but we still lost both games by a goal. It was definitely the end of an era."

CHAPTER ELEVEN

New Regime

Immediately after the Boston Bruins swept the Toronto Maple
Leafs in the first round of the 1969 playoffs, Leafs owner Stafford
Smythe fired the team's coach and general manager of the past
eleven years, Punch Imlach. "It was probably time," says Ron Ellis.
"I had total respect for Mr. Imlach, what he was able to do and the
team he brought together. He turned me pro, so I certainly
respect him from that perspective."

Imlach had joined the Toronto Maple Leafs as assistant general
manager in 1958, and soon afterwards was promoted to GM.
Twenty games into the 1958–59 season, Imlach fired coach Billy
Reay and assumed the bench duties himself. He held both port-
folios for the next eleven years, coaching 760 regular-season
games and chalking up a record of 365–270–125. Along the way,
the Maple Leafs celebrated four Stanley Cup championships.

"Punch was a great bench coach," Ron observes. "He was not
the best practice coach. Practices were very basic, very mechanical. We very seldom practised the power play. We never had a set
power play unit during the '60s. Punch's approach was to send out
whichever line was next up when a penalty was called. That's why
the Leafs never had a scoring leader; Punch wanted to have balanced scoring from all three lines. And it paid off. But if you had
put Frank Mahovlich or Davey Keon on the point during a power
play, they would have quickly moved into the top ten scoring
leaders.

"I tip my hat to Punch, though, because he was very seldom out-
coached. If he wanted to match lines, he got his way. He was a
good motivator and a good judge of talent. He could see the merit
in players that other teams had given up on. Punch was a better
general manager than a coach."

Bob Haggert weighs in with his opinion of the deposed Leafs coach. "Punch was a tough guy to work for, but I got along with him well. He let me do my job. He listened to what I had to say. But there was no question that he was the ultimate boss. When it came to letting you know who was in charge, Punch was a tyrant. I thought he was a good coach, but I thought he was a brilliant general manager and a brilliant motivator. He had a lot of gimmicks, but he made them interesting.

"In the days when we were travelling by train, Punch went up and down the aisle giving everybody on the team an autographed copy of Norman Vincent Peale's *Power of Positive Thinking*. I still have mine. He went out and bought thirty copies and said, 'Read this.' He was a master of thinking, 'We play eighty games — we can win eighty.' Great motivator."

In Imlach's place, Jim Gregory was named general manager while John McLellan was promoted from Tulsa to take over as coach. "I'd spent a lot of time travelling with the Leafs through the years and a lot of the Leaf players used to practise with the teams I coached [St. Mike's and the Marlboros] when they were injured and in rehab," Gregory says. "Between those players and the Leafs I coached in junior, I knew almost all of the team very well."

Dave Keon was named captain of the Toronto Maple Leafs, succeeding George Armstrong. "It was an honour to be the captain. I don't think I placed any more emphasis on that than I did on trying to be a good player," comments the classy Keon. Ron Ellis was made an alternate captain.

"I was very happy to see Jim Gregory come in," Ellis attests. "We certainly had our ties with the Marlies and we had kept up our friendship over the years."

Gregory explains his circuitous route to the general manager's office. "I left coaching with the beginning of the 1965–66 season on the advice of Stafford Smythe. He told me I should concentrate on being a manager. It hurt my feelings at the time, but it certainly was good advice. I stayed with the Marlboros until the 1966–67 season. We won the Memorial Cup that season. I was the general manager and Gus Bodnar was the coach. I went to coach the Vancouver Canucks of the Western Hockey League in '68–69, then I came back and scouted for the Maple Leafs for a couple months and was named manager of the Toronto Maple Leafs in April 1969.

John McLellan's ties to the Maple Leafs extended back as far as 1947, when he was part of the St. Michael's team that won the Memorial Cup. During the 1951–52 season, McLellan had been called up from Toronto's AHL affiliate, the Pittsburgh Hornets, to play in two games as a left winger for the Maple Leafs.

Ron calls McLellan "a wonderful, wonderful man. I liked Johnny. I think he was almost too nice to be an NHL coach. He handled the players well but let the press get the best of him.

"I thought he and Jim Gregory complemented each other well. There was certainly the knowledge that John and Jim worked closely together, whereas Punch and Harold didn't. Punch wanted to run his own show.

"There's one story about Johnny McLellan that I remember well," Ron says, snickering. "We usually had a tough time winning in Los Angeles. We looked at it as a bit of a break from a tough schedule — something a lot of teams did. Of course, Marcel Dionne and the boys were just waiting for us, because they knew that we were looking at it as a holiday, and they'd jump all over us. We were down 3–0 very quickly during one game against the Kings. I'm one of the veterans of the team, and Johnny said, 'Ron, I'm going to have to throw a tantrum here.' And that wasn't John's style. But he came into the dressing room and started ranting and raving about our efforts — and for emphasis, he kicked over the garbage can in the centre of the room.

"Out popped one of the players' six-pack of beer, wrapped in ice! We all looked at each other, then we all looked at John, and everybody started laughing. We came back and won the game," howls Ron.

Until this point, Ron had negotiated his own contracts, but in 1969 he retained Alan Eagleson as his agent. Eagleson had been close to the Toronto Maple Leafs since the early '60s, when he formed an investment club with Bob Pulford, Bob Baun, Carl Brewer, Billy Harris and an assortment of business acquaintances and associates.

"Bobby Haggert, who had been working on player endorsements after retiring as Leafs trainer, said, 'I've got two guys who would like to talk to you about representing them on their contracts,'" Eagleson says. "Paul Henderson and Ronnie Ellis came in together. That's when we started acting for Ronnie and Paul.

"I had three accountants. I put Paul with Marvin Goldblatt and

I put Ronnie with Graeme Clarke. I could assess their personalities and I knew which would work better with which accountant. Over the next twelve years, I negotiated Ronnie's contracts." Eagleson was not only a pioneer amongst player agents, but he was known as a shrewd negotiator. "Ronnie always underestimated his own abilities. It was my job to overestimate them. He was much better paid as a result of our intervention. I don't blame Imlach. His job was to get the players signed for the least amount of money. Mine was to get them the most."

Ron scored 7 goals in the team's first nine games, but couldn't buy a goal for several games after that. The slump broke, however, and by the time the mid-season All-Star voting results were announced on January 5, Ellis was the highest-scoring right winger in the NHL with 18 goals. Montreal Canadiens coach Claude Ruel named him to the East Division All-Star team, where he played on a line with Dave Keon and Bobby Hull. "I got a lot of static for picking Keon and Ellis," Ruel admitted at the time, "but I knew what I was doing. When I put them with Bobby Hull, I had a great line — almost perfect."

In a special article written for a Toronto newspaper, Punch Imlach wrote, "There is no question Ron Ellis is the best right winger in the league. He has a tougher job than [Gordie] Howe in a number of ways. He isn't usually on for power plays and is on a last-place team. That makes it harder to get chances for goals. Ellis is also a two-way hockey player."

The Toronto Maple Leafs finished last in the East Division in 1969–70. Only 7 points separated first-place Chicago from fifth-place Montreal. Toronto was a distant 21 points behind the fifth-place Canadiens, who also missed the playoffs. Ron led the Leafs in goals scored with a career-high 35. His 54 points placed him fourth on the Leafs that season.

"I remember I climbed onto the bus after one game," laments Ron. "Johnny McLellan was really giving it his all. He was really trying. I sat beside him and said, 'John, I feel bad. I let you down tonight. I could be playing better.' All John said was, 'Keep doing what you're doing.' We just didn't have the talent. We had a pretty dismal team.

"From a personal standpoint, it was a good season, but from a team point of view, it was brutal. I was really starting to question whether I was going to play much longer," Ellis says. "I was the kind of player who put too much pressure on himself. I know that. It's part of my makeup. I took the game home. I envied the guys who could leave the game at the rink. I replayed the game and I replayed my mistakes. There are pros and cons to that, but I took it too far, to the point that it was detrimental to my confidence. I loved the game, but those were real tough years. Playing in Toronto, the hockey Mecca, made it that much tougher."

A *Toronto Star* article from the period commented on the weight that seemed to rest heavily on Ron's shoulders during that forgettable season: "Things have been dismal with the Leafs this season. Most of the time, the Leafs' mood is that which befits a last-place team. Ellis, a strong team man, is especially prone to moodiness." The *Telegram* suggested, "There is only one fault Ellis has consistently displayed since he came into the NHL. He tries too hard."

A headline above a *Globe and Mail* story reported, "Ellis glum about hockey future in spite of his 35-goal season — enjoyment gone." The article said, "Ron Ellis, the top goal scorer of the Toronto Maple Leafs, calls the hockey season just completed the most miserable of his NHL career. A last-place team has odd effects on even its best players. 'I'm not sure about hockey anymore. I don't enjoy it like I did my first couple of seasons. It's just not something I want to spend fifteen years of my life on.'"

During the season, Ron Ellis showed another side of his talents. Brian McFarlane, the *Hockey Night in Canada* commentator, discovered that Ron had become quite an accomplished singer and guitarist, and arranged to tape a performance by Ron and some friends, to be aired between periods of a Wednesday-night telecast.

"Doug Moore was an engineer at the Gardens," Ron explains. "Dougie looked after the ice, and we had become friends. He taught me to play a few chords on the guitar in the boiler room. Brian McFarlane arranged for Doug, his son Louie and me to go to a retirement hom and entertain the folks there, and it was taped for *Hockey Night in Canada*. We played 'King of the Road' and 'Green, Green Grass of Home.' We had fun doing it."

The *Globe and Mail* marvelled that the shy winger would make such an appearance. "Ron Ellis is not your average athlete. He's quiet, very polite and self-effacing. It is a toss-up which would embarrass him more — singing in public or saying something nice about himself. It took the *Hockey Night in Canada* people a long time to convince Ron to record the song."

Another writer suggested, with tongue planted firmly in cheek, that Ron might have to change his name: "Buck Ellis. Or Cowboy Ellis, or Rompin' Ronnie Ellis, even. And he'll need some musical backing, too. Stan Obodiac, the publicity man, could beat the drum. Mike Walton could blow his own horn."

"Doug was the kind of guy you'd invite to a house party, and he'd end up pulling out his guitar and singing a few songs. He used to perform a song he wrote called 'Swingin' Right Winger.' It was about me, and he got most of the boys' names into the song," Ron laughs.

"My two brothers, Roger and Randy, are very talented musicians," Ron continues. "When we had the camp, we would have a singalong every Saturday night. We all played. One brother played the banjo, the other played lead and I plunked away at the bass. The guests really looked forward to it every Saturday night. And this wasn't just a few people. When you have a camp and cottages, two or three hundred people might show up. We held the event in the rec hall and invited our guests to take part in an impromptu amateur show. It was amazing how much talent came forward to help us out. I have good memories of those singalongs."

As the 1970–71 season, Toronto again struggled. Of their first six games, the Leafs won but one — the home opener against St. Louis. Ron had yet to score to that point in the season. But life got a lot brighter for Ron Ellis on October 28, 1970.

In a home game that evening against Montreal, Ron scored his first goal of the season, the winning goal in a 6–2 romp over the Canadiens. He also added a pair of assists. But more importantly, Ron and Jan Ellis received word that the baby they planned to adopt would be ready to be picked up the next day.

In the January 2, 1971, edition of *Weekend* magazine, Harry Sinden, who had coached the Bruins to a Stanley Cup title in 1970, chose his personal all-star team. His selections differed substantially from those made by the NHL Writers' Association, who chose the official All-Star Teams. Sinden and the writers were of one mind in choosing Bobby Orr, Phil Esposito and Bobby Hull, but Sinden chose Leafs goaltender Jacques Plante instead of Tony Esposito, Jacques Laperriere in place of Brad Park and Ron Ellis over Gordie Howe.

"I have always watched Howe with awe, but the choice is being made in terms of now and not for the wonderful years Howe has given the game," Sinden wrote. "You won't find many left wingers who will argue over my choice of Ellis at right wing. Ellis is awful hard to check and he hurts with his own checking. As for offensive ability, what was the matter with 35 goals with the last-place Toronto Maple Leafs?"

The Leafs improved from 71 points in 1969–70 to 82 in 1970–71, finishing the season in fourth place in the revamped East Division. (The league's second expansion in three years had added the Buffalo Sabres and the Vancouver Canucks to the East, while the established Chicago Blackhawks moved to the West Division.) Ron Ellis finished the season in fourth place in team scoring, contributing 24 goals, 29 assists and 53 points. Linemates Ullman and Henderson added 85 and 60 points respectively. But while the team was winning and his linemates were scoring, Ellis went through a stretch where he didn't score for fourteen games. He thought of quitting and talked about it actively with Jan. "It was the most frustrating year I ever had," says Ron. "The only reason he rejected jumping off the roof of Maple Leaf Gardens was that he was afraid he might not hit the ground," the *Telegram* cracked. Coach John McLellan was quoted as saying, "I could never fault Ellis all year. He always tries so hard. He never quits."

Darryl Sittler debuted as a Maple Leaf in 1970–71, scoring 10 goals and 8 assists. "I knew all about Ronnie Ellis from watching him on *Hockey Night in Canada* when I was growing up in St. Jacob's, Ontario. Even though I was a Canadiens fan, I respected Ron and thought he was a classy guy," smiles Sittler.

"The draft in 1970 was not the big media deal that it is today," Sittler continues. "Today, it's a public relations event. But in 1970, I was working away — building swimming pools — and I heard that I'd been drafted on the radio that Saturday morning. That's how I found out I was the Leafs' first pick. It wasn't until two days later that I talked to some of the folks with the Leafs. I was honoured to be going to Toronto.

"At my first training camp, which was held at Maple Leaf Gardens, Jim Gregory walked me into the dressing room and pointed out my stall. A Leaf sweater with Number 27 was hanging there. I knew what that number meant to the fans of Toronto and to the Maple Leafs. Frank Mahovlich had worn that number and he had been a star through the '60s, so when they gave me 27, it was significant."

Another newcomer to the Maple Leafs was Brian Spencer. An immediate fan favourite, the eight-year NHL veteran began his career with two seasons in Toronto. But tragedy seemed to follow Spencer. On December 9, 1970, the Leafs beat Montreal and, shortly after the game, Spencer's wife gave birth to a baby girl. Excited, Spencer called his parents in Fort St. James, British Columbia to tell them the news, and added that he was going to be featured on the telecast of Toronto's game against the Chicago Blackhawks on Saturday, December 12. Brian's father Roy discovered shortly before game time that the Leafs game was not going to be broadcast by the CBC's Prince George affiliate, which had decided instead to carry the Vancouver Canucks–California Golden Seals contest. Incensed, Roy Spencer drove the 150 kilometres to the station, armed and argumentative, and when the station wouldn't switch to the Toronto game, Spencer took several station employees hostage. The Mounties arrived, and when the argument turned violent, Roy Spencer fired at the police. He was immediately shot and killed outside the TV station. That same night, Brian Spencer was named one of the game's three stars, assisting on both goals in a 2–1 victory over the Hawks.

After retiring from hockey, Brian Spencer never really settled down. He became a mechanic in Florida and in 1982, was implicated in a murder. While incarcerated in a Florida prison on the first-degree murder charge, Brian wrote, "I remember my days as a Toronto Maple Leaf with a lot of pride. Every time I would skate out to a game in Maple Leaf Gardens, my heart would pump twice as fast. 'The Spin' [Spencer's nickname was "Spinner"] gave his heart, and I couldn't wait to get to the rink every day. The fans were so good to me." Although acquitted of the murder charge, a point-blank gunshot blast ended Spencer's life on June 3, 1988. Wistfully, Ron recalls, "I got along with Brian. We had a rapport. As one of the veterans, I took it upon myself to make him feel part of the team. When he asked for my opinion on something, I tried to advise him the best that I could."

That spring of 1971, Toronto faced the powerful New York Rangers in the quarterfinals. New York had finished second in the East with 109 points. The Rangers pushed the Leafs aside in six games, with former Leaf Bob Nevin scoring an overtime goal in game six to clinch the series for the Rangers.

* * *

During the off-season, the Ontario Ministry of the Attorney General concluded a two-year investigation of Toronto Maple Leaf owners Stafford Smythe and Harold Ballard, during which special prosecutor Clayton Powell interviewed 180 people. The investigation discovered that cheques written between 1964 and 1969 by the Ontario Hockey Association to the Toronto Marlboro Hockey Club had been deposited in a separate account under the name S.H. Marlie. The "S" stood for Stafford, the "H" for Harold. Only Ballard and Smythe had access to this account, and they used the money to cover personal expenses. In addition, the two had hired Cloke Construction to do extensive remodelling of Maple Leaf Gardens — and to carry out renovations on their own homes. All invoices were charged back to Maple Leaf Gardens.

In July 1969, the federal government had charged Ballard and Smythe with tax evasion. Ballard was charged with failing to declare $134,685 in income, while Smythe was alleged to have pocketed $278,919. In June 1971, the Attorney General of Ontario charged Smythe and Ballard with the theft of $146,000. Both were also charged with fraud; in Ballard's case, worth $83,000 and Smythe in the amount of $249,000.

The pair were scheduled to face trial on October 25, 1971, but Smythe became gravely ill and died on October 13. The Leafs' game against Detroit, which had been scheduled for that evening, was postponed until November 1.

* * *

After Tim Horton was traded to the New York Rangers in the spring of 1970 and George Armstrong retired after the 1970–71 season, "All of a sudden, I jumped in seniority to number two behind Keon," Ron says. "It was just an indication of the major facelift the Leafs had undergone in a very short time." Ron was just 26 years old and was entering his eighth season as a Toronto Maple Leaf as the 1971–72 season opened.

"Davey Keon was our captain and he did a great job," Ellis says. "He led by example. I was still trying to find my way. I was reserved and pretty quiet. I just went about my job. My whole way of trying to lead as a veteran and assistant captain was through my work ethic. He wasn't very vocal, either, but when he spoke, you would be wise to listen because he had a great hockey mind. If you had to name a 'rah-rah' guy in the room, Michael Walton was a bit of one. Although Davey and I were not especially close off the ice, we had a mutual respect."

"Ronnie was a very good player. He worked really hard, he really cared about winning and he cared about his own play," Keon says. "When you came through the system, there were certain ideas that were planted in you that the team was really important and then, after the team is successful, you'll be successful, as opposed to 'I'll be successful and then the team will be successful.' The team concept always came first. And Ronnie was very diligent in working at that. He was no different than myself — when we didn't play well, we weren't happy. When we played well, we were happy, but there was still work to be done. He was a professional and that's how he approached it."

By the time the Leafs played the rescheduled game against Detroit, they had posted a disappointing record of 2–5–3. The match on November 1 was the first Monday-night game in the history of Maple Leaf Gardens. Paced by Ron Ellis's third career hat trick — to which he added an assist — Toronto whipped the Wings 6–1. It was one of the few highlights in a challenging year for the Maple Leafs. Nevertheless, Toronto earned 80 points to secure a fourth-place finish in the East Division. Ron scored 23 goals and 24 assists for 47 points. Linemate Norm Ullman led the Leafs with 73 points, while Paul Henderson was Toronto's top goal scorer with 38. It was the highest total Henderson achieved in his professional hockey career.

The playoffs pitted the Maple Leafs against the high-flying Boston Bruins, who had finished first overall in 1971–72 with 119 points. Their 330 goals scored were 121 more than Toronto had mustered during the regular season. Boston finished off the Leafs in five games to advance to the semifinals.

* * *

Ballard's trial was set for May 1972, but in the meantime, Harold repaid the money taken from Maple Leaf Gardens and paid the income tax demanded by the government. As a result, the tax evasion charges were dropped, but Clayton Powell proceeded with the theft and fraud charges. After one piece of damning evidence after another had been presented, the judge convicted Harold Ballard on forty-seven of the forty-nine charges of fraud or theft of money, goods and services in the amount of $205,000.

Sentencing was scheduled for September 7, 1972, but Alan Eagleson interceded and was able to get the date postponed so Ballard could attend the 1972 Canada-USSR Summit Series. On October 20, Ballard was sentenced to two concurrent three-year sentences — one for theft and one for fraud. He was taken to Millhaven Correctional Institute, a minimum-security prison near Kingston, Ontario.

Ballard was released from prison after serving nine months. And by this time he was the principal owner of Maple Leaf Gardens and the Toronto Maple Leafs, having purchased his deceased partner's shares.

Ron gets noticeably sad when he remembers this dark period of Toronto Maple Leafs history. "The only things we knew were those things written in the papers. We didn't have access to people who could fill us in with further details. Harold had a pretty close-knit and close-mouthed group around him, so we didn't get inside information — at least, I certainly didn't. But we knew there was something happening.

"I've got to be honest — it was embarrassing. It really tainted the image of the Maple Leafs. I was so proud to be a Maple Leaf. This was my team. Toronto was where I wanted to play. It was very important for me to finish my career in Toronto. I took a lot less money along the way to make that happen because I wanted to be known as a Leaf.

"It was a huge day for me when I played my 1,000th game as a Maple Leaf. They can never take that away from me. A lot of guys played for the Leafs, but I'm fifth in line for most games played as a Toronto Maple Leaf. I played 1,034 games. Only George Armstrong, Tim Horton, Borje Salming and Dave Keon played more games for Toronto than I did. I'm very proud of that. So, for me to feel that way about the Toronto Maple Leafs and then to have the owner in jail was hard to swallow."

Ellis admits it was hard on his teammates. "We had to put up with all the write-ups and talk shows. But once you're on the ice and the puck's dropped, you focus. That's just part of being a professional. You know what your job is and you do it to the best of your ability every night. It was frustrating to read all the news about Harold, especially his running the Gardens from a jail cell. I respected the Toronto Maple Leaf tradition so much that this bothered me a lot.

"I wish it had never happened.

"When Harold Ballard, Stafford Smythe and John Bassett ran the team together, there were checks and balances. When Harold took over the Gardens solely, there was a change. It was strictly one man's personality, one man's stubbornness and one man's lack of vision. Decisions were made that were personal and the good of the team was not taken into consideration. And I had to play through that. The fans were upset and it was the players who had to take the abuse.

"Harold didn't seem to care," Ron scowls. "They couldn't get near him, but they sure could boo the hell out of us."

CHAPTER TWELVE

Da Da Canada

Over the course of a couple of weeks in the autumn of 1972, what had been billed as a friendly international match turned into a quest to defend the honour of Canadian hockey — and indeed, the Canadian way of life.

"The Stanley Cup championship was my career highlight while wearing the blue and white. However, winning the Summit Series while wearing the red leaf was the highlight of my career," beams Ron Ellis.

"Again, the timing was right, as I was fortunate to be at the peak of my skills just at the time they were constructing the team. I was 26 years old and at the top of my game. It was such an honour to represent my country in that series."

Alan Eagleson was the driving force behind the tournament. "In 1969, Hockey Canada said, 'Why don't you go to the World Championships and see what you can organize with the other countries?' I met with the Russians, the Czechs, the Swedes, the Finns and the Germans. Out of that, my relationship with these countries was very solid. In fairness, my job in the negotiations for the eight-game series was to make sure we got the players there. I met the Russians, so I knew they were interested."

Eagleson explains the genesis of the 1972 Summit Series. "We sent a team to Russia in 1969. Wayne Carleton played, and so did Jim McKenny and five or six other NHL players. We played seven or eight games against Russian teams and did very well — won four out of seven, as I recall. That turned the Russians off. Watching our minor-league players, with seven NHLers thrown in, do well against them made the Russians think that they may not be ready yet. As a result of that, they wouldn't allow an open team for the 1970 World Championships." The Worlds were scheduled to be played in Winnipeg in 1970, hence the desire for an "open" team that would include NHL players, who had so far been banned from the competition. When the International Ice Hockey Federation gave the proposal a thumbs-down, Canada withdrew from the World Championships. "We had to do it to stand up to the Russians," Eagleson maintains.

In the spring of 1972, Doug Fisher, an important cog in the Hockey Canada machine, insisted that Eagleson fly immediately to Prague. "My wife Nancy and I flew to Frankfurt that night. I asked General Motors for a car, so when I got to Frankfurt, there was a car waiting for me, and we drove to Prague. The Cold War was at its height. The lineup at the border was forty or fifty cars long. I couldn't wait, so I left Nancy in the car and walked up to the front of the line.

"I said, 'Hey, I gotta get through!'

"'What are you doing?' the guy said in broken English.

"I said, 'Hockey. Canada.'

"The guy acknowledged. 'Oh, Canada.' So I took him back to my car and I opened up my trunk. I had lots of stuff with pictures of Bobby Orr and Phil Esposito. I was flabbergasted! This guy knew every NHL player! He brought me up to the front of the line and away we went."

Alan remembers the result of the trip. "By the time we got to Prague, Charlie Hay, the chairman of Hockey Canada; Lou Lefaive, the head of Sport Canada; and Joe Kryczka, the president of the Canadian Amateur Hockey Association, were coming out of a meeting and told me they'd made a deal with the Russians. But they needed my assurance that I could deliver the players.

"I didn't like the deal. They'd agreed to eight games — I wanted seven. The first four would be in Canada, the last four in Russia. The Russians didn't want NHL referees — they had to be IIHF referees.

"I said, 'This is a bad deal.' But it was a done deal at that point.

"In fairness, just like every other Canadian, I thought we'd win all eight games 10–1," smirks Eagleson. "But Hockey Canada was formed to get our best against their best, and we'd been working on this for many years, so what the hell?"

On April 20, 1972, Hockey Canada and the Soviet hockey authorities announced an eight-game exhibition series between all-stars from the world's two most powerful hockey nations. The series would take place in September — as Eagleson pointed out, four games would be played in Canada and four in the Soviet Union. A share of the Canadian team's proceeds was pledged to the National Hockey League players' pension plan.

The Soviet National Team was a juggernaut, having won gold medals in hockey at the 1964, 1968 and 1972 Winter Olympic Games. They had also won the World Championships every year between 1963 and 1970.

"We made the announcement that Canada and Russia were going to play. Then, NHL president Clarence Campbell made the announcement that no NHL players would be permitted to play," sighs Alan. "So, as soon as I got back, I met with Bill Wirtz, who was chairman of the NHL board of governors. I said, 'Billy, I'm telling you right now, if the NHL says no, I've got enough clients — we'll play.' I had 150 clients in the NHL at that time. 'We'll play,' I said, 'but we don't want to play without the sanction of the NHL.'

"Wirtz was terrific. He persuaded Clarence Campbell to lay off. Then he asked, 'Who are you going to get to run the team?' I knew Harry Sinden from Bobby Orr's days in Boston. Harry was out of hockey; he was building homes in Rochester and was looking to get back into hockey. He said he'd do it." When Eagleson met with Sinden, the latter man said the first person he wanted to recruit was John Ferguson, the Montreal Canadiens' tough guy. "We wanted him to be a playing coach. Harry and Fergie didn't really even know each other, but there was a great deal of respect there. I knew Fergie well. When we met with him, he said, 'Harry and Al, I'll do anything you want, but I'm not playing.'" Ferguson had just retired. "He said, 'I can't play anymore and I won't play anymore. As long as you understand that I'm not here as a player, I'd be happy to coach.'"

Eagleson formed a management group referred to as "Team 5," which was made up of himself, Sinden, Ferguson, Bob Haggert and Mike Cannon. Haggert, the former trainer for the Toronto Maple Leafs, had retired after the 1967–68 NHL season and immediately got into the player representation business, handling product endorsements. Cannon was the National Hockey League Players' Association's director of operations. This group began the process of winnowing out the roster that would take on the

Soviets' best. "We went over the lists of all 500 players playing on the sixteen NHL teams at that time," remembers Haggert.

"The first fifteen players were automatic," Eagleson observes. "After discussion, we got down to twenty-five guys or so. Then, we knew we needed five or six guys as cannon fodder. They might play in exhibition games, but that was about all.

"The last three forwards picked were probably Henderson, Ellis and Clarke," Eagleson remembers. "The last centre spot was a choice between Dave Keon and Bob Clarke." As Eagleson remembers it, Sinden was very much in favour of Keon, while Ferguson was a Clarke booster. "The only input of any consequence that I contributed was when they asked me what I thought. I said, 'Take a look at the statistical data.'" Clarke had 81 points in 1971–72, while Keon had 48.

In all, thirty-five NHL players were invited to Team Canada's training camp, along with three players who had been drafted but had yet to turn pro: Billy Harris, John Van Boxmeer and Michel Larocque. "That made it thirty-eight players, which enabled us to play intra-squad games," Haggert recalls. "When we got into the series with the Russians, [Harris, Van Boxmeer and Larocque] went to their NHL teams." In Harris's case, it was the New York Islanders, while the other two were Canadiens prospects.

"The only player to turn us down was Dallas Smith," Eagleson reveals. "Nobody knew what this series was going to become at that stage, and Dallas wanted to bring in the crop on his farm."

One of Ellis's teammates was the beneficiary of that decision. "I thank God every day of my life for Dallas Smith choosing not to play for Team Canada in '72," smiles former defenceman Brian Glennie.

One of those who would miss the chance to play for Team Canada, but not by choice, was Eagleson's most famous client, Bobby Orr. "We wanted to be able to have him if he could play," Eagleson says. "But he had just gone through the big operation on his knee that summer, and then he put on about thirty or forty pounds that year. He warmed up in a scrimmage in Russia. It was great for the players to know that Orr was there, and it was a great public relations advantage to have him involved."

On July 12, 1972, Harry Sinden announced the names of the thirty-five Canadian-born NHLers who would be reporting for training camp at Maple Leaf Gardens on August 14.

"I thought there was an outside possibility they might need a player like me, particularly with thirty-five guys on the roster," admits Ellis. "I would have been happy to be one of those thirty-five guys. I didn't know this for many years, but my understanding is that John Ferguson is the guy who really lobbied for me. He knew what I could do and I guess he felt my skills might be helpful.

"When I played against John, he knew I could play both ends of the ice. At Team Canada's twenty-fifth anniversary celebration, I went up to John and said, 'I've heard you were responsible for my being here today, and I just want you to know I appreciate it.' And John said something like, 'Well, you deserved it.'

"John is a good man — a great team player and a good hockey man."

"Harry and Fergie picked a very good team," acknowledges Alan Eagleson. "They didn't pick thirty-five all-stars. They had their choice of everybody in the league, and there were a lot of very good players left off the team. And conversely, there were guys like Hadfield, Gilbert and Ratelle who were automatic choices, but by the time the series was underway, Hadfield wasn't happy because he couldn't play against that competition.

"He's blamed me forever. But I had nothing to do with it. Harry said, 'You're on the team. If you want to quit, you quit!'"

Ron Ellis doesn't have to think too long to come up with one of his fondest memories of the Summit Series. "It would be the first day we skated on the ice at training camp, and I realized that here I am, skating on the ice with the best Canadian-born players in the world. It was a real eye-opener. I was thrilled to be invited to the training camp, but it really didn't hit me until that first day when I was skating around with Esposito, Gilbert, Dryden, Lapointe, and on and on and on. That will be a memory I cherish for a long time."

"Just being chosen to play on this team was a pretty big thrill," Henderson agrees. "This was the elite of the NHL."

Ron hesitates and begins to smile. "It was strange to be skating around with guys you played against and butted heads with. Don Awrey and I used to have a good competition. He was playing for Boston at the time. Don's a good, hard player — a solid NHLer. I came down on him many, many nights. He gave me trouble because he was such a great skater. He had the habit of sticking that butt end out to pull you back. We respected each other greatly, but we didn't like playing against each other very much. I remember I skated up beside him at that first practice and said, 'It's kind of nice to be on the same team with you for a change!' Those memories are very special to me."

Brian Glennie comments on Team Canada's experience. "I got chosen as one of the thirty-five, although I was a spectator against the Russians. It was great to watch Henny [Paul Henderson], Clarkie [Bobby Clarke] and Ronnie play. Hell, they were supposed to be the checking line. I couldn't believe how well Ronnie played — there was nobody on the team who could skate like him."

Ron's mood takes a turn for the serious. "One of the problems we had to overcome on the team was that there were guys who didn't like each other. People didn't realize that. It took a while. In fact, it wasn't until we got to Sweden that we became a team. We were at a team meeting and Phil Esposito was spearheading it, but somebody said, 'Hey, guys — put the egos and animosity on the back burner! We've got a job to do here!'

"Players didn't fraternize in those days. That was just the way it was — you were butting heads with these guys game after game after game. A lot of old animosities were there."

"I appreciated how great a leader Phil Esposito was," Glennie says. "To be honest, I didn't like him when I first met him at training camp, but I learned to really care for the guy."

"In those days, players did not socialize with the opposition," says Rod Seiling, Ellis's teammate on the 1964 Memorial Cup–winning Marlboros squad, who was selected from the New York Rangers to play with Team Canada '72. "But if you knew someone, you certainly didn't ignore them. All the years I was playing in New York, I certainly didn't lose any respect for Ron. And we would have occasion to bump into one another, not just on the ice, and we'd talk and reacquaint ourselves. In those days, we had no fraternization, but we had a lot more respect for each other than the guys do today.

"Coming to Team Canada's training camp, it was great to know Ron was there and to know that you had a friend already trying out for the team along with you," Seiling continues. "From that perspective alone, having someone you know being part of the process always makes it a lot easier. Being able to become a teammate again and reacquaint myself with Ron and Jan was great."

The members of Team Canada worked out for a week, then

played three intra-squad games. It was the only game action the team would see before the series began. "We stayed at the Sutton Place Hotel and trained a couple of times a day," Ron recalls. "We had a good training camp. It may not have been as strenuous as a normal Maple Leaf training camp, but we worked hard."

Ellis dismisses the fact that Team Canada didn't prepare properly. "There was very little opportunity to prepare against the Russians. There were no game films to review. What we got were some highlights — we couldn't watch a whole game. Our coaches were certainly restricted in that area. We sent Bob Davidson and John McLellan, from the Leaf staff, over to scout the Russians. They saw Tretiak play a game or two and he got bombed, so they reported what they saw. They weren't given proper information."

The Canadian scouts spent just four days in Russia. Tretiak did, in fact, let in 8 goals in one exhibition game attended by Davidson and McLellan; but what the two advance men didn't know at the time was that the goaltender was getting married the next day and was battling a hangover as much as he was battling the puck. The Soviet scouts, on the other hand, spent two weeks in Canada, watching each of Team Canada's practices and intra-squad games. Still, Alan Eagleson says, "I don't think the Russians scouted us any more than we scouted them."

"I thought we had the firepower to win, no question," admits Ron. "I think, as a whole, the Canadian team went into the series very confidently. I remember Bobby Clarke being interviewed one time and he said, 'I look around and see the quality of the players here and wonder who can beat us.' He made a good point. Personally, however, I must say I was not quite as enthusiastic as my teammates that we would win the series easily. The Russians certainly were Olympic champions and had been World Champions and they had been defeating some pretty good hockey clubs, including some top amateur Canadian teams — with former pros in the lineup — that we'd sent over for international competition."

Ron thinks back to his previous experience playing the Soviets. "I had a chance to play against the Russians in 1963, when I was a junior. We had a great all-star team, and they whipped us 6–0 and didn't even break a sweat. It was embarrassing. And that was a number of years prior to 1972. So there was no question in my mind that the Russians were developing as a hockey power. I was prepared for a pretty good series. I doubted we'd win all eight games by a landslide. That was a question mark for me."

Bob Clarke, who is the general manager of the Philadelphia Flyers today, but a linemate of Ellis's in 1972, agrees. "I think there was a lot of arrogance on our part that we were going to beat the Russians eight straight games. As hard as the coaches tried to prepare us, many of our players weren't in very good shape at the start. They hadn't worked too hard through camp and some of them felt like they were making a huge sacrifice just to give up their summers to be there. Guys like Henderson and Ellis and myself, if we were going to play any games, we had to work exceptionally hard, so our conditioning was probably better than a lot of the guys. Not all of them; some were like us in that they had to work exceptionally hard, but we had some players who didn't work very hard and then, when the series started, they just weren't ready for it."

In the days leading up to the series, the North American media painted a picture of Team Canada's members as virtual Supermen — invincible to anything the Soviets could throw against them. "The NHL team will slaughter them in eight straight," predicted the *New York Times*. *Sports Illustrated* predicted that Canada would win seven of eight. The Southam News Service predicted, "Canada will win seven, with one game tied on Russian ice." Johnny Esaw, who was working for CTV at the time, was quoted as saying, "The Russians will win one here, one in Russia," for a 6–2 outcome. The *Toronto Star* predicted, "Canada will win handily. Say, 7–1."

Even sports celebrities expected Canada to dominate. "Eight straight for Canada," the legendary goaltender Jacques Plante said confidently. Former NHL referee Red Storey agreed, but said the toughest win would be in game one. Alan Eagleson, although hardly objective as the key organizer of the Summit Series, declared, "We gotta win in eight games. Anything less than an unblemished sweep of the Russians would bring shame down upon the heads of the players and the national pride."

One of those who did not share the pundits' confidence was Harry Sinden, Team Canada's coach. "I just didn't know how good this Russian team was, or what to really expect from it," he wrote in his book, *Hockey Showdown*. "Frankly, I started to be a little afraid. I knew we weren't in the condition they were, and I had the feeling maybe we were not quite as good as I thought we were. My main worry was the pace they played at."

"We just tried to put together the best team we had and the best units we could," Ellis says. "You put together a line of Phil Esposito, Yvan Cournoyer and Frank Mahovlich and you're going to say, 'Wow!' In the NHL, that line would have been phenomenal. Against the Russians, that line had trouble. They're all offensive-minded guys who weren't called on to play defensive roles to any great degree. We realized we had to develop a team that could do everything. We needed players who could play in both ends of the rink. We needed power-play specialists and we needed penalty killers. We needed toughness and finesse. We couldn't go with just the goal scorers."

Harry Sinden wrote, "The best line in training camp was the one that had Bobby Clarke of Philadelphia centring for Ron Ellis and Paul Henderson of the Toronto Maple Leafs."

"We were very fortunate that they put Clarke with Ronnie and me right off the bat," Paul Henderson says. "Maybe because we were underdogs, but we worked our buns off. We came to camp in pretty good shape and we worked like crazy, but there was chemistry there. Some of the other guys who were put together just couldn't find the right chemistry. Great hockey players, but you have to be able to complement each other out there. You have to play off each other's strengths.

"Bobby Clarke was like a younger Norm Ullman. Their styles were similar. Ronnie and I didn't have to make a lot of adjustments, and Bobby was very good at getting the puck to me so it worked out really, really well. We were probably a 'thrown together' line, but we were fortunate because we clicked right off the bat."

Henderson recalls that he started scoring right away. "We had a Red-White game — an intra-squad contest — and I scored 2 goals in that. It didn't matter who we played against, we just went out there and dominated them. You get your confidence up that way. The better the hockey players I play with, the better I'm going to look. I could shoot the puck and I had good speed. You give the puck to somebody and you break into the open and they'll get it back to you. If you play with a lesser hockey player, they can't get the puck back to you — they don't anticipate well. I really looked forward to this series because of the skill level of the players I was going to be playing with.

"Ronnie, Bobby and I were good defensive hockey players, too," Henderson continues. "We were good in our own end. We were good without the puck. I was really anticipating the larger ice surface in Moscow. I thought, 'This is where I will look as good as I ever have,' and it turned out to be prophetic. I scored 5 goals in the four games over there."

The members of Team Canada were not paid to play in the eight games that changed history. The agreement with the NHL Players' Association gave each player $500 for each of the six exhibition games — three intra-squad games, a pair against Sweden, and one against Czechoslovakia to be played after the Summit Series was over. The only other money the players received was $17 a day to cover incidental expenses. There was one other perq: the players were invited to bring their wives to Moscow for the four games there.

The first game was played at the Montreal Forum on September 2, 1972. Alan Eagleson describes seeing the Soviets take the ice for the first time: "They looked like a bunch of ragtags."

Phil Esposito opened the scoring at the 30-second mark of the first period, with Paul Henderson adding a second goal at 6:32. "The worst thing that happened was that we got off to a quick start," admits Ellis. "We got a quick two-goal lead. We players were starting to think, 'Maybe all the sportswriters were right!'

"I do recall how tough it was — the first big game, plus nerves and tension. I was struggling. I looked okay, but my legs were burning and my chest was heaving. I remember coming back to the bench after one shift, and Paul Henderson and I were sitting on the bench looking at each other, huffing and puffing, and Paul said, 'This is gonna be a long series.' I nodded my head, unable to respond as I was gasping for air. The Russians were just dancing, and a lot of us were sucking wind despite being up 2–0!"

Slowly, the Russians took over the game. By the end of the first period, the Russians had tied the score at two. "I knew we were in trouble," says Eagleson, shaking his head.

"I was hurt in game one," says Ellis, grimacing. "It was frightening. The play was in the middle of the ice. The puck was between me and Poladjev, the Russian defenceman. We both were going for the puck, and I got tripped from behind. I started falling forward; I went down, and the back of my head hit the Russian defenceman's thigh pad. It just wrenched everything. My immediate thought was, 'I'm hurt and I might not be able to play again. Ever.'

"I thought, 'I'm finished. The series is over for me.' That's how bad I thought it was."

Then Ron's professional pride kicked in. "There was no way I was going to let the Soviets think I was hurt. A delay in the game to get me off the ice might give them even more momentum.

"You never show weakness," Ellis asserts. "Somehow, I got off the ice. They took me into the dressing room and I was going in and out of consciousness. I lay there for a while. They gave me the smelling salts and finally, they asked me how I was. I said, 'I'm ready to go back.' Of course, the adrenaline was flowing and I did not want to miss any action. I was able to go back out and finish the game. I took a few hits and our line was effective. Clarkie scored in the third, and Paul and I assisted."

On the strength of 3 unanswered Soviet goals in the third period, the game ended with the visitors on the winning end of a 7–3 score. The Canadians, tired, angry and uninformed, left the ice without the traditional postgame handshakes. "One of the greatest dreams of my life turned into a nightmare in two and a half hours," states Ellis. "We lost. We got spanked. The next day, the newspapers wrote, 'Canada Shocked.'"

Alan Eagleson remembers a vote of confidence the team received after the game. "There was just Harry, Fergie and me down in the dressing room at the end of the game. Everybody else had gone. A knock came at the door, and in came Tommy Ivan — Chicago's general manager — and Sam Pollock, the Montreal GM. Both of them said, 'Hey, it's one game. It's not over — it's one game. A lot of teams win the first game but they don't win the series.' That was very good advice."

Ron Ellis woke up the next morning to another shock. "I couldn't move my neck. We just didn't have the same medical staff and equipment that the teams have today. This is not an indictment of the care I got; it's just a fact. I remember telling the trainer — our Leaf trainer, Joe Sgro — 'I'm in trouble. I can't turn my neck. Please tell Harry that I don't think I can go.'

"I couldn't shoot the puck. I started to regain that ability towards the end of the series, but I couldn't shoot the puck effectively during the next few games. I had chances, but I couldn't put anything behind the puck. Harry came to me and asked whether I could still skate. 'Can you shut Kharlamov down?' he asked. I said, 'I can do that.' I thought, 'This is one way I can make a contribution.' And that's how I stayed in the lineup." Valeri Kharlamov had played brilliantly in game one, scoring two goals in the second period.

Harry Sinden liked the work ethic that Ron's line displayed. "From the first day of training camp, Paul Henderson never had a bad practice or game," he wrote. "The guys on his line, Ellis and Clarke, were just as dedicated. Ellis [didn't say] two words since we put the team together, but [he was] our best defensive forward. We put him on Kharlamov, and Ellis grudgingly gave him 1 goal over the final seven games." Ron chuckles when he hears that, and issues a correction: "I was actually on the bench when Kharlamov got that goal."

"I would love to have scored a goal," admits Ron. "I just wasn't able to convert. I was frustrated, but Paul certainly made up for anything I wasn't able to do. I knew I did my job defensively. But when we had our ten-year reunion, we played games against the Russians at home. I was finally able to snap one past Tretiak. In fact, I got two or three, and I thought to myself, 'All right!'" Ron laughs contentedly.

The Canadians returned to Maple Leaf Gardens for game two on September 4. It appeared that Team Canada was comfortable in their unofficial home on Carlton Street. "Secretly, Paul and I were hoping the team would play well in Toronto," Ron says. "And we did. We had a solid game, no doubt about it. Everybody did their job.

"Two highlights that come to mind are Yvan Cournoyer's power-play goal from Brad Park in the second period, and Pete Mahovlich's shorthanded goal later in that period." Marcel Dionne later called Mahovlich's goal "one of the prettiest goals I've ever seen." Team Canada defeated the Soviets 4–1. "It was a good win for us. It got us back in the series and helped us establish ourselves," remembers Ellis.

Ron gets philosophical when he tells the story of game three, which took place on September 6 in Winnipeg. "This was one of the most critical games to the final outcome. We had a 4–2 lead in the second period, and we let them get 2 quick goals at the end of the period to tie it up."

Why was it a critical game? Ron continues: "If we had won that game, we could have gone into Vancouver with some positive momentum. Vancouver might have turned out differently, and then the whole series would have been different. By allowing them to come back and tie the game, we lost the momentum we picked up in Toronto." The game ended in a 4–4 tie. Ron assisted on Henderson's second goal of the tournament in the second period.

"Another key element of that game was that Bobby Hull was in the stands watching the game, instead of playing for Canada," Ellis recalls. It had been ruled that only those players signed to NHL contracts by the time training camp opened were eligible to play for Team Canada. By that time, Hull had signed with the fledgling World Hockey Association, and was declared ineligible to participate. "It wasn't a Canadian team, it was Team NHL," states Hull. "It was the most disappointing time of my career."

"The low point of the series was the game in Vancouver," grimaces Ellis. On September 8, the teams met for the fourth and final time on Canadian soil, at Vancouver's Pacific Coliseum. "We went into Vancouver and did not play well. We really got ourselves in a jackpot. It wasn't for lack of effort; we just didn't bring it together. It was an off game, for whatever reason, and the fans were tough on us. We got booed off the ice by our own Canadian fans.

"Now that I've had time to reflect on it, I certainly don't hold anything against the fans in Vancouver. They were frustrated just as much as we were. They were reading the newspapers the whole week prior to the series and they thought they would be watching our fourth straight victory. Here we were with just one victory in four games. They took their frustrations out on us, unfortunately. That was definitely a disappointment and the lowest of lows in my hockey career."

After the game, a devastating 5–3 loss, Phil Esposito did a television interview on the ice, in which he chastised the Canadian fans for their treatment of Team Canada.

> To the people across Canada, we tried, we gave it
> our best. To the people that booed us, geez, all of
> us guys are really disheartened and we're disillu-
> sioned and we're disappointed in some of the
> people. We cannot believe the bad press we've

got; the booing we've gotten in our own buildings. If the Russians boo their players like some of
the Canadian fans, then I'll come back and I'll
apologize to each one of the Canadians, but I
don't think they will. I'm really disappointed.

I am completely disappointed. I cannot believe
it. Some of our guys are really really down in the
dumps. We're trying. Hell, we're doing the best
we can. They got a good team and let's face facts.
It doesn't mean that we're not giving it our 150
percent because we certainly are. They can throw
the money for the pension fund out the window.
They can throw anything they want out the window. We came because we love Canada. Even
though we play in the United States and we earn
money in the United States, Canada is still our
home and that's the only reason we came. I don't
think it's fair that we should be booed.

Esposito's speech would prove to be the pivotal moment in the
series. "Phil's speech was very important to the team. A lot of us
didn't see it — we just heard about it," Ron recalls. "We had a
pretty good idea what Phil was saying. He came back to the dressing room and shared what he had said. You could tell he meant
every word because he was so emotional about it.

"It was Phil's speech that really forced people to make their
own decisions," Ron continues. "They certainly picked the right
guy to represent the team that night. I think that any of the players who had been interviewed that night would have said something along the same lines, but not with the passion that Phil
Esposito expressed. I really think the fans over the next couple of
days talked about that speech at the breakfast table and said,
'Wow! Maybe this Russian team is better than we thought and our
team has been caught off guard. Maybe it's time to get behind our
guys.' Over the next few days, Canadian hockey fans did just that."

* * *

After the Vancouver game, the Team Canada contingent flew
back to Toronto, where they would spend the night before setting

out for Sweden. "There was no one at the airport to see us off. That was quite disappointing, because the guys were really putting out," Ron Ellis says. "The guys were there for one reason, and that was to represent Canada. We were low, low, low, low, low. We were lower than whale poo."

During the brief hiatus between the games played in Canada and in Moscow, the Canadian team was slated to play a pair of exhibition games against the Swedish National Team. "After we played the four games in Canada, it became very obvious that, given the speed and conditioning of the Russians, a number of guys picked for Team Canada just couldn't do it at this stage of the season. After we left Canada, we went to Sweden and played the Swedish National Team to get used to the bigger ice surface and to acclimatize ourselves to the time change."

At that crucial time, coach Harry Sinden was adamant that Ron Ellis would continue playing on the team. "People forget that guys like Ellis and Henderson had to go through two steps," Haggert points out. "The first was to get invited to the initial training camp. The second was to make the final cut for the four games in Russia."

According to Ron, it is impossible to overstate the importance of the games in Sweden to the eventual outcome of the series. "If we had gone straight into Moscow from Vancouver, we would have had big problems. Sweden was originally supposed to be a holiday. We were supposed to be up 4–0 in the series by that point." Instead, the two games helped the team gel, while affording the NHLers the chance to get used to the bigger international rink. "I had never played on an international ice surface before," Ellis observes. "Personally, I loved the extra room, but it definitely took us a while to get used to the long pass up to the other blue line. Sweden was also the first time I saw Borje Salming, who came to Toronto the next year. Borje was the outstanding player for the Swedes in both games. That was the one thing I came back to the Leafs with. I said, 'Guys, wait'll next year. We've got a great one coming!'

"We really became a team in Sweden," states Ellis. "We played well against the Swedes; we beat them 4–1 in the first game and tied them 4–4 in the second. And they were pretty rough games. The Swedish papers just maligned us, talking about what thugs we were. Lars-Erik Sjoberg got nicked on the nose and, of course, it bled. I can remember it to this day: he skated around the rink three or four times to show the fans the blood. But the Swedish papers didn't talk about Wayne Cashman's tongue getting split open. He almost died; he could hardly breathe, it swelled up so much."

"I've seen a lot of terrible things happen on the ice during a hockey game," Harry Sinden wrote. "But none of those incidents were as vicious as the one in our second and, thank God, last game with the Swedes. Ulf Sterner nearly skewered Cash's tongue. He did it deliberately, no two ways about it."

"We lost Wayne because of that," fumes Ron. "He would have played a major role in Moscow.

"We put the animosities behind us in Sweden," Ron continues. "The egos were put on the back burner. We all agreed that it didn't matter who scored or who got the credit, we were in this together. We had a job to do.' Sweden is where we became a team."

Alan Eagleson agrees. "More important even than playing on the larger ice surface in Sweden was getting our act together. When you lose, there are a lot of reasons to be upset with each other. It's always someone else's fault. But we were going through a lot at that time. Frank Mahovlich was having a tough time emotionally. We told him, 'Frank, don't even come to Sweden. Take the time off.' We picked him up in Russia again."

There was also dissension in the Team Canada ranks. "In Sweden, I got a call from a player who I cannot name. He said, 'Al, I've got to talk to you.' The guy came to see me and he's got eight, maybe nine guys who were concerned about the direction of the team. Eight or nine out of a contingent of thirty is pretty considerable. He said, 'The way things are going, we're concerned that the team isn't going to win another game. We don't think Harry and Fergie are taking this seriously. They're out on the town at the Chat Noir.' I said, 'We'll address the issues, but if you want to quit, it's up to you. I'm not changing anything. I'm committed to Sinden and Ferguson and they're committed to you.'

So the next day, we were leaving for Russia at four in the afternoon, and we had a practice at ten. I said, 'Harry, as soon as everybody's changed, I want Team 50 (the players, management and support staff) in that room. We're going to have coffee, a sandwich and some discussion.' I didn't tell him what had happened earlier. I got up in front of the room and said, 'We don't have any time to fight each other. We've got an old rowboat that's leaking like a sieve. At the moment, we've got a lot of guys hitting each other over the head with the oars. If enough of us use those oars and start rowing, and the rest of start bailing, we're going to make it. If we don't, we're all going down together. If you want to get out, speak up now and get out now. If you want to stick with us, we're going to make it. I'm not looking for any rebuttal. The meeting's over. We're going to the airport.'

"The next day at practice, Harry said, 'You'd better talk to Hadfield.' This is during practice! Hadfield said, 'Eagle, get me outta here.' I said, 'Vic, what's all this about?' 'Ah, I'm on the fourth line and nobody else on this team got 50 goals last year.' So I said, 'The only guy who can get you back on this team is you.' But Vic wouldn't hear of it. 'Get me outta here,' he said.

"The next thing I see, he's grabbed Dennis Hull. He was trying to convince Hull he should get out, too. But gee, they're both left wingers. I told Dennis, 'Vic's gotta do what he's gotta do. I know you haven't been playing, but we might need you. You can't go. We can't have this happening.' Hadfield left."

Next, it was Punch Imlach's turn to interfere. In 1972, he was the general manager of the Buffalo Sabres. "He saw that Rick Martin wasn't playing and told him if he wasn't playing, he should report to the Sabres' training camp," Eagleson says. "Next thing I know, Jocelyn Guevremont's gone too, so there's three of them heading home. After the first game in Russia, Gilbert Perreault left — he had been playing well.

"Imlach did not help us."

Another problem — one that put the rest of the series in jeopardy — arose before the team had left Sweden. "One of the carrots they held out to us when they invited us to training camp in Toronto was that if you came, your wife could fly over and be with you in Moscow," Ron says. "We were going to stay at the same hotel and everything was going to be great. Well, Eagleson phoned over to Moscow the day before we left Sweden, just to make sure everything was under control. The guy Al was dealing with from the other side said, 'We've got one problem.'"

In a 1997 article in the Vancouver *Province*, Eagleson elaborated: "We got a message from the Russians that there was some sort of political conference filling the hotel, that the wives couldn't come as had been promised because instead of fifty rooms we were getting twenty-five and the players would have to double up."

"Al came back to us and told us the situation," Ron continues. "We had a team meeting and a vote, and the vote was 100 percent in favour of getting on the Air Canada flight the next morning and going home if they didn't change the arrangements back to what had been negotiated.

"This is why I respect Al: he was strong enough to deliver that message. A few minutes later, he got a call: 'Everything's okay, Mr. Eagleson.' He was absolutely a factor in our victory."

When the members of Team Canada touched down in Moscow, they were greeted by their wives, the tournament organizers and about 10,000 telegrams from Canada wishing them good luck. Phil Esposito's speech in Vancouver after game four had had a profound effect on Canadians. Also on hand were 3,200 Canadian fans who had made the trip to Moscow to see games five through eight.

"We didn't really get a chance to see much of Moscow," Ron recalls. "They didn't allow us to go anywhere on our own. We always went where they wanted to take us.

"The buses were always late," he complains. "I remember when we went to the Bolshoi Theatre, we were late — as usual — and had to go in and find our seats during the performance. The Russians in the theatre voiced their disapproval, but really, being tourists was the furthest thing from our minds.

"We went into Moscow with confidence, ready to play one game at a time," explains Ron. The first game in Moscow, the fifth in the series, took place on September 22. Like all the games in the Soviet Union, it was played at the Luzhniki Sports Palace in Moscow. "We were controlling the game and got up to a 4–1 lead. And then a few things started to happen," Ron recalls. "Some of them were flukes, some weren't. There were some great plays by the Russians and a couple of bad bounces for us. They came back and beat us 5–4." Ellis earned two minor penalties in the game — one of which was an offsetting minor with Kharlamov. Once again, the Henderson-Ellis-Clarke line played well. Henderson collected 2 goals and an assist while Bobby Clarke had a goal and 2 helpers.

"We controlled that game for three-quarters of the contest," Ron observes. "That was a real positive. And we knew we could score on them. We knew it was our game, except for a couple of bad breaks and a couple of penalties. Give them credit — they capitalized and came back to beat us. But, more importantly, we still had a strong feeling that we could beat these guys."

Ron swells with pride when he remembers the atmosphere in the arena in Moscow. "It always comes up every time we have a reunion. When we skated off the ice, the 3,200 Canadian fans in Moscow gave us a standing ovation. We all remember it so well. That was important. They knew we had played well. They knew we controlled most of that game. That was a key for us." The Luzhniki Sports Palace held approximately 11,000 spectators, so the Canadian contingent represented a sizeable portion of the crowd. Whereas the Soviet fans would whistle, the Canadians were yelling and clapping, and the difference in volume gave the Canadian team a great sense of being supported.

Game six was played on September 24. "Great hockey game!" exclaims Ron. "It was the night Paul Henderson scored the first of his game-winning goals. We won 3–2. What I remember about that game was that there were two and a half minutes to go, we were leading 3–2, and who should get a penalty but Ron Ellis. It was a pretty questionable penalty — I'm not the kind of guy who's going to take a penalty at that time of the game. I'm usually the guy who *kills off* penalties. I don't know if the refs were just trying to give the Russians one last chance, or what was happening.

"So there I am, sitting on the penalty bench. It was probably the longest two minutes of my life. If they had tied the game, the last two games would have been meaningless. Pete Mahovlich and Phil Esposito killed most of the penalty. I squeaked out of that one! Paul has told me many times that he would look over at me in the box and he could tell that the whole weight of the world was on my shoulders."

Okay guys — we got one. Two more to go. According to Ron, that's what the players were thinking as they faced off two nights later for game seven. "All I remember is great hockey. It was just great, great hockey," Ron enthuses. "Up-and-down, tough, exciting hockey. Your body is just tingling by the end. You know you're involved in something very special. Paul got the winner again in this game. An unbelievable goal — he beat about three guys." Ron assisted on the first goal of the game, which was scored by Phil Esposito. It was the first of two on the night for the team's leader.

The stage was set for the eighth game, which took place at Luzhniki Sports Palace on September 28. Each team had three wins and a tie. A Canadian win gave them the series. Anything else — even a tie — would give the bragging rights to the Soviets, who had outscored Canada by a goal so far in the series. "We were feeling pretty good by this point, and we knew we were capable of winning the series. There were so many things going on behind the scenes, which we were aware of, but that didn't make matters any easier. When you think of all the distractions, our team overcame adversity like you wouldn't believe," states Ron Ellis with great pride.

The terribly one-sided display of refereeing put on by Josef Kompalla and Franz Baader of West Germany had marred game six and created such animosity that game eight almost went unplayed. Rudy Bata and Uwe Dahlberg were scheduled to referee, but Dahlberg suddenly — and mysteriously — took ill. It was reported that he was confined to his bed in his hotel room. The Soviets insisted that the duo of Kompalla and Baader step into the breach and officiate the final game of the series. Team Canada retorted with an emphatic *nyet*. The Soviets finally agreed to a compromise: each camp would choose one of the two referees. Canada put forth Bata's name, while the home team stubbornly selected Kompalla.

"Before game eight, the Swedish referee, who was supposedly too sick to ref, was up in the stands watching the game," Ellis recalls, shaking his head in disbelief. "It was obvious for the first five or ten minutes that the officials were going to do everything they could to give the Russians an advantage." Within seconds of each other, Bill White and Peter Mahovlich were both sent to the box for holding. The game was barely three minutes old and already Canada was trying to kill off a two-man disadvantage. At 3:35, the Soviets went ahead 1–0 on a power-play goal by Alexander Yakushev. Less than a minute later, Kompalla assessed an interference penalty against J.P. Parise, who lost his composure and was thrown out of the game. By the end of the second period, the Soviets led 5–3. Three of the Soviet goals had been scored on the power play.

It would be perfectly understandable for any team to fall apart at this point. "Most teams would have thrown in the towel," Ron observes, "but that's one of the beautiful memories I have of this series: the quiet confidence of our team between periods. It's hard to describe, even now. But it's something I'll never forget; the scene is forever imprinted in my mind. There was just a feeling in that room that we were going to do it. I can't explain it. I have only experienced this feeling a few times in my career." Ron stops to soak up the memory.

"We knew how to play against them, we knew how to win and we knew how to defend against them," explains Ellis. "We also knew we had to get a quick goal. Again, the main thing that comes to mind so clearly was the lack of frustration. Everybody stayed cool. I remember looking around the room. You'd catch somebody's eye and the expression on their face would say, 'I won't let you down.'"

Team Canada did get the "quick goal" they needed. Team leader Phil Esposito scored at 2:27 of the third period to narrow the gap to 5–4. "We were back in the game," states Ellis. "Now we've got a hockey game. I played over 1,000 games in the National Hockey League, and only in fifty or maybe seventy-five of them was the whole team 'in the zone.' We were in the zone in that third period. It's a blur, but I just remember it was outstanding, unbelievable hockey. Both teams played fantastic hockey."

With seven minutes to go, Yvan Cournoyer tied the score. "That was so special," Ron says. "We'd overcome the referees and finally they couldn't play their games anymore. Finally, they just let us play hockey. The last ten minutes of game eight was the best hockey I've ever been involved with in my life. For ten minutes, both teams gave everything they had. It was phenomenal. What a memory! No one can take that away from me. I am so grateful." Ron pauses for a few moments, a small smile tracing his lips.

The team kept up its torrid pace, gaining momentum with every shift. "Everybody was playing at an extremely high level," Ron continues. "I remember coming off around the two-minute mark. Things were getting a little tense. Harry Sinden thought our line was going well, so he said, 'Get ready. You guys are going right back on.' He had the Esposito line — Esposito, Cournoyer and Pete Mahovlich — out, and he was going to come right back with our line. With about a minute to go, I was starting to get myself ready for the line change. That's when Paul stood up and yelled at Peter for a line change. That's how Paul got on ahead of Clarkie and me. Peter came off and Paul skated right from our bench. Ten seconds later, the puck's in the net. That's how Paul scored his famous goal."

No one who watched the game on television could ever forget Foster Hewitt's play-by-play call:

> Cournoyer has it on that wing. Here's a shot.
> Henderson made a wild stab for it and fell.
> Here's another shot. Right in front. They score!
> Henderson has scored for Canada! Henderson —
> right in front of the net! The fans and the team
> are going wild!

"What I cherish is that Harry Sinden had the confidence in me to put me out for the final 34 seconds of the game. A lot can happen in 34 seconds! We were so happy to be ahead 6–5, but we had to get control of ourselves again and finish the game. After we settled down, Sinden sent Pete Mahovlich, Phil Esposito and me out to kill the clock. The Russians were trying to tie it, but I can assure you, my guy wasn't going to get a chance. Paul later told me many times, 'I was watching, and you had a hold on your guy. There's no way he was going to get anywhere!'" Ron laughs heartily. "It was very memorable for me just to be on the ice as the clock ticked down those last few seconds. This was something I was very proud of. And then it was over.

"We were thrilled, of course. In some ways, we couldn't believe we'd done it. We were jubilant. We went into the dressing room, but after a few high-fives and some whooping it up, we went to our seats and sat down. We were emotionally drained. You'd look across the room and exchange a little smile with a teammate, which meant, 'We did it!' It took us a couple of days before we could really celebrate and realize what we had accomplished.

"We got back to the hotel, but the hotel had shut down and closed everything. I don't know whether this was standard procedure or the Russian officials were responsible. But as a result, we didn't have anyplace to celebrate, so we ended up sitting on the floor in the hallway of the hotel with crackers, peanut butter, jam and Coke. That was it. I remember sitting in the hallway with Bobby Clarke and his wife.

"That's how we celebrated our win. Another vivid memory, though!"

The next morning, the members of Team Canada set out for Prague to play the game that had been arranged with the Czechoslovak National Team, the reigning World Champions. The players' wives stayed behind in Moscow to fly home with the rest of the Canadian contingent.

"We went into Prague and they were happy as hell. This was just after the tanks went into Prague, so they welcomed us with open arms," remembers Ron. The game took place that night, September 29. "Paul Henderson and I didn't play that night; they let a lot of the guys who hadn't played in the Russian series play the Czechs. The Czechs were good, but not as good as the Russians. With ten seconds left, they were winning 3–2. We certainly didn't want to lose, so we pulled the goalie, and after a lot of great work by Phil Esposito, Serge Savard scored to tie it 3–3 with four seconds left.

"I remember Stan Mikita had a strong game, and the guys felt good for him because it was his homecoming." Mikita had left Czechoslovakia as an 8-year-old, sent by his parents to Canada to live with an aunt and uncle.

"The NHL didn't want all the players to fly together in case the plane went down," says Eagleson." We had half the players going home via Frankfurt and the other half going via London. So I called a friend at Air Canada, and he told me I could get a charter, but I'd need somebody in authority from the government to approve it. So I called John Munro, the Minister of Sports at that time. I mean, hell, after what we had been through and what we had done, we needed a charter so that we could all fly together. I said, 'We're not separating. After what we've been through, one way or another, these guys are going on the same flight.' I got in trouble with Hockey Canada, but the team got its charter."

When the team landed in Montreal on October 1, "I remember being met by the mayor, Jean Drapeau and Prime Minister Pierre Trudeau, and we rode around the airport on fire engines," Ron says. A throng of 10,000 fans was on the tarmac to greet the conquering heroes. It was raining in Toronto that evening, as Team Canada touched down in its home base. A motorcade swept the players to City Hall, where they were greeted by an estimated 80,000 Canadians who had waited for hours in the rain.

Alan Eagleson reflects on the importance of Ron's line to Team Canada's success. "The only line that stayed intact from start to finish was Clarke, Henderson and Ellis. They were all hard workers and they could all skate. Because Ronnie was doing his job, Paul was getting the puck. And Clarkie was playing well. Ronnie was understated and underestimated, but very important. That's a good summation of his entire career."

Ron's pride at participating in this series is justified, as the team is still remembered with affection. In 2000, the Associated Press named Team Canada its Team of the Century, while the Hockey Hall of Fame erected a monument to the squad outside its building in downtown Toronto.

Ron recalls some of the players who stood out in his mind in the Summit Series. "On the Soviet side, I ended up spending most of my time on the ice covering a fellow by the name of Valeri Kharlamov. I was quite happy to take that role, as he was Russia's key player. Outstanding hockey player. In my career with the NHL, I had to shadow a number of superstars, Bobby Hull being one of them. I would certainly put Kharlamov on a par with Hull in terms of talent and ability. There is no doubt in my mind he would have been a star in the NHL.

"Close behind him was Alexander Yakushev. He was a Frank Mahovlich–type player — big reach, good shot and always just seemed to be in the right spot at the right time. He got some goals against us that were devastating. He kept producing through the entire series.

"Their goaltender, Vladislav Tretiak, would be another one I was impressed with. Our team put him in the Hockey Hall of Fame. We made him look pretty good. He was a wonderful goalie, and from that point on, he was a household name."

Now Ron's thoughts turn to his teammates. "Our coaching staff had to come up with the right ingredients. You couldn't just put the all-stars out there — we would have been killed because of the way the Russians could counterattack so quickly. Phil Esposito was our leader from day one. We rallied around him. It just seemed to happen very naturally. But we had so many guys who were impressive. Paul Henderson — I don't need to say any more. Both Phil and Paul scored seven goals in the series and they were all very important goals. The guys were picked co-MVPs.

"But we did have other players who came and answered the bell. A fellow who comes to mind very quickly would be Gary Bergman. Gary played in all eight games, and I think he was one of those fellows, like myself, who was invited to camp and thought he might only get into a game or two. But his style of hockey was what we needed against the Russians — somebody who looked after the defensive end and didn't get caught in the Russian counterattacks. He had a wonderful series.

"There were other guys that I thought played extremely well throughout the series: Pete Mahovlich and Rod Gilbert and some of our defencemen — Bill White and Pat Stapleton did a wonderful job, as did Guy Lapointe, Serge Savard and Brad Park. You can go down the whole roster of the guys who played the last three games. They had to be doing a good job to play in those games. But if I had to pick one guy who I was very happy for, that I think got a lot of respect from all the players, it'd have to be Gary Bergman — he'd be the guy."

Ron's Leaf teammate Brian Glennie, who played against Sweden and Czechoslovakia but not against the Soviets, has his own special memory of the series. "Team Canada '72 made me a much, much better hockey player," he says. "I got to practise with Bobby Orr every day. Believe me, if Bobby Orr could have played, it would have been a different series." Orr, who travelled and practised with the team, was unable to participate in game action because of knee injuries. "I have great respect for the guys who played," Glennie continues.

Anatoli Tarasov, the renowned coach of the Soviet hockey team, stated, "Our players were better conditioned physically and stronger in skills, but we could not match Canada in heart and desire. The Canadians battled with the ferocity and intensity of a caged animal."

When Rod Seiling looks back on the Summit Series, he says, "I believe the bonds established between the players on Team Canada '72 are the same as amongst a regiment that has gone to war. Those bonds have never been, and will never be, broken. After 1972, teammates would have a difficult time arguing if you happened to tap one of the Team Canada guys on the shinpads while you were skating around during the warmup. It was very easy to say, 'Look, we've been through something few people in their lifetime will ever experience and it's a friendship built on a sense of respect for one another and what we've accomplished together as well.'"

Ron Ellis agrees with his longtime friend. "To spend time with all those fellows and to almost go through war with them made a big difference. I certainly respected all of them very, very much before that series, but getting to know them a little better and meeting their families really created a bond amongst us all. The bond is very strong. I know that if somebody called me from that team and needed my support or help, I'd be there. And I know they'd do the same for me.

"But the series did something else for me that had an impact on my life. When it was all said and done, and I got home and had time to reflect, I realized it had done a lot for my confidence as a player. I could say to myself, 'I was on the ice with the best in the world and I was able to hold my own and contribute.' That did a lot for me when I went back to play in the National Hockey League. Team Canada showed me I could play a consistently high calibre of hockey. It gave me a little more peace of mind. I could accept the notion that I belonged and that it wasn't a fluke that I had been chosen for the team."

"I cherish the opportunity I had to be part of that team and represent Canada in something so special," Ron concludes. "We knew at the time that we were involved in a wonderful series, a unique series, but I don't think any of us expected it to live as long as it has. It just seems to continue. It is incredible to me that we celebrated the thirtieth anniversary of our victory in 2002. I'm so grateful that I was able to represent the Toronto Maple Leafs, the National Hockey League, my country and our way of life in the series of the century."

CHAPTER THIRTEEN

Return from Russia

Coach John McLellan of the Toronto Maple Leafs welcomed Ron Ellis, Paul Henderson and Brian Glennie back from their Team Canada sojourn, then promptly told them to take a rest. "Ronnie hasn't had a breather since reporting to Team Canada last August 12," stated McLellan at the time. "He came right home and pitched in to try and help us. He's a hell of a team man. He has to be mentally and physically beat up because of what he's been through, but nary a complaint. He comes in, puts on his suit and does his job."

"I was so pleased to represent the Leafs on that team," says Ron. "One of the more pleasant things that happened when we got back was a special ceremony before one of the games. Harold Ballard presented the three of us with some shares in Maple Leaf Gardens Ltd. and a beautiful set of cuff links with the maple leaf and a diamond on them."

"Yeah," Brian Glennie laughs, "somebody else is wearing my cuff links. I left them in a tuxedo shirt when I returned it!"

Ron describes the way the special bond between Team Canada warriors lasted beyond the team's return to Canada. "After the series, training camps had already started for all the NHL teams, so on our return home, we dispersed very quickly. The next time we saw each other, it was as opponents. We had to make a quick transition, yet there was something unique about playing against my Team Canada '72 teammates, something that lasted the rest of my career.

"It was mutual respect," Ron continues. "We still played hard against each other, we didn't let up on the checks, but there was that element of respect — you knew you weren't going to be fouled with any intent to injure from that group of players. There'd be the little wink or the little nod, but that would be the extent of the acknowledgement."

Ellis recalls that, while some players had to work to readjust to NHL action, "I was able to have my normal season that year. My stats didn't really change. I was never a player who was going after the scoring championship, and my style of play was conducive to being consistent. The series emphasized what I needed to do to have a long career. My consistency was important, as was my contribution to the team. If I wasn't scoring, I wanted to be able to contribute in other areas. My game is fairly solid, and that's probably one of the reasons I was selected to play in the Summit Series. I could play in both ends of the rink.

"Almost all of us come into the NHL as pretty good goal scorers. When you get to that level, you have to realize what your skill set is. And even more importantly, you have to figure out how to maximize your talents in order to give yourself the best opportunity to have a career in the NHL, not just a cup of coffee. I just came back and played my game, and I think that my 1972–73 season was quite consistent with other years I enjoyed.

"It was, however, a watershed experience for a number of guys. Players like Bobby Clarke went on from that series to be a superstar. A young player like Marcel Dionne — being around the guys jump-started his growth and maturity. He also went on to become a superstar and represent Canada very effectively in international play for many years."

Over the next few years, Glennie, Henderson and Ellis became very close friends. "Our team continued to wallow in mediocrity," Ron says, shaking his head. "The only letdown from the Summit Series for me was to go from the high calibre of that international hockey to a team that was constantly rebuilding. But I was still very proud to be a Maple Leaf."

"After Ballard took over, we were all just so sick and tired of the way the team was operating," Henderson adds candidly. "We couldn't compete with Boston or New York or Montreal. Playing in Toronto is a wonderful experience, but not when you don't have a good team. We lost a lot of our young defencemen to the WHA and we were struggling."

The World Hockey Association first reared its head in the spring of 1971, when Dennis Murphy and Gary Davidson, the co-founders of the American Basketball Association, formulated the premise for this new rebel league. The charismatic leaders very quickly found owners for twelve teams, and announced their intention to begin play in October 1972.

NHL owners underestimated the impact of the fledgling league — almost naïvely so. League president Clarence Campbell was quoted as saying, "In the unlikely event the WHA gets off the ground, it won't last until Christmas." It would in fact last seven years.

Still, in a move perhaps designed to thwart the upstart league, the 1972–73 season saw the National Hockey League grow to sixteen teams with the addition of the New York Islanders and Atlanta Flames. The expansion would provide employment for at least fifty additional players while securing two markets the WHA was pursuing.

On February 12 and 13, 1972, the WHA's first player draft was held in Anaheim, California. Former NHL referee Vern Buffey conducted the proceedings at the marathon session, in which more than 1,000 players from every level of hockey were claimed.

"I was picked by Houston," Ron mentions, adding that he even met with the Aeros' coach/general manager Bill Dineen. "I did it more for curiosity than anything. They were going to double my salary, and I would have had a chance to play with Howe." In 1973, the Houston Aeros made a splash by bringing Gordie Howe out of retirement so that he could play alongside sons Mark and Marty. "That was tempting, because he was my boyhood hero. But making a move to the WHA was not a priority for me. I had an innate desire to finish my career in Toronto. Yes, it cost me some money to do so, but so be it."

The first significant player to defect to the WHA was the Maple Leafs' goaltender, Bernie Parent, who signed a contract with the league's Miami franchise. "A short time ago, we were fighting with the Maple Leafs to get $40,000 a year," said Parent that summer. "Now the Miami Screaming Eagles were offering a five-year, personally guaranteed deal for $750,000 with a house, boat, car and all the frills. How could I say no?" By the beginning of the WHA's first season, the lack of an arena and money had forced the Screaming Eagles to withdraw; the short-lived Philadelphia Blazers, with Parent in goal, took their place.

The NHL's most prolific goal scorer among active players,

Bobby Hull of the Chicago Blackhawks, was drafted by the Winnipeg Jets, with whom he eventually signed for a $1 million signing bonus and a salary of $250,000 a year for five years. After his playing days were done, the deal called for him to serve as an executive with the club for five years at $100,000 a year. Each of the eleven other teams in the WHA contributed $100,000 to help pay Hull's salary.

Harold Ballard had shared Clarence Campbell's assessment that the league would never find its legs, and he was livid when Parent jumped leagues. The budding superstar would not be the last to desert Maple Leaf Gardens — not by a longshot. In short order, Jim Dorey, Jim Harrison, Rick Ley, Brad Selwood and Guy Trottier joined the rival league. As the WHA gained momentum, it secured the rights to several others who had been Leafs property, including Bruce Boudreau, Dave Dunn, Paul Henderson, Dave Keon, Mike Pelyk, Dale Smedsmo, Blaine Stoughton, Norm Ullman and Stan Weir.

Wayne Carleton, a former teammate of Ron Ellis's with the junior Marlboros and with the Leafs, enjoyed a strong WHA career during its seven-year run. Between 1972 and 1979, Carleton scored 312 points in 290 regular-season games. "The WHA helped a lot of guys," he says. "It really changed the game, but you had to have the guts to do it. It was a risk, but I feel fortunate that I was a part of it."

By the mid-1970s, team captain Dave Keon had grown disgruntled with the Toronto Maple Leafs front office. "They told me they were not going to renew my contract unless I waived my no-trade clause. I got the feeling that, if I signed with the Leafs, I'd be traded early in the 1975–76 season. I figured it was better to find employment somewhere else, so I got the numbers worked out with Minnesota." After fifteen years with the Leafs, Keon joined his former teammate Mike Walton with the Minnesota Fighting Saints. He played four years in the WHA, scoring 291 points in 301 regular-season games. Keon would return to the NHL in 1979, as a member of the Hartford Whalers, for whom he would line up alongside 51-year-old Gordie Howe.

Paul Henderson was another player who was frustrated by the shortsightedness of Leafs management. He jumped to the WHA's Toronto Toros in 1974. "It was wonderful. I just loved it," says Henderson fondly. "I felt the Leafs would never get it going on the ice as long as Ballard was there. I had given up my dream of winning the Stanley Cup with the Toronto Maple Leafs, and I was 32 at the time, so I was getting into the twilight of my career. The WHA was a breath of fresh air. There was no pressure anymore — no pressure whatsoever." Paul Henderson counted 283 points in his 360 WHA regular-season games between 1974 and 1979.

"The three of us [Henderson, Glennie and Ellis] were talking one day and said, 'Who needs this?' Brian said, 'Why don't the three of us buy a garbage truck? There's no aggravation. We get up in the morning, we pick up the garbage, we go home. There's no pressure.' The three of us were just sick of the aggravation and pressure." As the 1967 Cup championship receded further into memory, the pressure on the Leafs to win again was mounting. Meanwhile, the players knew they were far from being among the league's elite. "There's no way on God's green earth that you can compete. You'd look at the talent we had and then look at Boston, for example. They had Orr and Esposito. They had three great lines. They had defencemen who were solid as a rock. We had guys — nothing against them, because they were great guys, but they just weren't NHL hockey players."

Ron concurs. "It was tough playing in Toronto during those years. It was different going to the rink. The fans were expecting more every year and they weren't getting it. We players tried to give it to them, but we'd take one step forward and then two steps back. We just couldn't get to the next level. It's frustrating when you go to training camp, and you know from day one that it's going to be a long year."

Adds Henderson, "We were smart enough to know that with Ballard there, it was probably going to get worse before it got better. And it did."

* * *

It was around this time that Ron, noticing the game was changing around him, responded by adopting a new regimen: working out with weights. "Although I was strong, NHL defencemen were getting bigger and stronger. I found that I was getting moved out from in front of the net and had trouble holding off defencemen when I tried to go wide to the net."

"I met Ron at the gym," remembers Bob Ruffo, a personal trainer who was into power lifting. "I watched him train — he was very diligent. In fact, Ron was one of the most devoted athletes you would ever want to meet. I recognized Ron, introduced myself, and told him if he ever wanted some assistance, I'd be glad to help him out."

"Bob was great," Ron says. "Mike Pelyk joined us, and Bob gave us both programs that would help us increase our upper-body strength." Ruffo remembers another member of the group, one who put in only a brief appearance. "Yeah, Paul Henderson worked out one day with us, too. He was naturally strong. Paul was a scratch golfer, but after doing a session of weights, he shot a 94. 'That's it for me,' he said. 'You're screwing up my golf game.'

"But Ron really stuck with the program," remembers Ruffo. "He took instruction very well and his form was excellent. We worked a lot on his upper body, but didn't use weights on his legs because we didn't want to loosen the knee joints. Ron worked out extremely hard three or four days each week. He was in phenomenal shape when he went back to the Leafs that fall. He got quite muscular. We advised Ronnie not to continue during the season, though. The Leafs' on-ice workouts were very hard, so there was no need to train with weights, too. We kept in touch during the season, and sometimes we'd meet in the training room to work on a few areas. Ron got hit a lot playing his wing and had a bad shoulder for years. Ronnie lost some of his muscle by the end of the season. Otherwise, he could have been quite a good bodybuilder."

Ruffo observes that Ellis was ahead of his peers. "Even at that time, most players waited until they arrived at training camp to get in shape. Weight training was in its early stages for hockey players." Ron remarks on the contrast with the modern-day NHL: "Today, every dressing room has a top-notch weight room attached to it, and all the players spend time on programs year-round to keep their muscle mass. You simply have to in today's hockey."

Bob Ruffo recalls that Ron also wanted to learn to box, a desire that would seem at first glance to run counter to Ellis' level-headed demeanour. "We used to go up to his garage and spar a little bit, but I tried to make sure that Ron knew that fighting on the street and fighting on the ice are completely different things," Ruffo says. "Ron knew he was not a fighter on the ice, but he just wanted to have a few skills. You never know, do you?

"We became very good friends," Ruffo confides. "We had a lot in common, but we didn't talk a lot of hockey, as I recall. We would see each other socially. Ron and I would play golf from time to time, and we also played tennis together — although Ron is a better tennis player than I am.

"Later, when Ron was managing the golf course, he used to run four or five miles each day," Ruffo continues. "But I told him he should be riding a bike. Speed skaters use the bike for training. You use the same muscles, your quadriceps, in skating as you do in cycling. So Ron said, 'I'll give it a whirl.' He was living in Aurora at the time, and there were lots of hills. Ron would ride his bike, and I used to drive beside him."

Ron talks about a partnership he and Bob Ruffo formed. "For a couple of summers, we operated a training program for kids between 13 and 18. We held it at York University. Universal lent us equipment. The kids would pay a small fee, and have access to a program and equipment to work out with. Some junior players used the program to prepare themselves for the upcoming season."

"Doug Jarvis was playing for Peterborough at the time," Ruffo adds, "and we had him in a program to help get him ready for the World Junior Championships in 1974." That year, the Peterborough Petes of the OHL were designated to represent Canada at the first-ever World Junior Championships, which were held in Russia. The hosts took the gold medal, while Canada claimed the bronze.

* * *

In 1972–73, Darryl Sittler discovered his stride and led the Leafs in scoring with 29 goals and 48 assists for 77 points. Keon topped the club in goal scoring with 37. Ron Ellis displayed the consistency he alluded to earlier, contributing 22 goals and 29 assists for 51 points. Toronto finished fifth in the East Division, missing the playoffs once again. Their 64 points placed them thirteenth overall, ahead of only the three-year-old Vancouver Canucks (53 points), the woeful California Golden Seals (48) and the first-year New York Islanders (30). Even the new Atlanta Flames team finished higher, with 65 points.

But Toronto improved substantially in 1973–74. Ironically, the autumn of 1973 marked Harold Ballard's return to Maple Leaf Gardens. Coach John McLellan, who was suffering from ulcers, was promoted to assistant general manager, and was replaced by Red Kelly, who had played for the Leafs between 1960 and 1967. Six years later, only Keon and Ellis remained of the team that Kelly had left when he retired to coach the L.A. Kings.

The team took a quantum leap forward in the standings, from 64 points to 86. Sittler, with 38 goals and 46 assists, was firmly established as a bona fide star. His 84 points placed him eighth in league scoring. Rookie Lanny McDonald provided a hint of his future excellence, scoring 14 goals and adding 16 assists.

Two other newcomers to Toronto also made their presence felt in 1973 — Borje Salming and Inge Hammarstrom. Both had played on the Swedish National Team that Ron Ellis and Team Canada faced in the fall of 1972. Leaf scout Gerry McNamara had signed the two Swedes and arranged for their move to Canada. Unfortunately, Hammarstrom, then a 25-year-old winger, is remembered less for his play than for the derision that Leafs owner Harold Ballard directed his way. Ballard said Hammarstrom, whose game was built on finesse, could skate into the corner with his pockets full of eggs and emerge with every last shell intact. Still, Hammarstrom scored a very respectable 85 goals and 82 assists in his four seasons with Toronto before he was shuffled off to St. Louis. Salming, on the other hand, earned his ticket to the Hockey Hall of Fame by putting in 16 seasons on the Leaf blueline, playing in 1,099 games and scoring 148 goals and 620 assists for 768 points. In an era when the list of blue-ribbon defencemen also included such names as Orr, Park, Robinson, Savard, Lapointe and Potvin, Salming was named to the NHL's First All-Star Team once, in 1977, and to the Second Team five times.

The old guard continued to produce. Eddie Shack returned to Toronto after being bought from the Penguins, and contributed 7 goals in a limited role. Paul Henderson, playing his last games as a Leaf, scored 24 goals and 31 assists. Dave Keon enjoyed the eleventh and last of his 20-goal seasons as a Maple Leaf, with 25. Norm Ullman, with 22, also had the last of his 20-goal seasons in a Toronto uniform. And, steady as a rock, Ron Ellis scored 23 goals and 25 assists for 48 points. It was the eighth consecutive season in which Ron had cracked the 20-goal barrier.

Despite the improvement during the regular season, the 1974 playoffs followed a script that was familiar to the Leaf faithful, as they surrendered to the Boston Bruins in four straight games in the quarterfinals. Since winning the Stanley Cup in 1967, the Toronto Maple Leafs missed the playoffs entirely in 1968; were knocked out of the quarterfinals in four straight games in '69; failed to qualify in 1970; were beaten by the Rangers in the 1971 quarterfinals; lost to the Bruins in the quarterfinals of 1972; and missed the playoffs in '73 and were again bounced by Boston in '74. It would not be until Darryl Sittler, Lanny McDonald and Borje Salming emerged to lead the team during the 1974–75 season that the Maple Leaf franchise would regain some of its past success.

CHAPTER FOURTEEN

Personal Commitment

"There were four of us from the Leafs who hung out together," Ron recalls. "Paul Henderson was rooming with Garry Monahan on the road, and I was rooming with Brian Glennie. Around 1971, when the opportunity arose, the four of us would go to church together. We had a common interest. I'm not saying we went to church every Sunday, but there was definitely some interest.

"When we were on the road in New York City, we'd go to hear Norman Vincent Peale speak. What a treat that was!

"In my discussions with other players, it seems that the ten-year mark of a career causes some introspection. You start asking yourself, 'What's life about? How did I get here? Where am I going? What is my purpose?' After Team Canada '72 was history, its impact on Paul and me was beginning to surface, no question," admits Ellis. "Paul came back and really started questioning life — 'What more can I accomplish in the game of hockey?' Paul was searching."

"I started looking at spiritual things during the fall of '72," Henderson continues. "As a kid growing up, I always dreamed of having the good life. The ingredients were a good marriage, financial independence, a good career, and maybe the chance to prove to yourself and the rest of the world that you could compete in whatever career you had. "Well, I had a great marriage, I'd proved to myself that I could play on a fairly high level, and when the WHA came along and offered me a five-year contract the future looked even better. But when I was really reflective, there was a lot of anger and bitterness in my life, especially in my dealings with Harold Ballard. And there was worry, too. I didn't know how to drop that burden, and that started my search. I just wanted to be content. One of the things I took a look at was

Christianity. That was a two-and-a-half-year search."

During the 1972–73 season, Ellis and Henderson were intro-duced to a man who would play an integral role in both their lives. "Mel Stevens, from a place called Teen Ranch, phoned Harold Ballard. He said, 'Harold, I want to do something for the team. I want to give them a gift.' And Harold was very good with him on the phone and asked, 'What would that be?' And Mel said, 'I'd like to give them all a Bible.' My understanding is that Harold's late wife Dorothy was a strong believer. Harold basically said, 'Y'know, that would be good for my boys.' Mel then said, 'Mr. Ballard, I'd love to come down and provide lunch for your team. I'd like to tell them a little about Teen Ranch and what we stand for and give them the gifts.'

"I didn't know Mel Stevens, and neither did Paul," Ron says. "We had no idea what or where Teen Ranch was. But Mel is a real man of faith, and a true sports fan. His experience with profes-sional rodeo gave him an advantage when it came to understand-ing professional athletes. He was also the chaplain of the Toronto Argonauts football team, working with Chuck Ealey, Peter Muller and Zenon Andrusyshyn. Mel developed strong relationships with the Christian athletes on the football club."

Stevens's original plan to address the team went awry. "Mel ended up coming down while we were on the ice and giving the Bibles to the trainer. The trainer put the Bibles on the players' benches in the dressing room. The players had no idea what was going on," remember Ron. "Mel did a wonderful job on the Bibles. I still have mine at home. It's a blue leather-bound Bible with the Maple Leaf crest and my name inscribed on it. Every Maple Leaf got one that day. In fact, every Maple Leaf since then has received a Bible from Mel and Teen Ranch. Laurie Boschman arranged for the Oilers to get Bibles when he was playing in Edmonton, so Wayne Gretzky has one. Wayne really appreciated it — he told Mel it was one of the most treasured gifts he had ever received.

"Anyway, that was our introduction to Mel Stevens," Ron con-tinues. "We came in off the ice and found Bibles on our benches. Can you imagine the things that were said? 'Hey, so and so, you'll never be able to read this — there are no pictures in it!' My reac-tion was very quiet. I was searching. I remember taking the Bible and leafing through it. There was a pamphlet in it that said, 'If you're new to the Bible, here are some places to start.' I put it

Although born with a club foot, through the efforts of my doctor and the patience of my mom and dad, the problem was remedied. As I grew older, my skating style accommodated the lack of mobility in my foot. In this photo, I am wearing a device that helped straighten my foot.

(author's collection)

Here I am with my dad, Randy, testing the water. Although born in Brampton Ontario, my father moved to Lindsay with his family as a child.

(author's collection)

This is me with my mother, Helen. Mom was born in Lindsay Ontario.

(author's collection)

This photograph was taken in 1948 while Mom, Dad and I were living in Scotland. Dad was starring with the Dunfermline Vikings of the Scottish Hockey League at the time.
(author's collection)

A young boy discovers the "monkey in the mirror."
(author's collection)

In 1957, while playing in the Cradle league, the Ottawa All-Stars got the opportunity to play in the Montreal Forum. Mike Walton is in the second row, second from the left. I'm in the same row but second from the right. Jean Beliveau is standing, surrounded, in the back.

(author's collection)

I was so proud to be a Toronto Marlboro because my dad played two seasons for them, starting in 1941. Here's Dad at 18, a Marlboro rookie.

(author's collection)

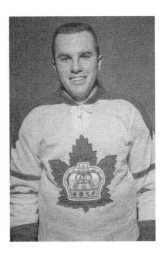

Two generations of Ellises were proud to wear the sweater of the Toronto Marlboros. In my third and final season with the Marlboros, we won the Memorial Cup.

(Graphic Artists/Hockey Hall of Fame)

There are seven years between me and my next oldest sibling, Roger. By the time of this photograph, I had already moved to Toronto to play Junior B with the Weston Dukes. Here are the five Ellis kids in 1960. From left to right, Rosemary, Roger, me holding Randy Jr. and Robin.

(author's collection)

Here are the Ellis brothers and sisters a couple of years later. This photo is from 1999, with Randy Jr. on the left, then Robin, Roger, Rosemary and me on the right.

(author's collection)

Our line had a blockbuster year with the Marlies during 1963-64. Wayne Carleton scored 42 goals, Pete Stemkowski scored 42 and I had 46. All of us went on to play with the Leafs. Here is our line in action during the Memorial Cup finals against the Edmonton Oil Kings.

(Graphic Artists/Hockey Hall of Fame)

Some writers have called the 1963-64 Toronto Marlboros one of the best junior teams ever assembled. We won the Memorial Cup that season. It was quite a team! Grant Moore was our captain, but can you pick out future NHLers Wayne Carleton, Rod Seiling, Peter Stemkowski, Gary Smith and Brit Selby?

(Graphic Artists/Hockey Hall of Fame)

You never forget your first goal. Mine came at home on October 17, 1964 in a game against the Boston Bruins. Eddie Johnston was the victim, and I kidded him about it when we played together on Team Canada in 1972.

(Graphic Artists/Hockey Hall of Fame)

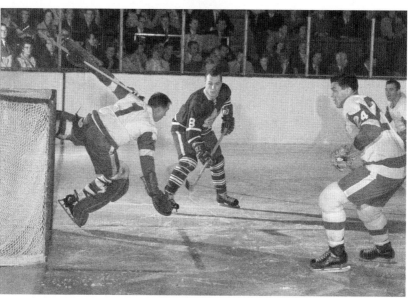

Roger Crozier of the Detroit Red Wings and I both broke into the NHL in 1964-65. The acrobatic netminder won the Calder Trophy as the NHL's rookie of the year, and I finished second.

(Graphic Artists/Hockey Hall of Fame)

Little did 9-year-old Janis Greenlaw realize when she met Ron Ellis in Grade 4 that some-day, she'd become a hockey wife and mother of two. This photo was taken in February 1963 when we were 18 years old. Jan and I celebrated wedding anniversary number thirty-six in 2002.

(author's collection)

On May 28, 1966, Jan and I were married at Rexdale United Church in Toronto. Brit Selby was in my wedding party, and the entire team, including Punch Imlach and King Clancy, came to the wedding. It was an outstanding day, and the beginning of a wonderful life together with Jan.

(author's collection)

As a boy, I dreamed of playing in the NHL and winning the Stanley Cup. In 1966-67, the Toronto Maple Leafs helped me realize both dreams. I'm beside our captain, George Armstrong, who is carrying the Stanley Cup.

(Graphic Artists/Hockey Hall of Fame)

In my third NHL season, the Toronto Maple Leafs won the Stanley Cup. Although my celebration was short, here I am in the parade, riding in front of Maple Leaf Gardens on our way to City Hall.

(Graphic Artists/Hockey Hall of Fame)

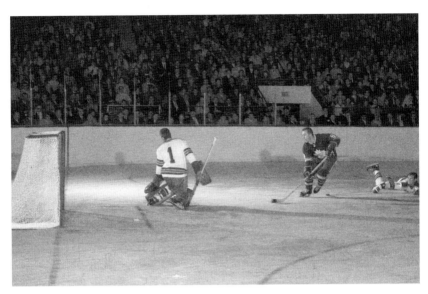

Whenever possible, I tried to use my speed to break past the opposing team's defensemen. Here I am in the clear against New York Ranger goaltender, Ed Giacomin.

(Graphic Artists/Hockey Hall of Fame)

When expansion took place before the 1967-68 season, it gave a number of players, like Bill White, their first opportunity to play in the NHL. Bill, here chasing me behind the Kings' net, is a prime example. We became teammates on Team Canada '72.

(Graphic Artists/Hockey Hall of Fame)

I was never more honoured than when Ace Bailey had his Number 6 taken out of retirement by the Leafs and presented to me. I wore his number with great pride. Ace suffered a career-ending head injury following an on-ice incident with Eddie Shore of the Boston Bruins on December 12, 1933. Here, Ace (left) and Shore shake hands before a Leafs/Bruins game in Boston late that same season on March 6, 1934.

(Hockey Hall of Fame)

Prior to the 1968-69 season, the Toronto Maple Leafs held a press conference where I was presented with the formerly retired Number 6 of Ace Bailey. I wore Number 6 for the remainder of my career. Here, Mr. Bailey himself is presenting me with my new sweater number in the Hot Stove Lounge of Maple Leaf Gardens.

(Graphic Artists/Hockey Hall of Fame)

Over the Boards

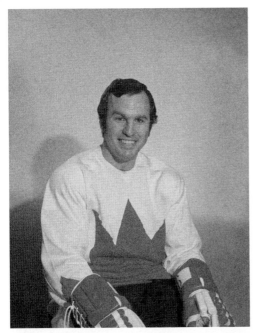

Participating in the 1972 Summit Series on behalf of my country not only gave me immense pride, but also gave me a confidence in my abilities that I hadn't known before. Although I injured my neck early on, I was still able to make my contribution to Team Canada on a line with Bobby Clarke and Paul Henderson.

(Graphic Artists/Hockey Hall of Fame)

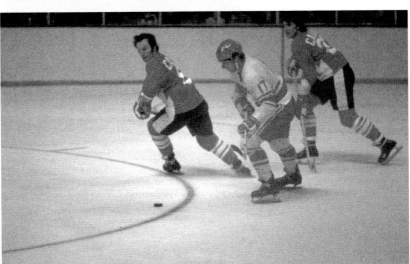

After game one of the Summit Series, my assigned role for Team Canada was to ensure that Valeri Kharlamov (Number 17) was kept off the scoresheet. I am proud to say that the only goal he scored after that first game in Montreal happened when I was on the bench. Kharlamov and I developed a great respect for each other, and I was saddened to hear of his death in 1981.

(Graphic Artists/Hockey Hall of Fame)

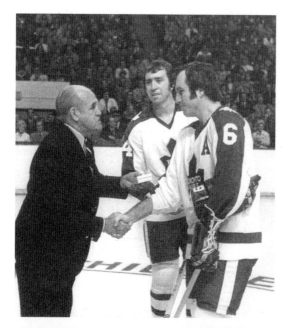

The Summit Series between Canada and the former Soviet Union had an immense impact on my life. We celebrated the thirtieth anniversary in 2002. Here, King Clancy, on behalf of the Toronto Maple Leafs Hockey Club, is presenting Brian Glennie and me with very special cufflinks to commemorate our victory in Russia.

(Graphic Artists/Hockey Hall of Fame)

On November 10, 2000 a monument to commemorate Team Canada '72 was unveiled outside the Hockey Hall of Fame. The team had been named "Team of the Century," an honour of which we were all immensely proud as both hockey players and Canadians. This photo shows me with teammates Yvan Cournoyer, Ken Dryden, Paul Henderson, Phil Esposito, Stan Mikita and Rod Seiling.

(Dave Sandford/Hockey Hall of Fame)

It was important for me to play well in both ends of the rink. Here, the Leafs play the Rangers. I'm carrying the puck out from behind Bruce Gamble while our defensemen, Mike Pelyk and Jim McKenny, look on.

(Graphic Artists/Hockey Hall of Fame)

RON ELLIS • R. WING

MAPLE LEAFS

After a two year hiatus away from the game, I played for Team Canada in 1977 and really realized how much I enjoyed playing hockey. This is my hockey card for the 1977-78 season. I look glad to be back, don't I?

(O-Pee-Chee/author's collection)

Although born with a club foot, I was able to develop a skating style that used my strength but allowed me to work around the lack of flexibility I had in the ankle.

(Miles Nadal/Hockey Hall of Fame)

I knew I just couldn't continue playing for the Leafs when I left before the 1975 season. But that didn't mean I gave up hockey. Left to right, it's me, my dad (the captain), my brothers Roger and Randy Junior playing for the Huntsville Huskies.

(author's collection)

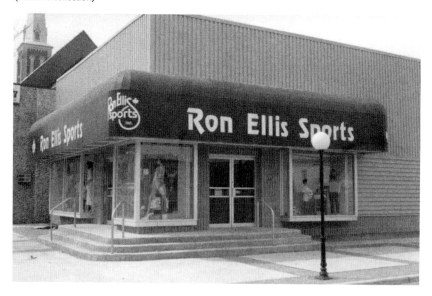

Some friends and I conceived an idea for a sporting goods store in Brampton. Ron Ellis Sports opened and did very well for awhile, but, unfortunately, between the economy and my depression, we were unable to keep the store going.

(author's collection)

Punch Imlach had quite an impact on the Leafs when I first joined the team in 1964-65, guiding Toronto to a fourth Stanley Cup in less than a decade during the spring of 1967. But his second era in Toronto, between 1979 and 1981, is remembered for the dissension that saw great players like Hockey Hall of Fame Honoured Members Darryl Sittler (centre) and Lanny McDonald (right) traded away, much to the dismay of teammates and to the horror of Maple Leaf fans.

(author's collection)

During my rookie season, the defense duo of Bobby Baun (left) and Carl Brewer (centre) was among the best in the NHL. But by my second season, Carl had tired of Punch Imlach and retired. The Leaf alumni always enjoy spending time together, and here are Bobby, Carl and me in September 2000. Sadly, Carl died on August 25, 2001.

(courtesy of John Cain, St. Catharines)

There is a very special bond tying together those who wore the blue and white. To this day, some of my dearest friends are those who skated on the home ice of Maple Leaf Gardens. During the beautiful summer of 2002, a group of us got together for a fishing trip off the coast of B.C. From left to right are Bob Baun, Andy Bathgate, me, Orland Kurtenbach, Darryl Sittler and Paul Henderson.

(courtesy of Michael Miller)

They're the lights of my life and, when things were dark in my life, they were the reason I was able to keep going. In this shot, Jan and I watch Kitty and R.J. at a Leaf family skate at Maple Leaf Gardens. Okay, so we all look a little different today, but you have to remember, this picture was taken in 1980.

(author's collection)

It was a special occasion during the summer of 2002 when four generations of Ellis men were able to get together for a visit. I'm on the left, with Dad in the centre holding Zachary and R.J. is on the right. Dad is 79. Zachary was born in March 2002.

(author's collection)

R.J. is married to Norma and lives in Belleville. Kitty and her husband Keith live in Bolton. We're all very close, but our home is a little more quiet now that it's just Jan, me and Caleb the German Shepherd.

(author's collection)

in my mailbox with no fuss."

It's a gorgeous day — sunshine raining down from a brilliant blue sky. Mile after mile of field and farm frame the highways that lead to Teen Ranch. Heritage homes and towns, seemingly untouched by the 21st century, are sprinkled along en route.

Teen Ranch is located northwest of Toronto, just outside the town of Orangeville. As you approach along Highway 10, the compound's sign is prominent on the left-hand side of the road. If you turn into the long driveway, the Ranch's property stretches out as far as the eye can see. Teen Ranch owns 150 acres, and the rural setting provides an overwhelming feeling of peace, even for those who might be unaware that Teen Ranch is a Christian camp.

The first building that comes into view is the Ice Corral, an Olympic-size arena set just off the path. Anyone who has spent a good deal of time around hockey rinks will quickly appreciate how fine a facility the Ice Corral is. All around the lobby are large, framed photographs of professional hockey players — Darryl Sittler, Mike Gartner, Jean Pronovost, Stu Grimson, Laurie Boschman, Dean Prentice, John Vanbiesbrouck, Ron Ellis, Mark Osborne, Paul Henderson and many more. A plaque indicates that this is Teen Ranch's "Hockey Hall of Faith." The inscription explains that the photos are of "NHL personnel who have expressed personal faith in Jesus Christ."

The large action photo of Ron Ellis in a Toronto Maple Leafs sweater is signed "To Teen Ranch." The caption reads, "In June 1975, I personally invited the Lord Jesus Christ into my life. From that time on in my pro career, I no longer measured my life by goals and assists. Accepting the fact that Jesus has a plan for me and realizing that my purpose in life is to bring honour to Him has made the difference in all aspects of my life." Below the caption is a Bible verse chosen by Ron Ellis:

> Train yourself in godliness, for while bodily training
> is of some value, godliness is of value in every way,
> as it holds promise for the present life and also
> for the life to come.
>
> 1 Timothy 4:8

Although the rink has been booked on this day for a father-and-son camp, the ice surface is empty. The participants, with whom

Ron scrimmaged on this particular blazing-hot summer morning, have only just stepped off the ice. Later in the same week, Paul Henderson will be visiting.

From the Ice Corral, the roadway leads past fences that corral beautiful horses to a series of what are later identified as bunkhouses for campers. Ron parks his GMC Jimmy and walks past a lovely waterfall fountain to the dining room. The walls are covered with barn wood and hung with objects identifying the room as part of a camp. It's noon, so the fathers and sons are gathering to enjoy a delicious buffet lunch. The lemonade and water on each table are consumed as quickly as they are poured.

Outside of the dining room lies Joey, the Teen Ranch dog. Resting quietly in the shade, Joey is loved by all, but has endured his own hardships en route to his nineteenth birthday. He's deaf and partially blind, has been struck by lightning, and was accidentally run over by Mel several years ago. Joey wags his tail vigorously at every passing camper.

Teen Ranch is rustic by design. Similar in design to the original Teen Ranch in Australia, Mel Stevens's dream perpetually evolves and grows. Not only are there hockey camps for both boys and girls, but also for Western and English horsemanship. There is also an "extreme adventure" camp that features canoeing, mountain biking, exploring caves, rock climbing and white-water kayaking. Just a few weeks before, the Ottawa Senators of the NHL had been in for four days of bonding and ice time. Roger Neilson, a Senators assistant coach, is a longtime friend of the ranch. Other teams that have made use of the facilities include national teams from Canada, Russia, Germany and Finland, as well as the St. Michael's Majors of the Ontario Hockey League.

Although Mel Stevens is slight of build, there is something about him that suggests great strength. He is quiet, yet commanding. There is no doubt that his word is law, yet his demeanour is calm and peaceful.

Stevens was born in Peterborough, Ontario, and lived in the country for much of his youth. After high school, he worked for the City of Peterborough in the tax assessment department before moving on to Toronto to work in sales. "I was very active in gospel music," he recalls. "I got active in People's Church and met a group of guys called the King's Men. To cut to the chase, we all headed for Australia. We went to help an Australian start a camp.

He couldn't get it going, and we figured, 'Well, maybe we can use our music to help him.'

"We sold everything we had and raised enough money together to pay our fares. My son was a month old. We had no job, no home, no car, no furniture — just $70. But the Lord provided for all that."

Their Australian contact put Mel and his friends on the radio. Six days a week, they did a half-hour gospel program, through which they told the story of Teen Ranch. "We did three concerts a week, church services and secular TV. After a year and seven months, we finally got enough money together to buy a piece of property. I had always gone to camp as a kid — they were Christian camps, and that was where I really got my spiritual life together, even though I was raised in a Christian home. Since I was the only guy with camp experience, I assumed the job of the director. Three of the guys and their families went home, but my wife and I stayed on for another five and a half years."

To make ends meet, Stevens operated a bulldozer part time, broke horses and even competed as a professional rodeo cowboy. "I did all these things because we had no salary and lived by faith all the years we were in Australia. I did whatever it took to help support us, and the Lord always provided. Then we decided to come back to Canada and start something here. By then, I had a wife and three children, eleven suitcases and $10 to get me through."

Mel and his family returned to Canada in 1967. Soon afterward, he founded the charity. "My brother was a pastor in Brampton, and he called the local newspaper on a Monday and said, 'My brother's here and he's going to start a camp in Caledon. Come and do an interview,'" he recalls. "They put a picture of me roping a calf on the front page and titled it, 'Cowboy to Start Christian Camp in Caledon.' After looking at sixty-five properties all over the province and down in the States, we came back to this one, which was the second one we looked at. I had a little master plan of what I wanted when I was in Australia, and I adapted it to this property. The land had nothing on it. Even the trees you see today, we planted. We put in the ponds, the roads, the buildings and the fences.

"We started with five kids the first week. The camp ran for five weeks, and we had a full house one week. We had one little bunkhouse with eight boys on one side and eight girls on the other. Horses were all we had at that time."

A smile comes over Mel's lips when he begins to talk about sports. "I played hockey and football, baseball and basketball, but hockey was my favourite. When I came back to Canada, the Leafs had just won the Stanley Cup that year. In 1971, I was at a Christian camping convention and I went to a basketball seminar. It was the last day, and I thought, 'Oh, no, I can't waste my money, I'd better go to something.' I sat in the back row, and as I sat there I realized there was no Christian hockey camp anywhere in the world. There was the Bobby Orr–Mike Walton camp, but people were telling me they were getting ripped off. Orr and Walton would show up and sign autographs for an hour. The kids would eat hamburger in different variations six days a week. All these stories kept coming back to me, so I thought, 'I'm a hockey man. I've got a good friend who's a university coach. Why don't I try a weekend?'"

Stevens held his first hockey camp on a Thanksgiving weekend. Out of that first group, he says, "One of the kids became a Christian and his father became a Christian. The kid went on and graduated from the University of Guelph, then went on to be a missionary in Haiti for a couple of years. Great things happened that first week.

"That summer we booked an arena in Brampton and started a summer camp. In 1973, I was the chaplain for the Argonauts and attended an Athletes in Action conference. I sat down in my room one day and sketched out an arena and a recreational complex. I wondered, 'Why can't we have something decent in a Christian atmosphere rather than sit in a hotel with a bar next door, with all the banging and crashing and loud music?'

"For fifteen years, I prayed about it, but was scared of it. I said, 'Lord, this will be to Your glory alone, and nobody's going to get an ego trip out of having our own arena.' Meanwhile, we found our program was dying. We were busing into Mississauga to get ice time. The kids would be on a bus two and a half hours every morning to get their two hours of ice time. And it was getting harder to get summer ice."

Finally, in the early 1980s, Stevens decided the time had come to build the rink. The project got off to a rough start. "The beams of the arena collapsed during construction, and neither the builder nor insurance covered the costs," Mel sighs.

"I was on the board of directors at the time," Ron Ellis adds. "We gave the go-ahead for Teen Ranch to build the arena. We didn't have all the money ourselves, so professional fundraisers were brought on board to help. A contractor was hired and the arena started going up. Huge beams were brought across Canada from British Columbia by train. The skeleton of the arena was in place, but then there was an accident. The beams came tumbling down like dominoes. Thank God it was on a Sunday and there were no workers around! The contractor didn't have the proper insurance, and there was a loophole in the contract that got them out of paying to rebuild the arena." It would take another half-million dollars to replace the original beams and Teen Ranch didn't have the money. The project was put on hold for a year until the necessary funds could be raised. "It was an exceptionally trying time," Ron says.

The trouble with the arena wasn't the only setback Teen Ranch encountered. "The things that went on at that time ... unbelievable!" Mel pauses and shakes his head. "A little girl died on the property. My wife died. My daughter was diagnosed with cancer. I had a malignant melanoma. There was a takeover bid by a former staff member. He tried to get rid of me — and succeeded in getting me out of the position of director. I'm usually a fighter, but I didn't fight then. The Lord turned that one around for us. All these things happened within about a two-year period. It just seemed like there was always something."

* * *

Mel Stevens explains how, as a sports fan, he got involved with NHL players. "I was watching Team Canada '72, and really felt a burden for two players in particular: Ron Ellis and Paul Henderson. I prayed for them, and noted their names in the journal I keep. I wondered how on earth I could ever get the message across that there was something missing in their lives, and it was the Lord. That was why they weren't content.

"The Lord gave me the idea that I should give Bibles to the players. It was a big investment, and we were a small charity — always struggling financially. The Bibles are about $70 apiece, and I covered all the players, the training staff, Ballard and everyone connected with the Leafs. Then I saw the testimony of Dean Prentice. He had recently become a Christian himself. I wrote a letter to Dean and asked him if he would be interested in coming to help at the first Christian hockey camp. He called me back and said he'd love to come. And he did, for several years." Dean Prentice was a solid NHL left winger for 22 seasons. Best known as a New York Ranger, with whom he was selected to the NHL's Second All-Star Team in 1960, Prentice later played with the Boston Bruins, Detroit Red Wings, Pittsburgh Penguins and Minnesota North Stars.

Stevens told Prentice about his concern for the two Leafs. "I was a teammate of Paul's in Detroit," Prentice said. "I know where he lives."

"I went to Paul Henderson's house unannounced one day, nervous as all get out," Mel says. "All he could do was to tell me to go away, I figured. I knocked on the door, and Paul's wife Eleanor answered. 'There's some man here to talk to you, Paul,' she said. Paul came to the door and was a little surly, but I asked him if he'd come up to Teen Ranch and be an instructor. And I think he asked me, 'How much?' Then I told him I was the man who'd left the Bible for him at Maple Leaf Gardens. Paul said, 'I've been meaning to write you a note.' He told me he had been reading the Bible and had some concerns. I didn't know Paul was searching for his spiritual reality."

Dean Prentice applied a little leverage, and Henderson finally agreed to come to the camp. "Paul had a lot of questions, and we started to meet on a regular basis," Mel says. "Sometimes it was once a week, twice a week, sometimes for three hours at a time. He had an insatiable curiosity."

"I drove him crazy asking questions," laughs Henderson. "He gave me some good books to read. And it was through the influence of Mel Stevens that, in March of 1975, I decided to become a follower of Jesus Christ."

Paul Henderson tells about the way he told his wife and friends about his search. "During the summer of '73, we were over in Switzerland — there was me and Eleanor and the Ellises — and we were sitting at the top of the Jungfraujoch in Interlochen, the highest railway station in the world. I looked around, and it was just incredible, and I said to them, 'I know there has got to be a God, and I'm going to find Him.' I had been on the periphery before, but that's when I really decided to get serious. Along the way, I had shared my struggles with Ronnie a bit, and told him what was going on — my discontentment with life. He and Janny were aware. When I became a Christian, I was nervous about sharing my faith. I basically talked to Mel Stevens and said, 'I need you to speak to these guys. I don't know how to share my faith in an intelligent way at this point.' And Mel said, 'Let's have a weekend.' So we invited Ronnie and Jan, plus a really good friend of mine, Paul Oliver, and his wife Jean, and Eleanor and I went up to Teen Ranch for a weekend. I had some conversations with Ronnie, but it was mainly Mel who explained it to all four of them."

"This was all happening during the hockey season, so of course, Paul talked about it all the time," continues Ron. "He started to share his thoughts with me. I'm his best buddy, and I was listening, but I'm stubborn. Then, I went up to the ranch and met Mel. We started talking. At the end of that season, Mel invited Paul and me and some other hockey players to an athletes' retreat. All the football players were there. Dean Prentice and Sandy Hucul, who were early Christian hockey players, also attended. Paul and his wife Eleanor really encouraged us to go up to Teen Ranch for that weekend, and Jan really wanted to go, so I went. We went horseback riding and did some really fun things, but then there were those devotional times.

"During those two or three days, I sat very quietly and listened. I was prepared to listen, I'll say that much. I didn't contribute very much, but I listened. I was still skeptical. I was listening to these other athletes who had the same pressures on them that I had experienced. It was obvious that they had something I didn't have — peace, contentment. I started to get the message.

"My wife and I went away from that weekend with some answers and many questions. Listening to other Christians was instrumental in our coming to the Lord. Ironically, our personal commitment to Jesus Christ came separately. I had gone up to the camp at Sand Lake, and Janny remained at home. When I came back, I remember saying, 'Jan, I've got something exciting to tell you,' and she said, 'Well, I have something exciting to tell you!' We had both made our commitment, pretty much at the same time, but separate from each other. It was likely better that way, as one didn't feel coerced by the other. From that moment on, I started living for the Lord. I started doing everything I could to honour and glorify Him."

That September, Ron retired. "When I think about it, being a young Christian did give me some courage to retire. I said, 'Okay, Lord, you're in control of my life — show me the way.'"

"We had Bible study at different homes," Stevens says. "Sometimes, Paul and Eleanor would host, and other times other people would host the evening. One time it was scheduled for Jan and Ronnie's house. They had a pool in the backyard. Well, Paul said, 'I want you to baptize me in Ronnie's pool.' When we got to Ron's, we told him what we wanted to do. He was so worried that the neighbours were going to wonder what was going on in his pool. But that's where Paul Henderson was baptized, in Ron and Jan's swimming pool."

"There's an old quarry on the property of Teen Ranch," Ron mentions, walking through a patch of cedar trees past a large fire pit surrounded by benches. In the nearby clearing, Ron points to a beautiful pond, where campers splash about playfully. "Mel Stevens and Ron Hembry, our pastors at the time, baptized Jan and me there in that pond." There is a very contented smile on Ron's face at that moment. "It was a quarry up until 1930," Mel adds. "We've never promoted it, but almost every year, somebody asks to be baptized there."

Mel Stevens talks candidly about his friend, Ron Ellis. "Ronnie oozes sincerity. The marvellous thing I've noticed about Ron is the openness and transparency and willingness to talk about anything. He's a very private individual, and for many, many years, you didn't get past that shield. But Ron is the most gentle, sincere gentle man that I've known — certainly in sports. He's highly respected all over the country. There's no pretence. He's just a beautiful, warm guy. In our new coach house, we named one room the Ron Ellis Room out of respect for him."

Stevens elaborates on Ron's insularity. "He was very private about his faith at first — extremely private. But as he gained confidence, he had a powerful influence on many of the guys on the team. It's interesting. Paul Henderson is a guy who is very aggressive about his faith, and Ron is very quiet. But because of Ron's sensitivity and the way he lives his life, he has a powerful influence on people.

"Once, he flew me to Montreal, then to Quebec City for chapel services with the Leafs. He didn't want somebody he didn't know personally to come in. He paid for the trips himself so that I could do the two chapel services. Laurie Boschman decided to come to one of them."

* * *

"I was born in Kerrobert, Saskatchewan, a town of 3,000, but my hometown was really Major," says Boschman, who joined the Leafs during the 1979–80 season. Major, with a population of only 150, wasn't large enough to have its own hospital. The nearest one was in Kerrobert.

"As I was growing up, I followed hockey like every other young kid. We only got two channels on TV, but we watched the Leaf games a lot as a family. I was certainly aware of Ron Ellis and the Maple Leafs of the time, but I found myself cheering for the Boston Bruins — Esposito, Hodge and Cashman."

Boschman played his junior hockey with the Brandon Wheat Kings of the Western Hockey League. He had hired Alan Eagleson to act as his agent, and Eagleson arranged for Boschman to play for the Canadian Olympic Team. "But right at that same time," Boschman says, "I was drafted by the Toronto Maple Leafs." Laurie was the Leafs' first choice, and the ninth pick overall in the 1979 draft. "Mr. Ballard called me to congratulate me, as did King Clancy and Dick Duff. I now had a huge decision to make — do I play in the 1980 Olympics or go to the Leafs training camp with no guarantee I was going to make the team?" Boschman decided to go to the Leafs camp.

"I had just turned 19, and I was in awe when I walked into Maple Leaf Gardens for the first time. I mean, watching TV back home, there were two Meccas — the Forum in Montreal and Maple Leaf Gardens.

"My roommate was Jiri Crha, the goaltender. He couldn't speak much English and I certainly couldn't speak Czech, so we communicated by way of a Czech-English dictionary. I just remember it being an unbelievable time. Toronto had so many character players at that time. They had Ronnie Ellis, Darryl Sittler, Lanny McDonald. They had Tiger Williams and Borje Salming. I learned an awful lot from these individuals.

"Floyd Smith came up to me and told me I had made the team. He told me to get a place in Toronto. I called my folks and told them how thrilled I was. I happened to sit beside Ronnie in the dressing room. I was 19, and he was 35 at the time — married with two kids. I didn't even have a girlfriend.

"I remember thinking, 'The guy's a fossil. He's so old!' I never told Ron that at the time, although we've talked about it since and had a good laugh. It's just how your perspective on life changes. All of sudden, I got to my late twenties and thought, 'Thirty-five-year-olds aren't that old.'

"Ron was one of those guys who were extremely well respected. He was the elder statesman on the hockey club. He was a confidant for many of the guys. Many of the guys, including myself, would go to him because he was a veteran player, had been on a Stanley Cup–winning team, had seen a lot of coaches come and go, and had a tremendous work ethic and a great perspective on hockey and on life. For a young rookie in the league, it was priceless to sit beside a guy who was so well grounded and, in my estimation, had a tremendous peace about him through the ups and downs of hockey.

"The three years I was in Toronto were quite tumultuous," Boschman admits. "They were the Punch Imlach and Harold Ballard years. For a young kid cutting his teeth in the NHL, it was invaluable to have guys like Ron around so that I could learn how to practise, to discover the work ethic that was needed, and how to deal with the media. I learned an awful lot sitting beside Ronnie and watching how he conducted himself.

"As a family, we used to go to church on a regular basis," Boschman continues, "but I just went because that's what we did. I wasn't really into understanding what the Bible had to say or if it did have anything to say to me in my life. That's another thing I learned through Ron.

"I was playing in the National Hockey League and things were going quite well for me, especially that first year, because I was playing regularly with John Anderson and Rocky Saganiuk. Growing up, I always thought my goal was to make it to the NHL. I never thought that it would actually happen. Once I had in fact made it, I was experiencing all these things that I had seen as a youngster — Madison Square Garden, Boston Garden, it was an absolute thrill! Being at Maple Leaf Gardens and being recognized on the streets of Toronto was pretty interesting for a 19-year-old kid from a small town.

"As a youngster, I thought that if I made it to the NHL, everything would be great and my life would be totally complete. Now, here I was playing in the NHL and experiencing all those things I had dreamed about, and yet I wondered, 'Is this all there is?' I felt that there was something missing in my life. My success didn't bring me the sense of joy and fulfillment that I thought it would," Laurie states.

"Ron was the sounding board that guys would go to, and I was no different. So one day I said to Ron, 'I've been watching how you conduct yourself with your wife and your kids and how you are in the dressing room whether we win or lose, and I noticed there's something different about you.'

"I asked him, 'What makes you tick? What makes you go?' And he said something I had never heard before. He said, 'Laurie, I'm a born-again Christian. I have a relationship with Jesus Christ and I use God's word in the Bible as a basis for my life.' I always thought it was up to the priest or the pastor or the minister to open up the Bible and tell us how to live. I had never before heard that I could actually look into the Bible myself and find some guidelines and some answers to life. It was really through Ron's example that I decided I wanted what he had, and that was a tremendous peace. That's what really attracted me to him and to the Bible and to a personal faith in Christ."

Boschman says that the early years of his NHL career were also difficult because of the strained relations between Toronto coach/general manager Punch Imlach and his players, especially team captain Darryl Sittler. "Punch tried to bring in some old-style management ideas that had gone by the wayside and there was a lot of butting heads amongst all of us players and management. And Harold Ballard didn't mind saying what he thought about this, that or the other thing."

After his first NHL season, Boschman decided to become a Christian. "We had a chapel on the day of a game in Quebec City. Ron invited me to attend, so I went up to the hotel room where the chapel was being held and realized I was a sinner and needed a saviour. And that's when I asked Christ into my heart." He smiles broadly. "I accepted the Lord right there. I realized that being a Christian was something that would be very helpful in my life. I recognized that I needed to make a decision about what role Christ would play in my life."

Boschman admits to being worried about how Leafs owner Harold Ballard would take the news. "I had been a first-rounder, and if I wasn't playing well, what would Mr. Ballard say?

"In my second year, I got into a fight with Robbie Ftorek in Quebec City. I gave him an uppercut and hit him right in the tooth. I chipped the index finger on my right hand. It was bleeding and the doctor sewed it up, but he failed to give me a tetanus shot. I guess the mouth is the dirtiest part of the body — it's got the most bacteria. I didn't think anything about it and finished the game. After we flew home, my hand swelled up and it started going up my arm." The young Leaf had come down with blood poisoning. He was admitted to hospital and administered an intravenous drip to get the infection under control. "It's interesting, because Robbie ended up being an assistant coach under John Cunniff when I played in New Jersey, so we had a chuckle about that incident," he says.

"Shortly after I came back, I got mononucleosis. I only played fifty-three games my second year. There was pressure on me to perform. In my third year, I got off to a slow start and thought, 'Oh, no! What's going on?' I was concerned about what my fate would be, and in what kind of light it would be played. We were playing against the Rangers in 1981. I guess Harold Ballard went on TV with Dick Beddoes on CHCH-TV between the second and third periods and said he was going to trade Boschman because I'd got too much religion. I didn't know about that. After the game at Madison Square Garden, we chartered back to Toronto and practised the next day. I was out on the ice and Darryl Sittler came up to me and said, 'Hey, Bosch, did you hear what happened last night?'"

Darryl filled in the blanks for his teammate, and said, "Laurie, get ready, because all the guys from the media are going to be asking you about this after practice."

"Ballard used to really get on Laurie's case," adds Mel Stevens. "He used to call him 'Born-Again Boschman.' The Leaf coach was Mike Nykoluk. He phoned Laurie's father and told him he had to get Laurie out of that cult at this ranch up there, north of Toronto. Laurie would be on the phone all upset. He was a 20-year-old kid and they just put him through hell. And as if there wasn't enough pressure on him already, he had mono at the same time. He used to come up to Teen Ranch to skate with me when he was recovering from mono. I had more stamina than he did!

"Ballard was really angry. Boschman, Ellis and Henderson and a few of the other boys were now Christians and he made an announcement that none of the players were allowed to give me tickets," Stevens says with a smirk. "Darryl Sittler wasn't a Christian at the time, but he challenged Ballard on an airplane one day. Ballard was up in first class, and Darryl went up and gave it to him. 'Do you realize that probably 20 to 25 percent of your season ticket subscribers are born again?' Ballard just grumbled. Borje Salming phoned me and said, 'Mel, no worries. Any time you want tickets, I'll leave them in my name for you. I don't care about Ballard.' And Ballard loved Borje."

"I didn't quite understand why Mr. Ballard would point to my Christian faith as the reason I wasn't playing well," continues Boschman. "I felt it was through his ignorance that he would even make that statement. He was a bombastic individual, and the statement was out there and there was quite a debate over whether you could be a Christian and play a physical game like hockey. By year three, I guess I wasn't living up to the expectations Toronto management had for me. It got to the point where it was very difficult to play under those circumstances, so I had to ask them to trade me."

Punch Imlach had suffered a heart attack, and Gerry McNamara had taken his place as general manager, while former Marlboro Mike Nykoluk was handed the coaching reins. "I had to find another team that was willing to take a chance on me," Boschman says. "That happened when Edmonton traded for me. I just needed an opportunity to start fresh. I was basically traded because of my faith. It had come to that point."

Dave Burrows is another Leaf who credits Ron Ellis with his decision to become a Christian. "When we retired, we built homes within fifteen minutes of each other and we started playing old-timer hockey together. We saw quite a bit of each other. Ron eventually invited me to a hockey tournament in Timmins. This team was made up of a bunch of Christian men. Because I knew Ron and Mel Stevens and a few of the other guys, I agreed to go along. For the first time, I heard the truth of the Gospel about Christ. I accepted Christ because of that weekend hockey tournament."

"I remember watching Ron Ellis when I began to get into hockey," says former Leaf Mark Osborne. "He was easily identifiable — he had that helmet and was always adjusting his elbow pads. But he really patrolled that right wing.

"I was born and raised in a family of regular church-goers. When I was 14 years old, my Uncle was hit by a car and passed away. Around that time, John Wesley White came to speak at our church. He was from the Billy Graham Ministries. At that time, I didn't know where I stood in God's eyes. I wanted a personal relationship with God. On the morning of November 2, 1975, I asked Christ to come into my life, and made that personal step of faith.

"I received an invitation as a 17-year-old to attend the Niagara Falls Flyers camp. In midget, I had been one of the smallest guys, but lo and behold, that summer, I grew six inches. I went from 5' 8" to 6' 2". I also spent the summer running and working with weights. I went to the Flyers camp and made the team as a walk-on. The timing was right, and I was determined.

"That was where the rubber met the road for me. I believed in my heart of hearts that, since the door to hockey was opened for me, I needed God to walk beside me to give me courage and to direct my path. I started to ask myself some questions. 'Who am I, and who am I amongst my peers?' If there was drinking, drugs or sex, how was I going to fit in? But I figured I would just live up to my personal convictions. I didn't know how my teammates were going to accept me. I was just one of twenty guys on the team. I didn't try to make my teammates feel guilty. If they were doing things I didn't agree with, well, that was their choice. I'm not any better than they are because I don't do certain things. Once I spent time with the guys, they accepted me for what I was. I just realized I had a responsibility to be a good role model, but also a good Christian role model.

"The next year, I started to hear that some of us might get drafted. It's one thing to get drafted, but that's just the first step — there's a lot of work ahead," Osborne continues. "In 1980, I was Detroit's second pick in the draft. After three years with the Niagara Falls Flyers, I was sent to Adirondack, Detroit's farm team, for the playoffs and we won the Calder Cup, the American league championship. It was a great learning experience. The following autumn, I made the Red Wings as a 19-year-old.

"Without a doubt, I was a Toronto Maple Leafs fan," chuckles Mark. "I was born and raised in Toronto, and would often go to the Gardens to watch games with my Dad. I had dreamed of wear-

146

ing that sweater. In 1987, the dream came true when I was traded to Toronto. That was the ultimate. And it gave me the chance to play at home in front of family and friends. It's a jersey with a rich tradition.

"It was ironic," suggests Osborne, "that I was going to Toronto, playing for an owner who claimed he'd never let another Christian play on his team. Laurie Boschman and Ronnie Ellis had stood up for their faith, and that gave me inspiration. In the '50s, '60s and most of the '70s, no one stepped out about their faith, but now Boschman, Ellis, Henderson, Burrows, Chico Resch, Mike Gartner and Ryan Walter were all open about it. They were all exceptional hockey players, with no lack of edge.

"I never got to play with Ronnie, but after all these years, we've gotten to know each other quite well. We've both been involved with Leaf alumni events and both been involved with ministry in the game of hockey.

"I have a lot of respect for Ron Ellis," declares Osborne. "I admire the fact he has made himself transparent as a human being, letting everyone know about his self-admitted struggles. With Ron, actions speak louder than words. He may be quiet in many respects, but he's a quality guy, a friend and someone who has given me great encouragement through the years."

* * *

"I'm genuinely humbled that the guys would allow us to get involved," says Stevens, shaking his head in wonderment. "Teen Ranch has been going since 1967. Every year, we bring thousands of kids up for a real adventure experience. Teen Ranch has positive role models and positive peer pressure built on a foundation of Christian faith and morality. It's a non-denominational Christian sports camp." Stevens says he has further plans in mind for Teen Ranch. "A pool, a gymnasium, a big weight room, more extensive riding facilities. In a world that seems to have gone mad, we encourage our guests to consider Biblical values.

"I'm not a religious man," explains Mel Stevens. "I have a relationship with God."

CHAPTER FIFTEEN

First Retirement

The 1974–75 season represented the best and worst of times for Ron Ellis.

On a personal level, he enjoyed an outstanding season, with 32 goals — only the second time he had reached the 30-goal plateau — and a career-high 61 points. But the line with which Ron had enjoyed the most success as a professional hockey player was in the midst of breaking up. Prior to the season, left winger Paul Henderson had jumped to the Toronto Toros of the WHA, with whom he scored 30 goals in fifty-eight games. The hero of the 1972 Summit Series was also on hand to represent his country for a second time in 1974, when a team of WHA stars took their turn challenging Team USSR. Henderson and his Toros teammate Frank Mahovlich were the only members of Team Canada '72 to play for the 1974 edition of the team. Four of the eight games ended in ties; of the other four, Canada won only once — at Toronto's Maple Leaf Gardens.

Meanwhile, centreman Norm Ullman saw his playing time cut back considerably. "I didn't play much at all that year," says Norm Ullman. "I could never really figure out why. I'd led the Leafs in assists the year before, and I'd been fifth in scoring at the All-Star break, yet I was only getting one or two shifts a game [in '74–75].

"Yeah, I was getting older [Ullman turned 39 during the season], but I was still producing. Red Kelly was the coach, but he never said why I wasn't getting more ice time." Ullman scored only 9 goals and 26 assists in his very limited role. The Edmonton Oilers of the WHA had made him their first selection in the massive 1972 draft, a fact to which Ullman had never given much thought. But when Toronto released him, he decided to return to his hometown. Edmonton was also where he had played junior and minor-pro hockey, as an Oil King and then a Flyer.

Dave Keon was another Leaf centre whose production dropped off in 1974–75. His 16 goals represented the second-fewest total of his fifteen-year NHL career. After the season, he jumped to the Minnesota Fighting Saints of the WHA.

"Ron Ellis was the only player from my Marlie days who was still playing on the Leafs when I returned in 1974," Rod Seiling points out. A look at the Toronto roster in 1974–75 bears out his observation. The team's best player was now 24-year-old Darryl Sittler, whose supporting cast included a handful of players who had yet to pass their twenty-fifth birthday: George Ferguson, Lanny McDonald, Errol Thompson, Blaine Stoughton, Borje Salming, Dave "Tiger" Williams, Bob Neely and Ian Turnbull. At 29, Ron Ellis was considered one of the team's elder statesmen.

Sittler had established himself as the team's most potent scoring threat, notching 36 goals and 44 assists to finish with 80 points and leading the Leafs in all three categories. "I played on a line with Darryl and Tiger Williams that year," recalls Ron. "We had a great line. It was the Leafs' number-one line."

Still, Ron was struggling with questions that refused to be answered. "From a professional point of view, the '74–75 season was very enjoyable. It was a very successful year and it was a thrill to play with those two guys. We balanced each other really well. But mentally, I was struggling with life. My original goal had been to play ten seasons. This was my eleventh. I was really wondering about, 'Where does Ron Ellis go from here?' In the back of my mind, there was always the reminder that I could have gone to university and got my degree. We still weren't making great money — that year, I made $100,000. There was a lot going on in my mind.

"In talking to a few other players, that ten-year mark was when you had to start making decisions. You've got to decide whether you're going to leave then, while you're healthy and fairly young, and move into that new career, or leave everything on the back burner and try to get in five more years.

"All those thoughts were consuming my thinking," Ron confesses. "A dark cloud was starting to come over me."

Ron still commanded his share of respect in the Leafs dressing room. Lanny McDonald, who was on the verge of becoming an

NHL scoring star, would pay tribute to the veteran in his autobi-ography, *Lanny*. "If there was an unsung leader of the Leafs at the time, that man was Ronnie Ellis. He didn't say much, but he let his actions on the ice speak for themselves. I tried to pick up all the good things he did. Not realizing he was as good as he was, he was never satisfied with himself. His legs were always moving, and I learned a tremendous amount just by watching him.

"[Ron] took time with the young players in Toronto," McDonald continues. "Ellis was a hero of mine when I was grow-ing up. I still looked upon Ellis that way when I played for the Maple Leafs. There are times in life when you expect too much from people, but Ellis was the type who gave and never stopped giving. I wanted to be just like him, and I still think of Ronnie as a hero."

"When Dave Keon left the Leafs in '75, Leafs management asked me to be captain," says Darryl Sittler. "But before they did, they went to Ronnie to talk to him about it. He had the seniority and the respect, and they wanted to make sure he was onside. Ronnie was in full agreement, and was very supportive, which was very important to me and the Leafs. The captain has to have the support and respect of the players, and I got lots of support from Ronnie, Lanny, Tiger and the rest of the guys."

"At one time, Punch had told me that he was grooming me for the captaincy," Ron recalls. "I would have been honoured to be captain of the Toronto Maple Leafs, even if it was only for one year. I could have taken it when it was offered, but I was so uncer-tain of my future and my health. The front office made the right decision in choosing Darryl and I was wise not to cause a problem. Darryl was ready to be the official leader."

* * *

In what was becoming a biennial tradition, the 1974–75 season was yet another expansion year. This time the NHL took on the Kansas City Scouts and Washington Capitals to increase its com-plement of teams to eighteen. The league was realigned into two conferences of two divisions each. The Toronto Maple Leafs were assigned to the Adams Division, which lined up in the Prince of Wales Conference, along with the Boston Bruins, Buffalo Sabres and California Golden Seals. Twelve teams would qualify for the revamped Stanley Cup playoffs; the four division winners earned byes into the quarterfinals, while the second- and third-place teams took part in a preliminary best-of-three series to compete for one of the four remaining second-round berths.

The Toronto Maple Leafs finished the season with 31 wins, 33 losses and 16 ties for a 78-point season — a drop of 8 from the season before — and a third-place finish behind the Sabres and Bruins. In the opening playoff round, Toronto faced the Los Angeles Kings, who had recorded 105 points, in what would prove to be an incredibly close series. Game one was played in L.A., and Mike Murphy — a future coach of the Leafs — scored in overtime to give the Kings a 3–2 win and a 1–0 series lead. Two nights later in Toronto, the home team matched the feat, as Blaine Stoughton scored in extra time to give the Leafs a 3–2 win and tie the series. The deciding game was played the following night in Los Angeles, and Toronto won a 2–1 squeaker to upset the Kings and move on to the quarterfinals.

The Leafs would not be as fortunate in the second round. Their opponents, the Philadelphia Flyers, were the defending Stanley Cup champions. With 113 points, the Flyers had finished in a three-way tie for first place overall with the Montreal Canadiens and Buffalo Sabres. They made short work of the Leafs, sweeping the best-of-seven series and going on to recapture the Stanley Cup.

"That summer, I got up to the resort to help out when I could," Ron says. "I also took a summer job just to get some experience in sales. I kept myself busy training and working. But I knew something wasn't right — I just couldn't put my finger on it. Physically, I looked strong. I was weight training and bench pressing over 300 pounds."

In retrospect, Ron concludes, "I was really having trouble mentally and I really believe depression was starting to get its hold on me."

Even so, Ron felt he could shake off his dark feelings. "I went to training camp, and felt good physically. I remember Jim Gregory telling me, 'Hey, Ron, you're having a real good camp!' I played in all the exhibition games. Then one day, towards the end of training camp, we were doing our stretches before practice and I said to Brian Glennie, 'Brian, I'm going to retire.' Brian couldn't believe what he was hearing. He was the closest guy to me on the team and wasn't aware of the turmoil I was going through.

"There was a feeling of heaviness, or a fog. I wasn't sleeping. I was withdrawing from everyone. I was able to get on the ice and perform, but after that, it was straight home. I knew if I had carried on, something was going to happen, something detrimental to myself, my wife and my kids, so I thought it was best to leave the game for a while."

Ron was coming off his best NHL season and was walking away from a new four-year contract that would pay him $140,000 per year.

"Can I explain the reasons? No, I can't. I just knew," says Ron, his voice dropping to a near whisper. "Something inside told me, 'You can't play this year.' I never completely closed the door to a return to the Leafs. But I knew that, for the time being, I couldn't play."

His decision made, Ron broke the news to the Leafs front office. "I went to Red Kelly, the coach, and said, 'Red, I can't play.' I don't remember the conversation. Red is a pretty quiet guy, but I think he just looked at me and said, 'Okay, Ron. You know best.'

"I tried to explain my decision to Jim Gregory. He said, 'Ron, we were in Ballard's Bunker [the owner's private box at the Gardens] last night during the exhibition game and we were just saying, 'Isn't it great to see Ellis out there?' Even when he told me that, all I could say was, 'Jim, I can't play.'"

"I had been keeping abreast of things," says Jim Gregory. "When you're living together for eight or nine months a year, you see things. I knew he was troubled and we talked often. But it was still a surprise when he announced his retirement."

Ron understands how his announcement would seem to have come out of left field. "Here was a guy who had just signed a four-year contract. Here was a guy who was coming off his best year. The team was starting to make noise. Sittler, McDonald and Williams were developing. And Darryl was very influential in getting some key players into Toronto — Pat Boutette, Dave Hutchison, Walt McKechnie, Dan Maloney. Darryl knew all these guys — he had played with them in junior. We were starting to get some character players. It was a breath of fresh air for Toronto. Even with these positives, I knew I couldn't contribute to the team's efforts in the short term. I didn't want to be a sideshow to a team that was becoming competitive.

"My sense was that, the way I was feeling, I might not be able to remain in the lineup consistently. I didn't want to be a drag on the Toronto Maple Leafs," he says with a sigh. "My sense of 'team' was a major factor. I prided myself on my consistency. In my eleven seasons with the Leafs to that point, I played every single game of the season in seven of them. And in '74–75, I only missed one game." Ron felt that, given his state of mind, he might not be able to uphold that standard of reliability. "I'd be a distraction to the team. That was one of the main thoughts that I remember.

"So I walked away. I didn't know what I was going to do. I didn't have any plans — no job offers, no nothing. I did have enough money saved to handle our affairs for a few months. That's how suddenly I made the decision."

Brian Glennie roomed with Ron for several years, and the two became very close friends. "When I came up to the Leafs in '69, my first roommate was Tim Horton," Glennie recalls. "Timmy was traded to the Rangers at the end of that season, and my second roommate was Ronnie. We roomed together for five or six years. Then, I guess the Leafs felt I was mature enough and I inherited Jim McKenny." He laughs.

"Ron had a lot of nicknames — Chuvalo, Chevy — but I'm the only one who calls him R.J. — Ronald John," says Glennie. "R.J. had so much natural ability. He had powerful legs — tree stumps for legs. Easy skater, but he couldn't always hit that upper right corner though he tried. He was a class individual, and maybe too quiet for his own good. He was very, very quiet. He just went about his business. Of course, back then, you didn't question management. They were the gods and they could send you down to the minors if you questioned them.

"R.J. was a great roommate. He is godfather to both my children. My daughter is a chiropractor in Toronto and my son is out in Halifax managing a bar. He must get it from his mother — he couldn't get it from me!

"Even though we were very close and I was with him every day, I never knew what Ron was going through. He was a very private individual. I didn't know he was suffering from depression until he retired.

"Personally, I felt it was the wrong thing for him to do. Then again, having gone through depression myself since, you don't ever really know what somebody is going through. I don't even know if he was aware that it was depression. Who knew about depression then? It certainly wasn't a common topic. R.J. probably didn't know what was bothering him. I'm not sure he could explain it to a doctor. Being the quiet kind of person that Ronnie is, how do you sit down and talk about your feelings of sadness? He never talked to me about it then. Since then, of course, we've talked about post-hockey problems. He's able to talk to me about his depression. We both have had bouts of it.

"At the time, I thought he just got tired of the game," recalls Glennie. "Playing for Punch could have made anybody depressed! He was a little general. I mean, I remember Johnny Bower, 45 years old, on a road trip to L.A. I knocked on the door and saw Johnny trying to hide a beer under the bed. He said, 'I thought you were Punch.' Johnny was 45 years old, for gawd's sake!"

Paul Henderson, Ron's closest friend, was aware that Ron was battling himself. "I knew Ronnie had always struggled, but now we know why. I didn't know it was depression, but I knew Ronnie struggled. Ron is a very moody guy and he lets things get to him. I just couldn't understand what the poor guy was going through. My faith was so new. 'Well, if you just give it to the Lord, you'll get over all this stuff. You're just not trusting the Lord.' Well, that was so simplistic it's a joke. But when you're new and immature to your faith, you think things like that. I'm a little more mature now and I realize life is very, very complicated. There are different personalities, and depression is a terrible, terrible thing. I don't understand it to this day, but I understand that it's very difficult. It's just oppressive. With my personality, I have not had to deal with depression at all."

Rod Seiling had played with Ron Ellis when the Marlboros won the Memorial Cup in 1964, and the two were again teammates ten years later after a trade with Washington brought Seiling back to Toronto. "I was aware of Ron's depression," he says. "Those are things we kept private, and keep private. We all have our problems we face in life and everyone faces them in different ways. It wasn't really a surprise when Ron announced his retirement at the end of that season. It was understandable, knowing what was going on."

Darryl Sittler remembers Ron's decision to step away from the game. "When the point comes that you're not enjoying the game, it's time to move on, and I think that's what happened when

Ronnie retired in 1975. You have to make a decision that's right for you personally and for your wife and kids. So when Ronnie retired, we all respected his decision. You have to respect anyone who makes a decision as hard as that one.

"Through all the crazy times, Ron was a man of honour and integrity. But where Ronnie and I differed was in our approach to the game. I tried to make sure the negative part of the game didn't affect me. Ron was a conscientious guy who worries a lot. He's still like that today. If he had chances but didn't score, he'd be frustrated. He'd feel he let himself and his team down. He was never satisfied with his game — he had very high expectations of himself.

"Ronnie always knew what his role was, and did whatever it took to do it to the best of his ability," Sittler concludes. "He was a real team player. And he tried to fulfill his role as best he could both on and off the ice. And when Ron decided to come back a couple of years later, we all thought that was great, too. I've never heard anyone say a bad word about Ronnie Ellis."

"I was surprised when I heard that Ron had retired," remembers former linemate, Norm Ullman. "I knew he was having some personal problems, but it still surprised me."

Brian Conacher, who had known Ron Ellis since the two played for the Toronto Marlboros in 1961, says, "Ronnie's personal challenges didn't become public until much later. Ronnie was very quiet — he wasn't flashy. Quietly confident. He was a very, very honest hockey player. He came to play. He wasn't outspoken. Perhaps the depression explains why Ronnie was so quiet. Ronnie Ellis was a very, very good hockey player. But maybe he didn't think he was."

"My teammates were shocked," Ellis remembers. "No one could understand, and I couldn't explain what was happening. They knew I wasn't myself. No one ever suggested that I go see a doctor. Few understood depression. No one talked about it, especially around macho athletes. Depression was associated with weakness, at least, that's what I thought. This is an example of the misunderstanding of depression.

"As the years have gone on, it has occurred to me that I should have told Jim Gregory, 'I'd like to see a doctor.' It never even occurred to me to ask. And the Leafs never suggested it. And I didn't say, 'Hey, would you just give me a few weeks off? I want to see the doctor to see if I can get my act back together.' But that's what happened.

"Whether it was the right decision or the wrong decision, it's in the past. It's history. I've had to make some tough decisions in my life — whether to turn pro or go to university, and whether to retire or not say anything and try to keep playing. Life puts us in the position where we have to make these decisions. And we have to live with those choices."

As soon as he retired, Ron says, "There was immediate relief. I missed the guys and I missed the team, but there was relief. Just like a piano had been taken off my back. For the first while, I rested, slept and spent time with the kids. The first few months were fantastic, but then I knew I had to move on."

Ron's thoughts reflect back on his retirement as a player. "As a professional athlete, I was always wondering what I would do when I was finished. There's always that concern. Having those two years away from the game, I realized that I could survive in the real world. I came back with a whole new outlook."

CHAPTER SIXTEEN

Life after the Leafs

"I made the announcement that I had retired at the end of September 1975," Ron Ellis recalls. "October and November were difficult, but I felt a good deal of relief. It was tough to watch the guys play — and I couldn't bear to go down to the rink — but I knew I had made a good short-term decision. It definitely seemed that a tremendous weight had been lifted off my shoulders."

Ron decided to retire so suddenly that he hadn't given any thought to what he would do next. "Then I got a call from an acquaintance I had met at a Christian men's dinner. He called me and said, 'Hey, Ron, you know I work for McClintock Homes. Well, we've just bought a golf course in King City, north of Toronto. Would you be interested in joining our company and running the golf course for us?'

"I said, 'I'd love to meet with you on that.' The McClintocks, who owned McClintock Homes, were a strong Christian family. They had built a great deal of the community of Agincourt, in Scarborough. The company was very well known and a highly respected developer. The golf course has now been turned into a beautiful estate development, but at that time it was a semi-private golf course called the King Valley Golf Club.

"We eventually met and I got excited about the opportunity. Within a month or so, we had come to an agreement. That's when I started managing the course." Under new ownership, the course was renamed the Carrying Place Golf and Country Club. The new name reflected the location's history. The Toronto Carrying Place was a trail used by the Iroquois to portage between the Humber River, which flowed into Lake Ontario, and the Holland River, which flowed into Lake Simcoe. From Lake Simcoe, it was possible to proceed along the Severn River into Georgian Bay. The trail would have run through land occupied by the golf course.

For the next two years, Ron served as manager of the complex. During that time, "Improvements were made on the course and we started a tennis club. I was enjoying my new position and I proved a lot to myself during those two years. I proved that Ron Ellis could survive in the real world. He had skills far beyond that of skating and shooting a puck.

"There was another positive aspect to my new position," states Ellis. "I was invited to attend a Bible study with the owner, the president and vice president once a week at the main office in Toronto. The gentleman who had hired me also lived in the area and we started attending a little church, the King Bible Church, in King City. My faith grew and I really feel in my heart that this was part of the Lord's plan.

"If I had been thrown back into the hockey world as a young Christian, who knows what might have happened? Paul Henderson was gone by then, and I would have been the only professing Christian on the Leafs. I might not have matured as a believer. By getting away from the game, meeting with these accomplished, successful men and joining a lovely church, my faith had a chance to grow. If I had continued to play, with the pressure of being a veteran and being expected to produce, maybe my Christianity would have been put on the back burner.

"I hadn't closed the door on going back to the Leafs, but I was enjoying the work and they were happy with my contribution. We had built a lovely home in the development, and our family was content. There were opportunities to grow with the company. During the two years I was out of the game, I was playing with the NHL Oldtimers and really enjoying it. Andy Bathgate was on the team. I was still young and in pretty good shape so I was having a lot of fun. We travelled around, playing hockey and raising money for charities. I was enjoying being around the guys.

"And then, I started to ask myself, 'I wonder if I could go back?'

"During my second year away, the announcement was made that the International Ice Hockey Federation had agreed to allow professionals to play in the World Championships for the first time. Talk about timing!"

CHAPTER SEVENTEEN

Return to the Leafs

In the early months of 1977, Ron Ellis heard that the International Ice Hockey Federation was planning to change its policy and allow professionals to take part in the World Championships, to be held that spring in Vienna. It meant that Canada, which had been absent from the tournament for eight years, would once again compete. The news excited Ron. "I made a phone call to Alan Eagleson, my lawyer at that time," he recalls. "I said, 'Al, I hear you're going to Vienna and using pros. I've been there, I've played international hockey; a lot of these players haven't. If I talk to my guys at work and can get the time off, can I help in any way? Can I come along as a cheerleader?'

"He said, 'Ron, do you think you could play?' I said, 'I beg your pardon?' I had been out of the NHL for two years and was playing oldtimer hockey. I hadn't played contact hockey for two years! Al repeated: 'Do you think you can play?'" Ron considered himself fairly content with a life that did not involve hockey, but admits that his desire to return to the National Hockey League was growing. "I gave the decision to the Lord. I said, 'Lord, this might be an opportunity to return to the game as a believer.' To Al, I said, 'Look, don't announce anything yet, but I'll think about it and talk to Jan.'"

Alan Eagleson offers his perspective. "Ron called me and said, 'Do you think I could get involved?' I can remember saying, 'Sure, how about as a player?' We needed bodies. I'd set up eight exhibition games and I needed everybody I could get because we knew we were going to get a front-end load and a back-end load." Because the tournament was taking place in the spring, during the NHL playoffs, the Canadian team would be made up of players whose teams hadn't made the playoffs — in 1977, the Cleveland Barons, Colorado Rockies, Detroit Red Wings, New York Rangers, Vancouver Canucks and Washington Capitals. As other clubs were eliminated from the opening playoff rounds, players would be parachuted into Vienna, fortifying Team Canada's roster. "I figured we'd get Ronnie there on the basis that he'd play the exhibition games, then be gone when an NHL player became available. I told him, 'You'll go over, and if you can't play, so what?'"

Ron continues: "I figured I would try to get myself in shape. No one knew, but every weekday morning for two months I went up to the little rink in Bradford and skated by myself. The cook at the golf club was a guy named Jim Muzelaar. His son was on the arena staff, and had played some goal in Tier II Junior A hockey. We made arrangements for Jim's son to come out, put on the goalie pads and help me with some shooting drills. Jim would come and blow the whistle for stops and starts. I did that for six to eight weeks.

It was freezing cold in that arena at seven in the morning. I'm doing stops and starts. One time, my skates went out from under me and I fell into the boards. I remember thinking, 'What are you doing, Ellis? This is crazy! What are you trying to prove?' There were days where I asked, 'Lord, do you want me to give it up?' But I continued on in private."

Ron had become a Christian in 1975, two years beforehand. "When I went to Bob West, my boss, and said I'd like to see if I could play again, he gave me his blessing. McClintock had spent a lot of time and money developing me, and here I was telling them I might not be part of their executive team. But Bob knew where I was coming from. I said, 'Bob, I'm giving this to the Lord. If it works, I'm going to give all praise to the Lord,'" smiles Ellis.

"They were going to announce the members of the team at a press conference downtown. What they were going to do is play two or three exhibition games and make four cuts. They were taking four or five extra guys. Al hadn't said anything, and I hadn't said anything. So I showed up at the press conference. They started announcing the players — Phil Esposito, Wilf Paiement, Walt McKechnie, Jean Pronovost. Then finally they said, 'Ron Ellis.' The press was astonished. They thought I was there to wish the boys well.

"I could just imagine the buzz," laughs Ron. "'What is Ellis doing on the team? He hasn't played in two years! What's going on?'

"It was the first time I said, 'Lord, I can't do this by myself. This is crazy. I'm going to go with this team and I'm going to play two exhibition games and try to make it.' The reason Alan Eagleson asked me to consider playing was that he knew which teams wouldn't make the playoffs. Al already knew they were going to have a weak team, so he really was hoping I'd accept," admits Ellis.

"We went to Germany and played a couple of games. Wouldn't you know it," smirks Ellis, "in my first game I get a goal. There was no training camp. I just went over, put on a sweater and played."

"Ronnie's father-in-law, an Air Canada pilot, came to one of the games with his crew," Eagleson adds. "Ronnie got into a fight that night. It's one of the few fights he ever had. Somebody cranked him into the boards and there was a melee with Ron in the middle."

"I guess I played fairly well in those two games because I was named to the team," Ron suggests.

"We were in Prague and were getting down to our final roster," says Eagleson. "Johnny Wilson was the coach, and I went to a meeting to hear the discussion on the final roster. The third right winger was Ronnie Ellis. Espo said, 'Ronnie's playing great! We're going to hang onto him until the next load of players comes over.'" But Ellis played well enough that it was impossible for him to be considered a placeholder. Instead, he remained on the roster throughout the tournament.

"We were over there and I was playing well and I was interviewed by one of the radio stations broadcasting back to Canada," Ron remembers. "It was a Sunday morning in Canada. My boss, Bob West, was on his way to church with his family when, on the radio, he hears me giving the Lord credit that I couldn't have done this on my own." Ron beams. "I guess he was just blown away."

The Soviet Union beat Canada twice during the tournament, and Canada's hopes of bringing home a medal were diminishing. "At a bit of a low point, there was a team meeting. Phil Esposito was our leader. He was the leader in '72, so why wouldn't he be the leader here? Phil was taking the lead, trying to get the guys together. Finally at the end, Phil said, 'We'll go around the room.'

Everybody put in their two cents' worth. I did, too. It came time for one of the defencemen to speak, and he said, 'I just can't believe what this coach is doing. He's got Ron Ellis on the power play. The guy hasn't played in two years. How can Ron Ellis be on the power play?'

"Most people, under those circumstances, would have jumped up and said, 'You're no Bobby Orr yourself!' But here I am, a new Christian. So I stood up and said, 'Look. I don't put the players on the power play. I'm here because I want to be part of this team. I'm here to do whatever I can. I'll play wherever the coach wants me to play.'"

One of those in the dressing room was Jean Pronovost of the Pittsburgh Penguins. "Years later, Jean and I became pretty good friends — he became a Christian, too. Jean brought the episode up one day and said, 'Ron, that impressed me so much.' I was surprised. I said, 'It did?' But it was a reminder that when you declare yourself a Christian, people will be observing your life," states Ron.

In a *Toronto Star* article at the time, Canadian coach Johnny Wilson pronounced, "Ellis has been my most pleasant surprise. I didn't see how he could possibly make it back. But he did make the team on merit and he has been improving steadily." Two years removed from NHL competition, Ron scored 5 goals and 4 assists in the ten-game tournament. "There was no official selection after that series in 1977, but after it was all over, our media guys selected Phil Esposito and me as co-MVPs." Ron was very pleased.

Canada finished in fourth place, missing a medal. "We didn't have an experienced team that year," says Ellis. "We played fairly well, except against the Russians. The Russians were at the top of their game and they beat us both times we played them. We handled the other clubs without too much problem." In fact, Canada whipped Czechoslovakia, who went on to win the title for the second year in a row, by a score of 8–2.

It wasn't long after the team returned from Vienna before Ron Ellis got a telephone call. "It was my old friend, Jim Gregory. The Leafs had heard that I played pretty well. Jim let me know that they had hired a new coach, Roger Neilson, and that Jim was calling me in part at Roger's request. He wanted me to come in and talk. So I went in, talked to Roger, liked what he had to say, and said, 'Okay.' I knew Roger was a Christian as well, and that was important to me."

"I always kept Ron's phone number in my pocket," admits Jim Gregory, who was then the Leafs' general manager. "I didn't just phone him once and he said 'yes.' I phoned him a few times. I used to call him just to keep in touch, and I would let him know that if he ever changed his mind, he had a job waiting for him.

"I remember we met for lunch in Woodbridge," Gregory continues. "We had a really terrific meeting. I came away from that meeting very happy. There weren't a lot of ways to get players with Ronnie's talents into your organization without a big sacrifice — without giving up draft choices or players. When Ronnie decided to come back to pro hockey, that was a very important day for the Maple Leafs."

When Ellis decided it was time to return to the NHL, he phoned George Gross, a friend from the *Toronto Sun*. "I told him, 'I'd like you to break the story.' I had a lot of respect for George Gross and knew he would handle the story properly."

Gross had been a friend to a number of the Leafs through the years. "I had close relationships with most of the Leafs," says the columnist, "but especially Red Kelly, Bob Baun, Carl Brewer and Ron Ellis. They respected my writing. I was not catering to players, but I was not kicking the daylights out of them, either. If the player had a good game, I said it. If the player played a poor game, I said it.

"I took a liking to Ron Ellis because of his general deportment. He was a decent fellow and a dedicated hockey player." Gross recalls a night when the two dropped their respective job descriptions and talked as friends. "Ron was always doubting his ability. I remember the Leafs playing an exhibition game in Quebec City against the Bruins. The night before the game, Ron told me he was going to pack it in. I said, 'Ron, I think we should talk.' We walked the streets of Quebec City for a couple of hours. I felt like a psychology major, but finally, Ron said, 'Okay, I'll give it another try.'"

The next day, George Gross's column appeared under the headline, "It's Back to Game Ellis Loves." Gross quoted Ron as saying, "Money was no problem. The problems were of a different variety when I retired two years ago. At that time, I found it difficult to handle the outside pressures of being a pro hockey player. I still believe I made the right decision two years ago for my sake and the sake of my family."

Rod Seiling was guardedly optimistic when he heard that Ron

was returning to the NHL. "By that time, I had moved on to St. Louis, but I knew what was behind the retirement and I also knew that Ron could still play, so his decision to come back certainly was no surprise. I had heard rumblings. My concern was whether Ron could handle it, not whether he could play."

Ron's reacquaintance with the NHL was smoother than he had expected. He scored 26 goals in his comeback season — it was the eleventh and final time Ellis would reach the 20-goal plateau. One of those goals held a special significance. "I was feeling pretty good about the Team Canada showing, but I got off to a slow start with the Leafs. I was late getting into training camp, then they threw me into the first game, but I wasn't ready. Ten games in, I started to question myself — 'Was this a good idea?'

"But during a trip out west, I started playing with Darryl Sittler and we just clicked. On March 4, 1978, I scored my 300th career goal against Vancouver. I was on the ice with Stan Weir. He carried the puck in over the blue line, then dropped the puck back to me. I took a slapshot along the ice that caught just inside the post. As soon as it went in, the boys came over the boards to congratulate me."

Sittler finished third in NHL scoring in 1977–78, collecting 117 points. Lanny McDonald came in tenth, with 87. His 47 goals were one short of the club record established by Frank Mahovlich in 1960–61. Outscoring all but those two forwards were defencemen Borje Salming and Ian Turnbull, who racked up 76 and 61 points respectively. Ellis was fifth in team scoring. (Dan Maloney, who came to the Leafs in a mid-season trade for Errol Thompson, totalled 52 points on the season, two more than Ellis, but most of his output had been generated with the Red Wings.)

The Maple Leafs skated to one of their finest seasons in recent memory. Their 41 wins tied the club record set in 1950–51, while their 92 points were second only to the '50–51 season's total of 95. Their 41–29–10 record put them sixth in the eighteen-team NHL, but even so, they finished in their customary third-place slot in the Adams Division, behind Boston and Buffalo.

Toronto swept its best-of-three preliminary round series against Los Angeles to set up a meeting with the New York Islanders in the quarterfinals. That series went the full seven games, but the miracle Leafs won the series on Lanny McDonald's overtime goal in game seven. In the semifinals, Toronto ran up against the Montreal Canadiens, who had lost only ten games during the regular season, had finished in first place overall with 129 points and were coming off back-to-back Stanley Cup championships. The Habs were all over the Leafs like a grizzly bear on a salmon, winning four straight and proceeding to the finals, where they claimed their third Cup title in as many years.

The trip to hockey's "final four" led to a hefty increase in the fans' expectations for 1978–79. And for the most part, Toronto didn't let their fans down. Again, Darryl Sittler led the Toronto offence with 87 points, but linemate Lanny McDonald nipped at his Tacks, finishing with 85. Turnbull and Salming maintained their offensive punch from the blue line. This year, the team was supplemented with veterans Walt McKechnie, Dave Hutchison and Dave Burrows. Toronto was the seventh NHL stop for the well-travelled McKechnie, who had played with Ron Ellis on Team Canada in 1977, and had been a teammate of Darryl Sittler's as a junior with the London Nationals. Dave Hutchison had also played with Sittler in London. He came to Toronto in a trade that sent Brian Glennie to Los Angeles.

"I almost didn't go to L.A.," Glennie announces. "I had two young children, and had just had my best year. Roger Neilson had been my coach from peewee to midget, and he had shown a lot of faith in me. Then he traded me! After I got over the shock, it was good for me in a way to go to another city. It gave me a different perspective on hockey. I knew Marcel Dionne from Team Canada in 1972, and I moved in with Charlie Simmer for a while. Hockey wasn't as big in L.A. as it was in Toronto, although the city was in love with the Triple Crown line of Dionne, Simmer and Dave Taylor. R.J. still had to live under the microscope in Toronto."

Also new to the team was Joel Quenneville, a native of Windsor, Ontario, who had just been drafted from his hometown Spitfires. "Everybody in Windsor was either a Leafs fan, a Red Wings fan or a Canadiens fan. I had to be different — I rooted for Chicago. There was no special reason — maybe because of Bobby Hull, I don't know.

"I remember watching Davey Keon, Lanny and Sit, Borje and all the guys on *Hockey Night in Canada* on Saturday nights. I remember Ronnie Ellis was always a very competitive guy. He'd give you everything he had every night. It was exciting when they became teammates of mine not long afterwards."

Joel quickly switched allegiances when Toronto made him their

165

first pick — the twenty-first player chosen overall — in the 1978 amateur draft. He was pressed into action almost immediately, making his debut with the Maple Leafs on October 22, 1978, against the New York Rangers at Madison Square Garden. "It was a nerve-wracking experience. The veterans all treated me well. They'd invite you to go out for a few pops with the guys. It made you feel like you were part of the team," remembers Quenneville.

The Leafs paired Joel, the youngest member of the team, with the eldest. "Ronnie was my roommate during training camp, which was pretty good. Because he lived in Toronto, he'd spend time with his family and only come to the room to sleep. We didn't chum around or anything. Ron was quiet — he didn't say much. I could tell he was very intelligent. I hadn't been too aware of Ronnie coming back from retirement. At the time, I was a young guy just observing everything around me."

Dave Burrows came from the Pittsburgh Penguins, and was ready to add some muscle to Toronto's blueline corps. "The Leafs had beaten the Islanders in the playoffs the year before I got there, and everybody was expecting things from the team that year," explains Burrows. "They made the trade for me and brought in Davie Hutchison. We had a nucleus of really good guys."

Dave Burrows already knew Ron Ellis from a distance, but the two became good friends. "Ron and I had a chance to get to know each other fairly quickly when I first got there because we were both injured in the same game. We both got knee injuries about six games into the season. We both went through rehab together for weeks, so we'd meet at the gym together. It was special for me to get to really know him. It was often away from team activities, so it was often just him and me. I got to know Ron a little better and a little quicker than I got to know most of the guys on the team."

Before he joined the Maple Leafs in a trade for Randy Carlyle and George Ferguson, Burrows played seven seasons in Pittsburgh. "Ron was a winger who always came down my side," he smirks. "He and I butted heads many times. I certainly got a respect for Ron for the type of player he was. When people think about Ron, they don't think about him as a tough player, but he was tough. He wasn't a dirty player, but he was strong. I was a lot taller than he was (6' 1" to Ron's 5' 10"), but I certainly knew he was very strong. He was a tremendous skater, which you had to look out for, but people don't realize how strong a player Ron was." Ironically, in a 1978 questionnaire, Ron was asked who his least favourite opponent was. He answered, "Dave Burrows was a fellow I didn't like playing against. He's almost impossible to beat one-on-one, so I'm glad he's with me now."

"Roger Neilson was the coach, and I still think he's the best coach I played under," says Burrows. "There were big things expected of us, but they were also the Harold Ballard years. There were problems between ownership and the coach and players. That turned into a major distraction. It was hard to keep your focus. I really believe it affected the way we played. As much as you try to keep that out of your mind and just play your game, it still had its effect on how you performed on the ice. Roger wasn't treated real well the years he was there and that had an effect on us, too."

In one of the most peculiar series of events to take place in one of the oddest eras in Toronto Maple Leafs history, Harold Ballard fired Roger Neilson on March 1, 1979, then rehired him two days later. Ballard had never warmed to Neilson or his ground-breaking coaching methods, which included intensive analysis of statistics and videotape. The Leafs encountered a minor slump and lost four games in a row at the end of February, prompting Ballard to threaten that Neilson would be fired if the Leafs did not return from Montreal with a victory on March 1. The players were unaware of the ultimatum. With star goaltender Mike Palmateer sidelined by a knee injury, Toronto led 1–0 late in the game, but Montreal scored twice against backup goalie Paul Harrison late in the game to win 2–1.

After the game, Ballard informed Dick Beddoes, a CHCH-TV sportscaster and noted Ballard crony, that Neilson was done. Beddoes immediately went on the air with the breaking story on his post-game show, *Overtime*. Neilson was not fired in person. He wasn't even fired by Jim Gregory, the general manager. Roger Neilson found out he was no longer coaching the Toronto Maple Leafs from the reports he heard about Beddoes' TV show.

In his haste, Ballard had failed to consider who would replace Neilson. He offered the job to Ed Johnston, the coach of the New Brunswick Hawks, an American Hockey League team the Leafs and Chicago Blackhawks shared. Johnston, who was under contract to the Blackhawks, declined. Ballard then asked John McLellan to return as coach, but he refused. The players, meanwhile, were lobbying the owner to reinstate Neilson. Time was of the essence: on March 3, the Leafs were scheduled to play the Philadelphia Flyers at home. And the playoffs were only four weeks away.

His back against the wall, Ballard acquiesced, agreeing to take Roger Neilson back. But he couldn't let the matter go without attempting a stroke of showmanship. His brainstorm: to steal a page from the TV game show *The Gong Show*, a spoof of talent shows that featured a recurring act known as "The Unknown Comic," a comedian who told lame jokes while wearing a paper bag over his head. Ballard thought it would be clever if Roger Neilson appeared behind the Leafs' bench in Saturday's game against the Flyers with a paper bag over *his* head and, just before the opening faceoff, tear off the bag to reveal the "new" Leaf coach's identity. And, of course, there would be a thunderous ovation from the Gardens' faithful.

Neilson flatly refused to have any part of the scheme. And strangely, Harold Ballard didn't push the issue. Neilson's return couldn't rescue the Leafs' season, however, as they finished with 81 points, down from the previous year's 92. On a personal level, it was also a disappointing season for Ron Ellis. "I got hurt early in the season, and it affected me all year long. When skating is a key to your game, any kind of knee injury takes its toll." Ron finished the season with 16 goals and 12 assists. "If I told you I wasn't disappointed, I'd be lying. Every season, I knew I was good for 20 to 25 goals. I prided myself on my consistency. Since I broke in with the Leafs, I had better than 20 goals in eleven of my twelve seasons, and the one season I missed, I was hurt and still hit 19. But my ice time was starting to be cut, and I wasn't playing on the specialty teams anymore."

Toronto again finished in third place in the Adams Division, behind Boston and Buffalo, earning them a ticket to the first round against the Atlanta Flames. The Leafs swept that series to advance to the quarterfinals; their opponents, the Montreal Canadiens, had registered 115 points during the regular season, one off the New York Islanders' league-best mark. For the second year in a row, the Canadiens whitewashed Toronto in four straight games. The Habs would go on to win their fourth Cup championship in a row.

Roger Neilson was fired, permanently this time, after the series ended. Jim Gregory, the Leafs' general manager for the previous ten seasons, was also fired shortly thereafter.

"I had been really enthused with our team in '77–78," Ron says. "The rest of the league started to show a bit of concern when they played us. The team had good balance — all three lines could score, we had toughness, a strong power play, good penalty killing. We were a player or two away from being a legitimate contender. Then, Harold fired Roger Neilson. I still don't know why.

"Roger made us believe in ourselves. He formed a player committee so that if anybody had any problems, they could go to the committee and talk things out, then the committee could go to management if necessary. Borje Salming, Lanny McDonald, Ian Turnbull, Darryl Sittler and I were on the committee. And then, it all came to a head with Harold. We all supported Roger. Darryl went to bat for Roger, and my role as a veteran was to support my captain. We were a close-knit team."

CHAPTER EIGHTEEN

The Impact of Punch

The hockey world was astonished in 1979 when the Toronto Maple Leafs announced that Jim Gregory's replacement as general manager would be none other than Punch Imlach. Punch promptly hired Floyd Smith as the new Toronto coach. A former Leaf, Smith had arrived in Toronto as part of the Frank Mahovlich trade. He played two seasons with the Maple Leafs, then was sold to Buffalo along with Brent Imlach. The coach and general manager of the Sabres at that time? Punch Imlach. Smith played one season as a Sabre, then was named coach of the team. Between 1974 and '77, he was an effective coach for the Sabres, and when Imlach returned to Toronto, so did Smith.

Dave Burrows talks about the new management team. "We all knew how much success Punch had in the '60s. And Ronnie knew how he had coached, so we were interested in finding out what kind of guy he was. But times had changed, although Punch still ruled with the iron fist. He was so different from Roger Neilson. But his effectiveness wasn't anywhere near what it had been during the Stanley Cup years."

"The Ballard years got to be pretty crazy at times," team captain Darryl Sittler confirms. "I had a lot of respect for Punch Imlach for winning the Stanley Cups and for being a successful hockey man, but I knew when he came back in 1979 that things weren't going to be the same. Punch had no use for the players' association and ended up suing Palmateer and me for appearing on 'Showdown.'"

"Showdown" was a between-periods feature that ran on *Hockey Night in Canada*. It was a friendly skills competition that pitted star forwards from across the league against some of the better NHL goaltenders. Imlach refused to allow any Leafs to take part. Sittler insisted it was his right to participate, as the NHL and its board of directors had approved the feature. But Imlach was adamant that *he* would decide whether or not Darryl would take part.

The impasse between Punch Imlach and Darryl Sittler festered. The fact that Sittler was a client of Alan Eagleson, the executive director of the NHL Players' Association, only incensed Imlach further. Imlach and Eagleson had butted heads in contract negotiations during Punch's first tour of duty as Leafs general manager. Leafs president Harold Ballard, never one to shy away from a confrontation, stood behind his GM. "If Sittler thinks he's going to run this hockey club, he's got another thing coming," Ballard barked. It became apparent to insiders that Imlach wanted to get rid of Sittler, but was hamstrung by a "no trade" clause in the captain's contract. So Punch did the next best — or, depending on how you look at it, worst — thing. He traded away those players whom he considered to be friends and supporters of Darryl Sittler, including Lanny McDonald, Tiger Williams, Pat Boutette, Walt McKechnie and Dave Hutchison.

The trades came quickly. On December 24, Boutette — a former teammate of Sittler's in London — was sent to Hartford for Bob Stephenson, a career minor leaguer. On the 29th, McDonald and Joel Quenneville were dispatched to the Colorado Rockies for Pat Hickey and Wilf Paiement.

Quenneville reflects on the tumultuous 1979–80 season. "We were all aware that changes were possible — it's part of the business. That part is not always fun. I was having fun just being there. I had great admiration for the administration around me, but you get to know that there is a negative side and that it can be political. You just learn to go with it. When Punch came back, he made some changes. I was part of that change."

Leaf fans were furious, and were not afraid to let management know. Protesters, hundreds of them, carried placards (with slogans like "Bad Punch spoils a party"), wore Lanny McDonald–style mustaches and chanted anti-Ballard and Imlach slogans outside Maple Leaf Gardens. Lanny McDonald was Sittler's closest friend, and it was glaringly obvious that Imlach was trying to aggravate the Leafs captain. Just before the team's December 29 game against the Winnipeg Jets, Darryl Sittler removed the captain's C from his Maple Leafs sweater. In an emotional speech to his teammates, Darryl explained his reasoning. Tiger Williams was the acting captain for that night's game.

The purge continued in the new year. On January 10, 1980, Hutchison, another friend of Sittler's from his London days, was sent to Chicago for Pat Ribble. On February 18, Williams, Darryl's linemate, was packaged with Jerry Butler and traded to Vancouver for Rick Vaive and Bill Derlago. On March 3, McKechnie — again, an alum of the London Nationals — was shipped to Colorado for a third-round draft pick.

Just before the end of the regular season, coach Floyd Smith was involved in a tragic automobile accident. Two people died, and Smith was hospitalized for an extended period. Dick Duff, who was a scout for the Leafs, took over behind the bench for two games. For the final ten games of the schedule, Punch Imlach was officially the coach, although Joe Crozier was behind the bench.

Considering the chaos, the Leafs had a respectable season. Toronto finished fourth in the Adams Division, and eleventh in the twenty-one-team NHL, with 75 points. Darryl Sittler finished ninth in the scoring race, collecting 97 points despite being harassed by the Leafs front office for the better part of the season. Ron Ellis scored 12 times, adding 11 assists for 23 points.

Joel Quenneville remembers playing against Ron. "When I went to Colorado, I was certainly aware of my former teammates when we played each other. I remember having an appreciation for Ronnie Ellis. He seemed to get better with age, like fine wine. He was still moving well down the wing. Ronnie was noticeable out there."

On March 22, 1980, Ron Ellis played in his 1,000th NHL game. Every one of those matches had been played — and proudly — in the blue and white of the Toronto Maple Leafs. "It was a wonderful milestone," admits Ron. "It was important to me to be a Maple Leaf. I felt that once I hit that thousand-game plateau, I would forever be remembered as a Toronto Maple Leaf." The Buffalo Sabres visited Toronto that night, and stole a 5–1 win to cloud Ron's celebration. "Not too long after that game, there was a ceremony and I got a trophy from the NHL to commemorate my 1,000th game." As he speaks, Ron is visibly proud.

The Maple Leafs met their Adams Division rivals, the Minnesota North Stars, in the first round of the playoffs. The Stars swept the Leafs in the best-of-five series by scores of 6–3, 7–2 and 4–3 to bring Toronto's season to a bitter end.

"To this day, I can't figure it out completely," says Ellis. "We had been a player or two away from great things, we all got along, and everybody fell in under Darryl's leadership. But it was the wrong time for Punch Imlach. When it all came to a head with Punch and Harold, we lost our core."

Alan Eagleson sums up the 1979–80 season: "It was a disaster. Ronnie was not up to it emotionally."

Ron is still emotional as he carries on: "It was such a sad time. I had been so proud to be a Toronto Maple Leaf. I was so proud of all the history and the heritage. And then we went through that, and all I could do was shake my head and wonder what was going on with this franchise."

Ellis evaluates what was not only a most unusual season, but one that was also challenging, virtually from start to finish. "When management considered everything that happened that season — the constant personnel changes, the three coaching changes and all the nonsense that surrounded the Leafs that year — they had to be pleased with what the team accomplished. I mean that. We won 35 games, and if the confusion could have been reduced a little, we would have won another ten.

"I had never been through anything like that in my life. It was no fun at all."

CHAPTER NINETEEN

Final Buzzer

"No, I'm not bitter about the way it ended. Just a little puzzled and disappointed," stated a wistful Ron Ellis on January 17, 1981 — his final day as a Toronto Maple Leaf.

"I never saw it coming," says Ron's wife, Jan. "I had already stopped going to games. If Ron wasn't going to play, there was no point in my sitting there frustrated for him. Besides, I was the oldest of the player wives and it was not fun — there was no one to hang out with at the games."

"It was a sad ending to a great career," comments Alan Eagleson.

When Ron arrived at the Gardens that day, he didn't know that he had played his final game in a Toronto Maple Leafs sweater. That happened three days earlier, on Wednesday, January 14, 1981 — a 7–4 loss to the Edmonton Oilers. It was game number 1,034 of his career.

"We had a game against the Canadiens on the Saturday," Ron says, "and I had been told earlier in the week that I was going to play."

Ron had not been seeing much playing time, but was excited to learn he'd be dressing for the game against Montreal. "When I walked into the dressing room at the Gardens, ready to play, I noticed right away that my stick rack was empty. I walked around the corner — my sweater wasn't up." Ron discovered that his nameplate had been removed from his stall in the dressing room. He was devastated. "I knew right away what was happening. They could have called me. Then the trainer, Joe Sgro, told me that Punch wanted to see me, and that just confirmed my fears."

"I was going to the game with Mel Stevens and his wife," Jan recalls. "We arrived just in time for the game. I looked down at the bench and didn't see Ronnie. I was concerned, hoping that nothing had happened to him. I ran into Wendy Sittler, who was my only real friend on the team that year. I said, 'Wendy, I can't see Ronnie! Was he hurt in the warmup?' She looked right at me and said, 'Jan, Al Eagleson is looking everywhere for you.' Right away, I started feeling nauseous.

"We waited for Ronnie after the game. We waited until every last person had left the building. Mel and his wife and I stood outside the dressing room for an hour and a half. Finally Ronnie came out. I said, 'What happened?' And Ronnie looked down and said, 'I'm finished.'"

"That was a very, very difficult time for the Toronto Maple Leafs," Ron says. "It didn't do the team any good when the players saw the way they treated me. Guys were saying, 'If they're treating Ellis like this, what the hell are they going to do to us?' I had been there 15 years, but I realized they'd done the same thing to George Armstrong; done the same thing to Dave Keon. You can go down the list. That's the sport. That's the message: if you're going to go into that game, you'd better understand what can happen. Don't expect things to be rosy, because they won't be. Instead of ending things with a little class, they do things that way.

"I've come to the point where I don't let those last two months of turmoil take away from the rest of a great career. But for a while, it overwhelmed me. I've now got it in perspective.

"There was so much pressure on everybody, Punch included. But the reason I was hurt so badly by being let go is that I had gone to see Punch before the season started."

Ron had remained good friends with his first NHL roommate, Andy Bathgate, who was a playing coach for a Swiss team between 1971 and 1974. During Ellis's first retirement, the two played old-timers' hockey together. "Andy shared stories about the time he spent in Europe, and what a great place it was. The money was good, there was much less pressure, and it sounded like it would be a great life experience. The more I talked to Andy about Europe, the more I thought that it might be a nice way to wrap up my career if the Leafs didn't have plans for me.

"I met with Punch and opened up the door to my future. I said, 'If I'm not in your plans, we can negotiate a settlement and I might look at this opportunity to go to Europe, play a year over there and say, 'Thanks very much!'

"But he said, 'No, we're very happy with what you're doing. We have plans for you this season.' When I wasn't playing, I was spending a lot of time with the young guys, trying to help them and work with them and encourage them. I was really enjoying that. Spot duty, working with the kids, and being able to say, 'This is my last year.' I would have been very happy with that. Punch said, 'We want you here and think you can help us. We don't want you going anywhere.'"

Ron was clear about his role with the Maple Leafs. On the right wing depth chart, Ellis stood behind Wilf Paiement, Rick Vaive and Rocky Saganiuk. "I knew it meant being a fourth liner and penalty killer. But I also knew I could help the team and the younger guys by passing something on to them. I was prepared to take on that role." As Leafs forward Terry Martin said at the time, "Ron Ellis really helped me because he's a dedicated man who always works hard to keep himself in top condition."

"The team got off to a dismal start," Ellis remembers. "We weren't competitive. People started to protect their butts and I got caught in the crossfire." Although used sparingly, when he did play, Ellis acquitted himself well, as headlines from the sports pages — "Old Fiddles Still Play a Fine Tune" and "Leafs' Old Boys Sparkle" — attest. Joe Crozier was coaching the team. "He and Punch were old army buddies, and just like Punch, Joe Crozier was old school," Ellis says. "Joe was a good man, but he wasn't right for the Leafs at that time. There was a lot of turmoil. It was sad.

"Before long, I wasn't dressing for games, and things were getting worse and worse. If the team had been playing competitively, it would have been different. Something had to give."

It certainly did.

"I was skating around the ice during practice one day, trying to get a sense from Crozier as to whether I was going to play or not. Joe said, 'I'm gone, and so are you.' In my meeting with Punch, he told me I had been waived through the league." The Leafs had put Ron Ellis on waivers, and not a single NHL team claimed him. This was by design. "Al Eagleson and I were pretty sure the Leafs were going to waive me," Ron reveals, "and we let teams know that I wasn't going to finish my career with any team but the Leafs.

"Punch said, 'Here's a ticket for Moncton' — the Leafs' farm team. Then, Crozier was fired and they brought in Mike Nykoluk.

"Mike said, 'I want Ellis.' He could see that I hadn't been used properly that season." But Nykoluk's vote of confidence would not have carried any weight with Punch Imlach. It had not been the GM's decision to hire Nykoluk. He preferred Doug Carpenter, the coach in New Brunswick. But Harold Ballard pulled rank and hired Nykoluk, a former Marlboro and Rochester American who had done some commentary on Leafs radio broadcasts. It was evident that Imlach needed to reassert his authority, and Ellis would be one of the casualties.

After waiving the winger through the league, Imlach gave Ellis an ultimatum. "I told him he could call the shot — either retire with a lump sum payment or go to the minors," he wrote in his book, *Heaven and Hell in the NHL*. "In this era of 18-year-old hockey players, there is no great demand for a 36-year-old with 2 goals in twenty-seven games." For Ron, the decision didn't require much thought. He had been a member of the Toronto Maple Leafs organization for more than twenty years, and had made the leap from the Marlboros to the NHL without ever playing a day in the minors. He knew that now was not the time to start riding a bus.

"Ron did a hell of a job for me when I was with the Leafs before," Imlach commented. "But I felt we had to make room for some of the younger players. I thought the best thing for him to do was retire, take a lump sum settlement and call it a day." The National Hockey League Players' Association called for a settlement amounting to one-third of the outstanding balance of the contract. In Ron's case, to buy out the last two years of his contract — at a salary of $140,000 — would have cost the Leafs just over $90,000. Alan Eagleson, Ron's agent, felt his client was owed the full $280,000, but informed Imlach he would settle for $180,000. Imlach, who held all the cards, refused at first to budge, then sweetened the pot to an even $100,000.

Ron met with Imlach to inform the general manager of his decision to retire. Alan Eagleson joined the two that evening and to witness their signatures on a buyout agreement. Punch got Harold Ballard's approval and had the accounting staff prepare a cheque.

In his book, Punch wrote about the classy veteran's retirement. "I think he understood all along that I had a job to do. I made sure my admiration for him and his contribution to the team over the years got into the statement about his retirement. When I handed him the cheque, I asked him to sign the club's copy of the settlement. He signed it: 'Punch. We started together and I'm happy we were able to end it all on a good note. Ron Ellis.'"

In addition to his regular-season stats, Ron had played seventy games in the playoffs, scoring 18 goals and 8 assists. A proud Leaf, he had won the Stanley Cup once and had represented his team and country at the Summit Series in 1972 and at the World Championships in 1977. Ron had played in four NHL All-Star Games. And now, after fifteen full seasons — plus four in the Leafs' junior system — it had all come to an end.

The local press was incredulous. "Ron is Punched Out," screamed the headline in the *Toronto Sun.* "Disappointment Marks the End for Leafs' Ellis," said the *Globe and Mail.* The *Toronto Star* led with "Ellis Bewildered by his Sudden Exit." Columnists commented on the departure: "Leafs Lose More Class," read the *Globe and Mail,* while the *Star* wrote, "Classy Ron Ellis Deserves Lot More than Humiliation."

Ron's teammates were stunned. "Ellis' Dunking Angers Leafs," the *Toronto Star* headline roared. Former Leaf Trevor Johansen, then playing in Colorado, said, "I couldn't believe the way one of the greatest gentleman ever to play the game was treated. They should have had a night for Ron Ellis, given him a new car and a batch of gifts."

Jan Ellis remembers the end of her husband's career with great bitterness. "My heart just broke for Ronnie. It wasn't like I was sad to see the end of hockey; it's just that it hurt me so much to see Ron treated in such a despicable way. Ronnie did everything the Leafs ever asked of him. There were times when he played with a temperature of 102. Then they treated him like a piece of meat."

Wayne Carleton feels Ron was betrayed. "Ron is a wonderful person. Imlach should never have treated Ronnie that way. [Ron's] loyalty to the Leafs came back to haunt him. It could have been handled so much better."

Brit Selby agrees: "I didn't think that the Leafs treated Ron very well. They didn't give him an option. I thought that Ron should have extended his career by going to another city. He would have seen how players were treated on different teams, and he might have had a more optimistic view of hockey."

Steve Paikin, the co-host of TVOntario's *Studio 2,* was, like so many others, a fan of both Ron Ellis and the Toronto Maple Leafs.

"Leaf management had made some kind of stupid decision, as, unfortunately, they were wont to do — to treat veteran players with disrespect. I found that appalling. I thought, given what this guy has meant to this team and what he had committed to this team — after all, he spent his entire career with this team — to think that that was how he was going to go out, I found that completely unfair."

"Ron and I had come through the sponsorship system," comments David Keon, pointing out that they represented the last of a dying breed. "It wasn't long before everybody who was coming to the team was drafted.

"Ron and I had a special bond. We were guys who had played Junior B and then Junior A and then come to the NHL, all in the Maple Leaf system." Neither Keon nor Ellis ever played a game in the minors. What would be an extraordinary accomplishment at any time was even more monumental in the 1960s, when each of the six existing NHL clubs carried only seventeen skaters. With only 102 possible jobs, and very little turnover, it was the rare individual who could make that leap without serving an apprentice in the American Hockey League or one of the other minor loops.

"It was pretty difficult because it didn't happen very often. You had to be a pretty good player to make that jump," confirms the modest Keon. "It also depended on what team you were with. It was even more difficult with teams that were successful, because there was a reluctance to break up a winning team. I've told Ronnie a number of times that he is the last real Toronto Maple Leaf. He's the last guy who went through the system and played for the team and played his whole career there."

Brian Conacher reflects on an outstanding career. "I came back into the Leaf system in the fall of 1965. Ronnie had always stayed in the system, and he had become one of those rare young players that was going to make the Maple Leafs. Ronnie clearly was a very good hockey player. He was very, very focused — he was very disciplined and he was a tremendous skater. But Ronnie made it from the inside. He was one of the guys who stayed on track. He never played in the minors. Not a game. It's a phenomenal thing. Back in those days, I think of all these guys who I played junior with, and virtually none of them made it cleanly to the NHL. That was a very rare occasion to jump straight from junior to the NHL, so Ronnie was clearly an exceptional player."

"The thing about Ronnie's career is that if you look back on it, he was one of the very, very few players who played his entire career with one team," Conacher concludes. "Ronnie really was quite an exceptional guy, and to have made the Toronto Maple Leafs at that time is a tribute to him not only as a player but also as an individual."

CHAPTER TWENTY

Life After Hockey

"The disappointment of how my career ended made it impossible to do anything for a while," Ron recalls. "I did some soul searching." The settlement the Leafs made to buy out Ron's contract spared him the financial pressure to rush into a post-hockey career. "For the rest of that season, I was at home."

Ron talks about preparing for life after hockey. "During the '70s, I was thinking ahead to life after hockey, and exploring business opportunities. I was living in Brampton, and had a personal friend named Jim Thomas who had been with Bic Pens and was opening his own pen company. Initially, I invested in Thomas Pen to help Jim get the company off the ground, but I later got involved in the sales end. I enjoyed talking to people and making sure they had sufficient stock. I was a salesman for two summers, but bowed out once Thomas Pen got off the ground.

"Other than Sandhurst, my family's resort, that was the first time I had worked outside of hockey since I delivered newspapers as a boy. It was encouraging to know that I had abilities in other areas. When you're playing hockey, you're so focused, you lose sight of other possibilities."

During his first retirement, Ron had managed the Carrying Place golf course. This time around, he wasn't sure what would come next. "We were attending Kennedy Road Tabernacle in Brampton, and they had a private Christian school. It was a fairly new school and they needed some help. I figured maybe that was something I could do," he says. "You don't teach in a private school for the money, but it would give me some time to sort out where I was going and what I was doing. That summer, I met with the school and decided I'd join the staff in September." At roughly the same time, a rumour was circulating that Ron Ellis was about to be named the next coach of the Toronto Marlboros. "I had just made an arrangement to join the school, and I remember they called me up and asked, 'Is this true?' I said, 'No. It's just hearsay.' The last thing I would have done is coach the Marlies at that stage.

"I stayed at Kennedy Road Christian School for the year," remembers Ron. "I enjoyed it for the most part. I taught phys. ed., health and Christian ed. for grades 6 through 10. It was hard, because there was no curriculum in place. I had to develop my own.

"I was not a young man — I was 35. It wasn't the right time to be starting as a phys. ed. teacher, because I was the sort who wanted to run and do things with the kids. We had a half-dozen great athletes and did pretty well for a small school. Because it was a Christian school, I didn't need a teaching certificate as I wasn't involved in the core curriculum. But I knew if I wanted to continue as a teacher, I would eventually need to get one." Ron was uncertain whether that was a step he was prepared to take.

"I was feeling the stress after that year," he recalls. "It was quite a lesson. Maybe if I had stayed for a second year, it might have been less stressful, because I would have had my lesson plan in place from the year before. But I was pretty sure it wasn't what I wanted to do with the rest of my life. Apparently, I had been a good school teacher. The staff was disappointed when I decided not to continue teaching."

By this time, Ron and Jan had built a home in Orangeville, Ontario. "A very good friend of mine, a Christian fellow, was involved in an insurance business in Guelph and had always wanted to open a branch office in Orangeville. He came to me and asked if I would consider it. I thought it sounded interesting, so I took the courses and started a branch of Daly Farnworth McGregor.

"I had a little office about a mile from my house. I worked away at the insurance business for about three years, building it up into a successful branch on my own. I did well. It's still there and still doing well today. In fact, they've amalgamated with another company and they're very successful. But part of the problem of adjusting after hockey is trying to find that niche — some place where you can be comfortable and feel productive." Despite the success, and realizing that he had acquired invaluable business and life skills, his restlessness still had not subsided.

"Just about then, two other Christian friends from church in Brampton came to me with an idea. They wanted to get into the sporting goods business. They wanted to build a high-end store and asked if I would be part of their group. At first, I said 'no.' It was a bit of an unknown quantity and was going to require some investment. I'm pretty tight with my money," Ron laughs.

"But the more we talked and the more we looked at the opportunity, and the goals that we had, the more I was convinced. We wanted to use profits from the store to help Christian work. I thought, 'This might be worth a go,' so we started to get the store off the ground. One partner was a very good businessman and the other was a very creative guy. We thought we had the right mix."

The partners bought a building in downtown Brampton, gutted it, and opened for business as Ron Ellis Sports. "It was a very nice store. We wanted it to be a high-end store — the best quality product, great service — but the timing was bad. It was 1986 and the economy had taken a downturn. A lot of people got hurt. Here we were trying to open a high-end sports store and we got into trouble. We found out very quickly that banks don't like it when you get behind in payments." Ron, feeling the pressure to turn the situation around, started to work extra hours and invest more money into the business. "We all worked very hard. Jan was involved. We really gave it a good shot — it wasn't for lack of trying. The pressure and intensity grew and grew. I had this immense fear that I was going to lose everything I had. Everything escalated until one day, it all crashed around me.

"The crisis at the store was just part of it. I was going through some things with my daughter at the time. My Mom was ill. You can only take so much. It was a combination of a number of very difficult life circumstances. It wasn't just the store."

Ron had had a few skirmishes with depression before, and always felt he had pulled through. This time, he was about to fight a major, prolonged battle with the illness, one that would last the next ten years.

* * *

"Through a good friend, I decided to join the staff at the YMCA," Ron recalls. "It was a mid-line position with some responsibility. There wasn't a lot of stress, but there was the opportunity to be creative. I could test myself and see how I was doing. I did that for over a year. It went well, and I think there could have been the potential for advancement had I wanted to stay. But it was around this time that Team Canada's participation in the 1991 Canada Cup was being discussed."

A year before the tournament, Ron got a call from Alan Eagleson asking if he'd be interested in joining the Canada Cup working committee. "Al Junior [Alan Eagleson Jr., also referred to as Young Al] would be the legal guy, Marv Goldblatt was the financial guy and I would be the operations guy. We would all report to Al."

"John Ziegler and I were trying to improve the alumni," says Eagleson. "Bob Goodenow was in the process of taking over the NHL Players' Association in January 1992, but he started working at the offices in 1990. So I would bounce things off him. We had Darcy Rota doing some work at the NHL offices, but I thought Ron Ellis would be a real positive addition to the Association.

"Before we did anything, in case I was wrong, I suggested we have McFadden and Tucker conduct a psychological test on Ronnie. We used to do those tests regularly. I didn't want anybody to say, 'Ahh, you're just hiring another client'; I wanted something to support my idea of bringing Ronnie on board. So I went in to Goodenow and said, 'Here's the stuff that we've done. I've talked to John Ziegler, the president of the NHL, and he thinks it's a good idea, and I think Ronnie would be perfect.' But almost before the words were out of my mouth, Goodenow said, 'I don't think he's aggressive enough.'

"He didn't even know Ronnie Ellis.

"That was about October 1990. I realized that there was plenty of work to be done in preparation for the 1991 Canada Cup, so I figured Ronnie could work with Young Al. I went to McFadden and Tucker and said, 'Cancel the bill to the Players' Association and send it to Hockey Canada.' I didn't want the NHLPA yapping about it — it only came to $1,000 or something like that. Hockey Canada paid the bill and we hired Ronnie.

"I was basing my decision on what I knew about Ron Ellis and what I needed. I needed somebody who was honest, reliable, straightforward and available. Ron was all of those things. He worked, worked, worked. He and my son got along famously. Everybody on my staff loved him. I was all over the world and these guys were carrying the load. I knew that Ron's assets far outweighed his liabilities.

"This story is so typical of Ronnie," recalls Eagleson. "I'm very demanding and I'm precise. If I say I want something done, I want it done. If it's not done, tell me you can't do it and I'll either do it myself or show you how. Ron worked very well. Everything was fine. Then, literally the day before the tournament was going to open, my secretary came to me and said, 'You'd better have a talk with Ronnie. He's worried and upset.' I went up to see him and Ron said, 'Al, it's not going to work. All these buses and all these players...'

"I said, 'Ron, have you done what I told you to do?' He said, 'Yeah.' I said, 'Have you got the dates and have you got the teams and have you got the hotels?' He said, 'Yes.'

"'Then it'll work,' I said. 'You've done the work. If it doesn't come together, it's not your fault!' So he says, 'Yeah, but what if the bus is late, Al?' It just got to the point where the hard work was over and Ron thought that if something went wrong, it'd be his fault."

Despite Ellis's apprehensions, the 1991 Canada Cup went off without a hitch, both on and off the ice. Team Canada captured the gold medal. Although injured by a Gary Suter crosscheck that had long-term effects, Wayne Gretzky was the leading scorer for the fourth consecutive tournament. Eric Lindros, who was just 18 and had yet to make his NHL debut, also played extremely well. Things were equally smooth behind the scenes. "We got through it," smiles Eagleson. "Ronnie did a good job and everything was a success. At the end of it, Ronnie told me he'd had a conversation with the Hockey Hall of Fame. I said, 'Fine,' and sent a letter to David Taylor at the Hall of Fame and to Ziegler and told them what I thought of him and the job he did. The rest is history."

Ron approached his supervisors at the Y and asked for a leave of absence. "I told them what I had been offered and they were very understanding. They said, 'Sure. Go ahead.'

"I really feel that Al Eagleson was trying to give Ron Ellis a chance to re-establish himself and prove to himself that he's a quality guy," Ron says. "I believe that in my heart. He could have hired others more qualified for that job. He could have hired an event manager. But he hired me, and I really didn't know much about that area. I had to learn from scratch. I guess Al knew I was a good worker and would bear down and get the job done. We've never discussed it, but I just know.

"And it worked. The opportunity gave me a chance to grow and start believing in myself again. I had forgotten that I could be productive, that I could perform, that I had intelligence. Those things had been robbed from me when I was going through my depression.

"I think Al was worried that my job at the YMCA was taking me out of the circle of influence. But the role with Team Canada would allow me to meet some of the people I played with, played against or worked with over the years, and some opportunities might evolve. And that's exactly what happened."

CHAPTER TWENTY-ONE

Courage to Come Back

It's a Monday afternoon in May. The sky is overcast, dull and grey, which seems oddly appropriate for a day when Ron Ellis is scheduled to speak to a roomful of health professionals about depression in the workplace.

The seminar takes place in a quiet room in Toronto's Delta Chelsea Hotel. When Ron arrives, a discussion, chaired by Dr. Edgardo Perez, is in progress. Dr. Perez is a charismatic man who also happens to be Ron's doctor. His list of credentials is lengthy: a graduate of Cornell University, medical degree at the State University of New York Health Science Centre, Master's degree in Public Health from Harvard and a degree in psychiatry from the University of Ottawa. He is the CEO and chief of medical staff of the privately owned Homewood Health Centre in Guelph, Ontario. Dr. Perez is also a professor of psychiatry at the University of Toronto, the University of Ottawa and McMaster University in Hamilton, Ontario. Ellis and Dr. Perez frequently work in tandem to discuss the issue of depression.

After a break for coffee and the stretching of legs, Ron Ellis is introduced and greeted warmly by the forty or so in attendance. Ron's specific focus is on the management of employee stress, mental health and the return to work. Ron Ellis today is a confident speaker. It is hard to imagine that he once stuttered terribly.

"One cold January, two buddies went ice fishing," he begins, to the amusement of the group.

> But the weather took a turn for the better and a warm spell came in. The ice got thin, and the two friends fell through the ice. It wasn't long afterwards that the buddies found themselves in Hell.

Everywhere the boys looked, there were fires
burning. The Devil came over and said,
"Welcome, boys. You must be terribly warm!"

"No, sir," they replied. "We're from Churchill,
Manitoba, and this is quite comfortable!"

The Devil skulked away and turned the heat up
even higher. When he came back, he found the
men stripped down to their underwear, enjoying
a barbecue.

Realizing he couldn't win with heat, the Devil
turned the temperature in Hell down to minus-
fifty degrees. Again, he returned, only to find the
two buddies jumping up and down, celebrating
with high-fives and whoops of delight. "What the
Hell is going on here?" asked Beelzebub.
"Yahoo!" they screamed. "Hell has frozen over, so
the Toronto Maple Leafs must have won the
Stanley Cup!'

The group laughs, nodding to each other with wide smiles. It's
playoff time in Toronto, and the city is caught up in Maple Leaf
Madness.

Ron continues:

Thirty-five years ago, in 1967, I had a dream
come true. Just like most Canadian boys, I had
dreamed of playing in the NHL. I also dreamed
of winning a Stanley Cup, and the Toronto Maple
Leafs won the Cup, beating the Montreal
Canadiens. It's the last Cup the Leafs have won.

The hockey gods smiled on me again in 1972 by
allowing me to be picked for Team Canada. It was
the first time Canadian professionals would get a
chance to play the Russians. Most of you likely
know the story, but in game eight, with just 34
seconds remaining, Paul Henderson's goal determined the winner and Canada won. In 2000, the
Canadian Press chose Team Canada '72 as its
Team of the Century. We brought all the players
and their families back to Toronto for the celebra-

tion. They unveiled a monument at the corner of Yonge and Front, in front of the Hockey Hall of Fame, to honour the players and the accomplishment.

But if that ceremony had happened five years earlier, I likely would have declined to attend.

Yes, that's true. I wouldn't have been able to force myself to participate in one of the greatest experiences of my life. You see, I was in the midst of a ten-year battle with clinical depression. You thought the Canada-Russia series was tough? My depression was the greatest challenge of my life.

You ask, "How? How can a professional athlete, who has enjoyed some of the great successes in his sport — how can he be depressed?" Well, the answer is simple: it can happen to anyone. Three million Canadians suffer from depression. Three million! The 35- to 50-year-old male seems to be especially prone to depression, especially those that fall into the "high contributors" group.

As a Toronto Maple Leaf, I suffered my share of injuries. One time, I hurt my knee and was out for six weeks. During that time, I was in a cast. Quickly, I learned how to drive my car while wearing the cast, and could still go to practices and interact with my teammates. Even though I had a physical injury, I still had a zest for life. Not so with mental illness; it can destroy people who are physically strong. It can also destroy their families.

In 1986, I opened a sporting goods store. Everything my wife and I owned was on the line. I was under unbelievable financial stress and was struggling to adapt to a new life after hockey. My daughter was battling an eating disorder and my mother was dying of cancer. It was a horrendous time. I found I couldn't concentrate. Simple duties became overwhelming. I became a file shuffler and was afraid to answer the phone. I withdrew from my friends and from most of my family. At my worst, while at work, I'd leave my office and sit in my car in the parking garage for hours. Just sit in my car!

I knew I was in big trouble, but other thoughts nagged me. "Real men don't get depressed. Just give it time — it'll go away." I had always been strong and very goal-oriented. I'd been a perfectionist. I was afraid that if I admitted I had a problem, people would think I was weak. I said to myself, "Ron, snap out of it. Pull up your socks," but at that point, I couldn't find my socks and didn't much care. In time, I refused to leave the house, and preferred just sitting in a dark room.

Pride and ignorance held me back. Pride, particularly for men, is a huge obstacle. It kept me from moving forward. I wasn't being a husband to Jan or a father to my kids. My wife couldn't hold the family together by herself.

Then, it was almost as if God said, "Ellis, if you're not going to get help, I'm going to shut you down." And he did. It was almost like a computer that crashes, but I couldn't reboot Ron Ellis.

I quickly realized the importance of a general practitioner. My family doctor identified the problem immediately and walked Jan and I through the steps towards recovery.

There are four areas of importance in recovery from depression.

Number one is family — in my case, my wife Jan. She stood by me during some very dark times, and I'm proud to tell you, we celebrated our thirty-sixth anniversary [on May 28, 2002]. The divorce rate among professional athletes is much higher than the general population, and when you couple that with a partner struggling through depression, you get a sense at how blessed I am to have my amazing wife Jan in my life.

Number two is having a good family doctor. I was fortunate. I've had the same family doctor for twenty-five years. He did extra study on depression, and I was so thankful. He even went so far as to have a weekly meeting with Jan to help her and to give her the strength to get through my depression.

Number three is a good hospital facility, if one is needed. I resisted for too long, and finally needed to be hospitalized. I went to a hospital called Homewood, and after settling in I took courses in stress management, anger management and self-esteem.

Finally, number four is the role of the employer. Do they have insurance that covers hospitalization for mental illness? When I joined the staff at the Hockey Hall of Fame, I didn't read the small print in the company insurance guide. Fortunately for me, the Hall had the proper insurance in place and that made it relatively easy to get the required help even to the point of having short-term disability available.

I have to tell you, when it was time to approach my employer, I was full of anxiety. I did not want to have that meeting. But a meeting was called with my boss — David Taylor, the president of the Hockey Hall of Fame — Jan and me, Dr. Perez and a representative from the insurance company. By the end of the meeting, my employer made me feel safe to take short-term disability. If they had not, I know I would have soldiered on [without treatment] even if it meant ultimately losing my family and my job.

The insurance company developed a back-to-work program in conjunction with Dr. Perez and me. It was extremely important to develop a back-to-work plan, so that the employee can gradually take on more responsibility over time. I made the mistake during a previous reoccurrence by trying to return to work before I was ready. I wanted everyone to think, "I'm back and productive."

There are a lot of parallels between a hockey

team and a business. Both require good team-work. Both need stars and the diggers who will plug away doing whatever is asked of them. Both need valued employees. Both need their players to get back into the lineup when sidelined so they can contribute once again.

It took me a long time to realize that depression is an illness, not a weakness. I also understood that the longer the depression is left untreated, the longer the recovery time. Now that I understand depression better, I realize that there were players on my team playing with depression. There are a number of players competing in the NHL right now trying to compete while coping with depression.

This is my final statement. After what the Hockey Hall of Fame has done for me, they have one *very* loyal employee. I'd go through a wall for them. I've been offered other jobs through the years, some with more perqs than I currently have, but each time, I said, "No way." I have a real loyalty to the Hockey Hall of Fame for all they've done for my family and me.

Warm and thoughtful applause greets Ron's words. It has taken a great deal of courage for him to be able to speak at functions like this. But Ron knows that what he faced during his darkest days is not something he wants others to have to endure, and he wants people to know that help is available.

"It all came to a head in 1986," says Ron. "I had retired in '81, and it's always hard for pro athletes to make the transition to the working world." Ron tried different jobs, searching in vain for a comfortable niche. Opening Ron Ellis Sports should have been a natural for a former professional athlete who was well known and well liked in the community. But instead of setting out on the road to success, Ellis was instead headed down a path that led to the depths of darkness. Ron wasn't prepared for the amount of time and money it would take to manage the store. "As a retired pro athlete, I was used to controlling my own destiny. I was having trouble handling the matters that were beyond my control. As the symptoms of clinical depression invaded my life, I began to magnify problems. The business was struggling, but not failing. However, in my mental state, I couldn't and wouldn't believe that that was not the case."

Ellis began to sink more and more of his time and resources into Ron Ellis Sports. "That was not the solution. Like most men, I just kept truckin', saying, 'If I just work longer and harder, we'll get out of this.' Well, unfortunately, it didn't turn out that way for me," sighs Ron.

"One day, I was going into the office and Jan said, 'No, Ron, you're not well enough to go.' I said, 'I have to.' My office was up high, and I looked down through my window over the whole store. I was just sitting there, then all of a sudden, I just lost control. The tears started. I had a mental crash. That was the time when everything came crashing in.

"However, when I look back, it was probably a ten-year process building up to that point. My body just said, 'No more, Ellis!' Mel Stevens was coming to meet me for lunch and found me with my head down on my desk, sobbing. On the pretence that we were going out for a coffee, Mel took me out through a back door so my staff wouldn't see me in that condition.

"After that day in my office, I saw what I was doing to my wife and my family. I knew I wasn't coping well on my own. I couldn't do anything productive in the office. I'd pick up the phone, flip through a file, move files from one side of my desk to the other. It's just so hard when you've lost your ability to do your job. That's pretty painful all by itself."

After seeking therapy, Ron was able to identify other times that he had felt overwhelmed by depression. "One that I can recall is when I retired from the Leafs for those two years in 1975. I had just come off my best year and signed a four-year contract, but felt that I couldn't carry on. It was just so hard to explain to people. No doubt, clinical depression was at work.

"At the end of each season, I'd be completely fatigued, my weight would be down and I'd be as white as a ghost. In the off-season, I had time to recover and that gave me an opportunity to get ready to go back the next year. If I had been in a stressful job twelve months of the year, I might have crashed sooner. It's hard to say."

Jan Ellis, Ron's loving and very supportive wife, looks back at her husband's emotional valleys. "I had noticed throughout our relationship that Ron could be very moody, but I knew nothing about depression. I did notice changes, but didn't recognize them as depression. I blamed hockey. I kept thinking that once Ron was finished playing, we'd be done with the withdrawal and the moodiness. I didn't understand what depression was doing to my husband."

"Fortunately for me, I have a terrific family doctor," Ron continues. "He had taken it upon himself to study depression. He's had a lot of clients with this problem. He prescribed medications for me and researched hospitals that could help people like me. He told me I had to take a break from the store. The staff was told that I was resting from burnout, and they picked up the slack. They were very understanding. For two months, I stayed home and improved somewhat, and then I started going back to the store. In no time at all, I hit rock bottom again. I realized I wasn't ready at all. My months away only delayed the inevitable." That's when Ron's family doctor recommended he be hospitalized. "Of course, I did not want to go to any hospital. I felt isolated. I didn't know anyone else who had suffered from depression."

Jan agrees on this point. "It would have been helpful to know someone who had been through depression in order to know how to get through each stage."

"When I look back, I didn't really understand what was wrong," Ron says. "I thought I was going to beat this thing all by myself, that I didn't need any help. I didn't think it was a mental illness at the time. I thought of it as a medical problem. In my professional hockey life, you didn't dare show any weakness to your teammates or your opponents." Ron thought that to admit he needed help would be a display of weakness. "If I hadn't been married, I wouldn't have sought the help," he maintains. "However, I could see what I was doing to my family. The possibility of losing my family was very real."

In October 1987, Ron finally agreed to hospital treatment. "I checked into the Homewood Health Centre in Guelph. The centre specializes in behavioural and psychiatric services. Admitting that I needed to be hospitalized was unbearable. It was hard enough just to admit that I was struggling with depression, but to think that I needed to be hospitalized was tough — real tough. I had my fears about where I was going. No one had really told me what goes on in these places. I feared the worst. But without question, it was the best move I've made in my life. The hospital environment provides protection from the sources of stress. In a short period of time, you begin to calm down and have a chance to allow the medications to work."

His stay at Homewood convinced him that his condition wasn't unique. "I was in the hospital with CEOs, doctors, school teachers — all people who had done well in their professions. It's about bonds. It's about trust. You start to identify with what people have gone through in their childhood and careers, and all of a sudden a light goes on: 'That's what happened with me, too.'

"When I was in the hospital, I would say that the majority of people in the ward were between 45 and 50 years old. That's when everything comes crashing in on you. You're at the peak of your career, you realize you're not going any further, your kids are growing up and parents are starting to pass away. That was a common theme. Another common theme was that these were successful, driven people."

Another lesson Ron had to learn was that it is a long, challenging path to come back from depression. "I was looking for the quick fix," he admits. "My first stay in the hospital was helpful, but I didn't give it my all. I was looking for that quick fix so I could return to work as quickly as possible. Most male patients think that way. They want to get back out there and be productive again. I'd start feeling better and would stop taking my medication. When I came out of the hospital the first time, I immediately returned to the store and started spending the same long hours I had put in before. Within a year, I had deteriorated to shuffling files around again."

Ron negotiated a settlement with his partners in the sporting goods store. "I was prepared to walk away from my investment and not ask for anything in return. I realized that the retail industry was not a good match for my personality; I was inclined to take everything personally, particularly because my name was on the door."

Ron continued to see his family doctor, who detected a gradual slide in his mood. Ellis was readmitted to hospital. "The second time, I went back to the hospital with a whole new mindset. I didn't expect the quick fix. I realized I needed to do everything I could to learn about this disease, to understand and accept what

I have to do to be productive and to get back to a normal, balanced life. I learned that I had to get a handle on the coping skills that I needed to combat depression.

"There were a lot of things that I had to put in place in my life. I had to accept the fact that I would be on medication for the rest of my life. That wasn't easy. I'm happy to say that it doesn't bother me anymore. I was very fortunate that I had support in place — first of all, my family, my wife in particular, my family doctor, a hospital and an understanding employer. I like to refer to this support as 'the four pillars of recovery.' Some of my fellow patients did not have a lot of family support, which made their recovery more difficult and made it take longer. Finally, I had to accept that I must be accountable to my wife, my doctors and the patient friends I made in the hospital.

"I had to take more control of my personal schedule. And believe it or not, by taking time for family and leisure, I find myself more productive in the workplace," Ron observes.

"I still have to keep on him about that," Jan says. "He has trouble saying no. We have an update talk every month."

Ron talks about the importance of a support network. "I'd certainly recommend finding a family doctor who understands depression and has the ability to refer patients to the proper hospital care. And your employer has to be involved in the process, too. The last two times I was hospitalized, I was working for the Hockey Hall of Fame. They made it very clear they were behind me and that they wanted me to return and be part of the team again. As a man suffering with depression, you tend to think the worst — 'If they let me go, I will not be able to look after my family.' I saw patients getting pink slips while in the hospital. You spiral down into the ground with such thoughts. It was extremely important that I knew my job was safe while I concentrated on my battle with depression.

"All of these areas of support are important," emphasizes Ellis. "If you don't have one or two in place, it's going to be almost impossible to make a full recovery."

* * *

Ralph Waldo Emerson said, "Courage consists of the power of self-recovery." Ron Ellis knows a lot about courage. He has not only battled his clinical depression to the point that he now has it in check, but he has chosen to step forward and speak candidly about his depression, in hopes of helping to shake the stigma that surrounds mental illness. "I could have kept my condition quiet for the rest of my life, but I decided that speaking up might help others."

The list of celebrities who have publicly acknowledged their own depression is startling — British statesman Sir Winston Churchill, astronaut Buzz Aldrin, recording artist Billy Joel, comedian Louie Anderson, author Kurt Vonnegut, TV personality Marie Osmond, actress Margot Kidder, TV host Rosie O'Donnell — the list goes on and on. To those on the outside, being a celebrity must seem like an idyllic existence — a comfortable lifestyle, public recognition. But the burden of depression can be every bit as debilitating to those in the public eye as it can be for the average citizen. In fact, it can be worse. Public expectations and the scrutiny of the media can make depression loom that much larger for a celebrity. "There's always that image out there of the athlete with no problems, and that's so far from the truth," says Ellis.

Andy Bathgate, a former teammate of Ron's, was surprised to hear about Ron's depression. "It's sad to see what stress can do to a person. It can be a long, lingering thing. It sure was with Frank Mahovlich, and he ended up having a breakdown.

"We were brought up in a time when we were taught to think we were invincible," Bathgate continues. "Even if we were badly hurt, we would find a way to get off the ice. I can never remember being helped to the bench. You don't want the other fellow to think he hurt you. You played through terrible injuries. And it was the same with mental problems. They didn't want anyone to know what they were going through. They hid it. As a result, friends and teammates can't help because they don't know that there's a problem. When I heard about Ronnie, I was concerned about his illness."

Wayne Carleton was also surprised to hear the word "depression" associated with his former teammate. "Based on the things I now know about Ronnie, I realize he's gone through a lot. Life hasn't been as easy as a lot of people think, but Ron has battled through his problems.

"Hockey is in Ron's blood," Carleton continues. "When hockey was finished for me, I made a decision that enough was enough, and I had to get away from it. There are other things I do now. I'm involved in the finance industry. Since the Air Canada Centre opened, I've only been to one game. I'm not caught up in being an ex-player. Life is short enough as it is.

"In my life, I've found things that make me happy," Carleton concludes. "It makes life a little easier when you're doing something you enjoy. I'm always glad to see Ron. Over the last five years, Ronnie has been as happy as I've ever seen him."

Darryl Sittler comments on Ron's depression. "We've all been put on pedestals as hockey players, and people often forget that we're all human beings. We suffer through the emotions of everyday life just the same as anyone else. Ron took a courageous step forward when he decided to tell people about his challenges. He wanted to help other people facing the same problems."

* * *

"I met Ron in 1993 when I was working as a psychiatrist in a program called 'Course of Recovery' at Homewood," begins Dr. Edgardo Perez. The program was designed to help people with depression and anxiety. "I was the psychiatrist who developed a specialized program for men who suffered from depression or anxiety. Ron was part of a specialized program we had at Homewood.

"I never really was involved in sports," chuckles Dr. Perez. "I went to school at Cornell University. I knew they had a hockey team, but that was it. I might have gone to a game once, but I never really paid too much attention to hockey. So after I started at Homewood, they said, 'Ron Ellis is here,' I said, 'Okay, that's fine.' I didn't know who he was. I just continued in my informal way like I tend to do with everybody. Afterwards, one of the male nurses asked, 'Do you know who he is?' and I said, 'He's a nice man.' It wasn't until after my first contact with Ron that I learned who he was!"

Dr. Perez identifies depression and its causes. "Depression is the difficulty to control your moods. You tend to feel sad, unable to cope, unable to concentrate and have difficulty reaching the goals you want to accomplish in your life. You are easily overwhelmed. The major component is feeling sadness, feeling helpless, and at times, feeling that there is no way out of the hole that you're in.

"Any depression will feature a chemical imbalance. The question is, why is there an imbalance? That can be answered in a few ways. You may have a predisposition to a chemical imbalance. It might be in your family, so you have the imbalance biologically. At least 30 percent of those who develop major depression have a family history of depression. Secondly, you may have had a major trauma or stressful event. And what is stressful to you may not be stressful to me. If you have a predisposition for depression, you might trigger that depression sooner than later. Or, if you have no genetic background for depression, you may have experienced a major loss in your life. You might develop chemical changes in your brain because of that major trauma."

Dr. Perez says that there are many signs that can indicate depression. These include persistent sad or anxious moods, feelings of hopelessness, feelings of worthlessness, diminished pleasure in activities that were once enjoyed, persistent fatigue, insomnia or lethargy to the point of sleeping much of the day, diminished ability to concentrate, significant weight loss or gain, irritability and recurring thoughts of death.

"To get to Homewood, usually a family doctor makes a referral, but it could be your employer or your employee assistance program that makes the referral — there are many avenues to get here. Ron came from a referral by his family doctor. He's an excellent physician. He tried to do everything he could for Ron, but more importantly he was well aware of the resources available to help his patients.

"Before you arrive at Homewood, we obtain as much information as possible relating to who you are — your demographic characteristics, clinical information, the psychiatric information, what kind of treatment you received prior to arriving at Homewood and the reason for the referral. We get all that information, then we look for the best possible program that we have to be able to fit you in. That's a very important component for us.

"Then, some people come for a visit and look at the facilities. They may ask further questions. When you come in, you spend much of the first week in assessment. The assessment is more than just trying to determine what your problems are. It prepares you to participate in your treatment program — we try to make you understand what it's like to be in a psychiatric hospital. It's not this scary place that people used to think of from the movies. It's a very healing environment, a beautiful physical environment. We try to help you understand your responsibilities. We try to help you understand how to work in a group — we do a lot of our work in group therapies. It's a way we get to know you and you get to know us. After a few days, you may say, 'This is not for me,' and that's fine. There is that element of dual assessment.

"For someone like Ron who has depression, the treatment period is usually six to eight weeks," Dr. Perez explains.

"First off, we assess your physical state to make sure you don't have any medical conditions that may lead to depression, like thyroid conditions or hormone difficulties or cancer. Next, we try to find the best possible medication from what we see. Then you are engaged in a series of group therapies. You would have process groups — looking at issues that may have precipitated your depression or your stresses. We try to help you understand how you relate to others, because we see a lot of relationship issues. We also have groups related to how you deal with stresses. We use principles of cognitive therapy to help you see life in a different way. People tend to be very negative when they get depressed, so we try to teach you how to look at situations in life without becoming too negative. We also look at the spiritual dimensions of life. Not religion, but the spiritual dimensions. What is the purpose of life?

"Some people need to be more assertive without being aggressive. Some people may need to learn how to manage their anger. [In some cases, we] use horticulture therapy — working with plants. We use anything we can to get individuals to talk about themselves. We also use art therapy. It doesn't have to be artistic, but they do drawings or paintings. It's fascinating to see the evolution of somebody who comes depressed — dark colours all the way — to the changes in colours and figures.

"Having some sort of beliefs, whether they be Christian or not, is very important," states Dr. Perez. "We teach that the individual is part of something bigger than themselves, and that's the basis of spirituality. That was really important in Ron's recovery. Eventually, as part of the recovery process, we ask people to do things for others. The more you do for others... it has a lot of healing power.

"The role of the family is essential. Early on, when Ron came, we did some work in that area. We've formalized it. We used to have a group for the spouses at the same time as we had the follow-up group for the patients. That was really helpful. We have to make sure that the spouses are not left out. Ron has a very supportive wife who is there for him, and that was very helpful."

Dr. Perez acknowledges that people being treated for depression are often under pressure from employers or insurance companies to return to work as soon as possible. "People already feel that maybe they have been a failure because they are depressed so they 'slide to health,'" he says. "What that means is that the person is feeling a little bit better and they don't want to be labelled as 'crazy.' 'I better go and show everybody that I can manage; I'm going to go back to work next week.'" Ron Ellis fit into this category; according to Dr. Perez, 30 to 40 percent of the people he sees are in the same straits.

"But in my opinion, there is a group of individuals who may need some time away from work. For Ron, this was very difficult, because he had very high standards. I remember very clearly sitting in the community mental health clinic with the case manager from the insurance company, and how difficult it was for Ron to accept the idea that he had to take time away from the Hockey Hall of Fame. Sometimes we feel that if we accept that, we are not productive. It was hard to convince Ron that he was going to be *more* productive by being able to take the time off and by eventually making a gradual re-entry to work. It really paid off for Ron."

Dr. Perez says that it is not uncommon for someone like Ron Ellis, who has been a professional athlete — and one who put great pressure on himself to excel and be productive — to worry about how they are perceived by others. "But we have to give a lot of credit to Ron's employer, the Hockey Hall of Fame. They were excellent in reassuring Ron that he could take the time off work and that he could eventually return to work gradually."

"Each case has its own unique circumstances," admits Hockey Hall of Fame president Jeff Denomme. "Depression is a reality and it hits a much larger percentage of the population than one may realize. Ron is big on building awareness on these issues. At the time, David Taylor was the president of the Hall. He took a proactive role on behalf of the Hall and really reassured Ronnie that he had his employer's support. He even went out to see Dr. Perez along with Ron and Jan. It gave Ron a comfort level that the Hall of Fame was behind him.

Denomme points out that, in the early 1990s when the Hall of Fame moved to its new quarters at Yonge and Front streets in Toronto, "There was an enormous pressure on the senior management to get the place up and running. There might have been a little bit too much structure for Ron at the time.

"When Ron was on his leave, the Hall went through a transition period," Denomme says. Prior to his being appointed president, the job had been vacant for two years. "I took Ron under my wing and that benefited Ron. He didn't try to rush back into the Hall and we didn't try to rush him. I knew Ron had an important role to play, and I knew that if I was going to get the opportunity to become president of the Hockey Hall of Fame, Ron was going to be valuable to me. I'm more hands-on technically and financially, and I knew Ronnie would be a key person in my management team.

"We're a small group at the Hall, but if anybody in this organization fell ill the way Ron did, we'd do the same thing as we did for Ron. There's the human element of the business here. We'd want to let that person know that the employer is 100 percent behind them and that they don't have to rush back into things.

"But we do have a business to run, and you've got to tend to that," Denomme maintains. "Ronnie has these intangibles that he brings to the job. When he was away, there was a gap to be filled, but it wasn't making or breaking the business. You have to take the person's position into account. Every case has its own unique circumstances.

"Ron's a hard worker," concludes Jeff Denomme. "Since he's come back, I know at times he has to step back. I can tell he may be taking on too many things sometimes. But I think he's obviously managing things much better. He's got it under control. I wanted Ron to have a lot of latitude to manage his own time. Ron doesn't flourish with too much structure and too much accountability." An ingredient that has also helped Ron is the ability to work from his home in Collingwood, Ontario, two or three days a week.

Dr. Perez points out that returning to work is one of the more difficult steps for someone who has been treated for depression. "Many companies and physicians don't spend the time doing this step. You have to take the job description, look at it and determine what elements can be done, and which ones should be delayed. After week two, more responsibilities are added. With each week, more elements are added, but it has to be a well-defined process.

"It is important to work with the patient, the employer and the insurance company. We did that for Ron, and it paid off. We were all accountable. In my opinion, that kind of planning is sadly lacking in health care and in organizations. That's where people tend to fail, and if they fail and get depressed again, the more difficult it is for me to administer treatment in the future. We need to prevent relapses.

"In the maintenance program, we usually continue with some counselling or psychotherapy and medication." Dr. Perez says it has been demonstrated that, in situations where there are relapses or treatment takes a longer time, certain chemicals in the brain begin to change, making it more difficult to treat the individual with medication.

"About two years ago, Dr. Perez asked me if I would assist him with seminars from time to time," mentions Ron. "I told him I'd be happy to, if he thought it might help somebody or if it helped erase the stigma around mental illness for some people."

"His contribution has been very helpful," confirms Dr. Perez. "When I approached him about speaking at some seminars, he was very eager. In fact, one day, Ron suggested we rent a mini-bus and travel across Ontario to give presentations. I would like to do that, if we only had the resources." Dr. Perez thinks for a moment. "It is very congruent with Ron's Christian philosophy. Go out and share with others and help others."

Dr. Perez comments that depression is more commonly found in women than men, but that, as a result of social pressures, adult men are less forthcoming about the condition. "Ron's celebrity status has helped create awareness about the prevalence of depression in adult men and to address the fact that depression can occur in people from any walk of life. Five to six percent of the population will develop a major depression at some point in their life. Ron has also helped convey the message that employers need to accommodate people who are suffering from mental illnesses. But it has also made people aware of Homewood, and that facilities like ours are not the scary places that have been depicted in the movies."

On May 4, 2000, Ron Ellis was presented with the Courage to

Come Back Award in the celebrity category. The awards, presented annually by the Centre for Addiction and Mental Health Foundation, recognize and honour the courage of individuals who are overcoming the challenges of living with either a mental illness or addiction, and who have chosen to use their experiences to contribute to their community.

"I see courage as something that provides the grit that gives the strength to accept and the staying power to endure," Ellis says. "I don't think you ever beat depression. It's always a challenge, and I know if I don't take care of myself, it could come back with a vengeance."

CHAPTER TWENTY-TWO

Hockey Hall of Fame

The Hockey Hall of Fame is located in BCE Place, an office/commercial complex at the northwest corner of Yonge and Front streets in the heart of downtown Toronto. The focal point of the museum is the extraordinary Great Hall, which houses the Stanely Cup, the NHL's annual merit trophies and the images of every Honoured Member. This unique space occupies what was once a branch of the Bank of Montreal. The heritage building, constructed in 1885, housed the bank until 1983. After the bank moved out, there was talk about turning the building into a museum of photography, but nothing came of it. On June 18, 1993, after more than three decades in its former home on the grounds of the Canadian National Exhibition, the Hockey Hall of Fame opened its doors in this location.

The idea of a hall of fame to honour hockey's legends had been discussed as early as the 1930s. One of the first to suggest that such an institution was required was hockey great Cyclone Taylor. From his home in Vancouver, Taylor stated that hockey's traditions should be recognized in a style comparable to the Baseball Hall of Fame in Cooperstown, New York. In the November 29, 1940, edition of the *Toronto Star*, sports editor Andy Lytle wrote: "I mentioned the idea to Conn Smythe and he favoured it with customary enthusiasm. He went a step further and characteristically thought of Maple Leaf Gardens as the shrine, the hallowed hall in which the living great and the dead but remembered ghosts could rest in a hockey Valhalla. Such a centre could be developed into a hockey museum national in scope."

Another thrust for a Hockey Hall of Fame was spearheaded by Captain James Sutherland, who had been president of the

Ontario Hockey Association beginning in 1915 and was named president of the Canadian Amateur Hockey Association in 1919. Captain Sutherland envisioned a permanent home for the hall in his hometown of Kingston, Ontario, which many have cited as the birthplace of hockey. Sutherland, along with W.A. Hewitt, secretary of the Ontario Hockey Association for 58 years, successfully lobbied the CAHA and the NHL to form a committee that would regularly select players and officials to be included in such a shrine. It was further agreed that a committee be struck to find a permanent home for this array of hockey greats and artifacts of the history of the game.

The first selections to the Hockey Hall of Fame were made in 1945. Dan Bain, Hobey Baker, Russell Bowie, Charlie Gardiner, Eddie Gerard, Frank McGee, Howie Morenz, Tommy Phillips, Harvey Pulford, Art Ross, Hod Stuart and Georges Vezina were the first twelve players to be named Honoured Members of the Hall. Two builders of the game, Lord Stanley of Preston and Sir Montagu Allan, were also among the first to be enshrined. But the Hockey Hall of Fame would remain an entity in name only for another fifteen years. The city of Kingston initially promised to provide a permanent home, but procrastination, fundraising concerns and the death of Captain Sutherland in 1955 combined to scuttle those plans. Nevertheless, further names were added to the honour roll in 1947, and selections were made annually beginning in 1958. Finally, the NHL appointed Frank Selke and Clarence Campbell to see that the brightest stars of hockey's history were properly recognized. Selke had been managing director of the Montreal Canadiens, while Campbell was then president of the National Hockey League. By 1959, the committee had secured both a location and an architect.

The Hockey Hall of Fame's first true home was at Exhibition Place — the grounds of the Canadian National Exhibition in Toronto. Cyclone Taylor and Conn Smythe did the honours at a ground-breaking ceremony, and on August 26, 1961, the Hall was officially opened. Prime Minister John Diefenbaker joined Livingston Merchant, the United States' ambassador to Canada, in cutting the ribbon.

When Ron Ellis relates how he became an employee of the Hockey Hall of Fame, he says, "After retirement, I went through a few years of trying to find my niche." He taught for a year at

Kennedy Road Christian School, then joined a friend's insurance business and established a branch office in Orangeville, Ontario. Next came the ill-starred sporting goods store that bore his name. Finally, an opportunity came for him to once again become involved in hockey.

It was while he was working on the organizing committee for the 1991 Canada Cup tournament that he met Ian "Scotty" Morrison, the former referee-in-chief of the NHL who had been given the mandate of finding the Hall its new home. "It was during that Canada Cup series that Scotty held a reception in the bank building that would become the Great Hall," Ron says. "The purpose of the reception was to show the plans and announce the new location to the corporate world, the media and a lot of other people affiliated with hockey.

"Scotty happened to invite the committee from Team Canada. I was quite happy to come down, and I'm glad that I did, because I really got excited about what I saw," continues Ellis. "Something hit me. Usually, I'm hesitant to step up, but something told me I *had* to talk to Scotty before I left that evening. There was a moment when Scotty was standing by himself, and I said, 'This is exciting! Do you have your staff in place?' And Scotty said, 'No. We've just hired David Taylor as our president, and he's in the process of hiring a director of marketing. Ron, why don't you give Dave a call?'

"I called Dave Taylor, and he told me he was about to hire someone for the marketing position, but that as soon as that guy came on board, Taylor wanted to have lunch with the three of us. Phil Denyes, who was hired as the director of marketing, thought I was the kind of person they needed to give a player's perspective on certain developments. I ended up joining the Hockey Hall of Fame staff as a consultant during the transition from the old Hall to the new location at the corner of Yonge and Front. When we got into the new building, they asked me to stay on, and I've been there ever since. And I have been enjoying it immensely. My title is Director of Public Relations and Assistant to the President."

"The Hall was going to be moving to the new building and we needed more player contact," says Phil Pritchard, the curator of the Hockey Hall of Fame. "What Scotty Morrison wanted ideally was a Toronto-area player, someone who was well respected and well liked, and who could relate well to both older and younger players. Ronnie had played in the '60s, '70s and in 1980, and had been involved with many of the current NHL players who would have been at the beginning of their careers when he was at the latter part of his.

"When he retired, Ron got into teaching, and one of the goals we had for the Hall was the education program," Pritchard continues. "Ronnie Ellis was a perfect fit. We had never had a player involved in the hands-on, day-to-day operation of the Hockey Hall of Fame."

"Ron came on board in May 1992," recalls Jeff Denomme, the president of the Hockey Hall of Fame. "David Taylor, the president at the time, hired Ron. His role going in was to develop the education program and the grassroots hockey — creating awareness throughout the Greater Toronto Hockey League and getting minor hockey teams to participate. I know Ron worked closely with the Centre of Excellence. I was in charge of finance and building at the time, so Ron wasn't really under my domain, but I thought he was a good choice. Ron was instrumental in developing and selling the educational program. He did a lot of legwork getting in front of the boards of education and going out to the schools and working with the London Life people, who are the key sponsors."

"There are certain positions at the Hockey Hall of Fame that are essential and there are people you just have to have, and Ronnie is one of those people," says Pritchard. "Ronnie has the respect of everyone as a co-worker, but we also have respect for him as a hockey player and the people he knows. In business, there are many doors you need to open. Ronnie has the ability to know the right people who can open those doors, not only because he played with the Leafs and with Team Canada in '72, which was a highlight for every Canadian growing up at that time, but Ron was a businessman after he retired, too. He knows people, and helps the Hall with sponsorships, as well as with artifacts and displays. But every bit as important is the fact he's a great public relations person. He puts a face on the Hockey Hall of Fame."

Denomme continues: "When I became president of the Hockey Hall of Fame in 1998, Ron was named Director of Public Relations and Assistant to the President. I guess you could say he is my right-hand man — my right winger. I'm a hands-on, day-to-day guy and Ron could help me in various other roles — speaking engagements, representation at events, charitable initiatives and continuing with his roles with minor hockey initiatives and the education program. He wears several hats, from NHL Alumni to Team Canada '72 to his involvement with the Toronto Maple Leaf organization. He has handled these things very professionally, knowing where his priorities are at in representing each group.

"As an example, when we developed the monument for Team Canada '72 in front of the Hall, Ron certainly had input from the Hockey Hall of Fame's point of view, but he was also on the other side representing Team Canada '72.

"I think he is a great conduit in dealing with the various groups he's associated with. As my assistant, he's a confidant. He's always somebody I can seek advice from, whether it's dealing with personnel issues or public relations issues or even offering input to exhibits at the Hockey Hall of Fame. As a former player, Ron can bring a perspective that I think is important.

"On the other side, Ron is definitely valuable in networking with the sponsors and conducting VIP tours for NHL owners and general managers," continues Denomme. "Ronnie is so positive, and has so much passion for the game and for people, that he's a natural to take people through the Hall and open the door to the Hockey Hall of Fame for new and potential sponsors. That's where his value is most significant."

"Ron's a great team player here and he's respected by all staff," concludes Jeff Denomme. "And I think he's a positive reinforcement for our staff at the Hockey Hall of Fame. He's a veteran, and our elder statesman, but everybody knows he's someone they can confide in. I do that myself. It's good to have someone like that on the team."

The staff of the Hockey Hall of Fame, with the addition of some friends as needed, rents the Moss Park Arena in Toronto every Friday at noon during the hockey season. Phil Pritchard talks about the times Ron Ellis has come out to play, usually to shake off the cobwebs before an alumni game. "I remember the first time Ronnie came out to play hockey with us. We think we're pretty good hockey players, but when Ronnie stepped onto the ice, we realized where we stood. It was like Ronnie never lost 'it.' His passes were bang-on. With NHL players, once you're there, you always have it.

"One of the things I'll always remember was going into the corner with the puck one week," laughs Pritchard. "Ron hammered me. Just hammered me. Flattened. Puck's gone. Ronnie skated back over and said, 'That'll just teach you to keep your head up.' He's done it so many other times with other guys, but it's an important lesson. If you're going to play, keep your head up. Otherwise, that's what happens.

"I've watched Ron in oldtimer games and in the All-Star alumni games and he's still a brilliant skater. Even now that he's in his fifties, his skating is textbook. Just so precise." Phil Pritchard shakes his head and smiles.

Under the arc of a magnificent stained-glass dome sits the Stanley Cup, which bears the name of Ron Ellis as a member of the 1966–67 Toronto Maple Leafs. The dome features mythological figures and the provincial emblems of the seven provinces that were part of Confederation in 1885.

Off to one side of the Great Hall sits an unmistakable reminder of the previous occupant: a bank vault, inside which rests the most significant relic of hockey's incredible past. It is the original Stanley Cup, the silver trophy that Lord Stanley of Preston purchased in 1892 and which has come to symbolize hockey dominance.

There is another, less obvious souvenir from the Bank of Montreal's tenure in this building. In the early 1900s — so the legend goes — a young bank teller named Dorothy was having an affair with a married co-worker at the bank. When the affair ended, the rejected and distraught teller ran upstairs to the washroom on the second floor of the bank and shot herself with the bank's revolver. She died instantly. Legend has it that the ghost of Dorothy still haunts the building. Through the years, employees and visitors have reported seeing the image of a woman wearing a long, flowing white dress, even though the area was in fact unoccupied. Others claim to have witnessed lights turning themselves off and on, discovering open doors that they were certain had been locked, and feeling sudden gusts of cold air for no rational reason.

Staff at the Hockey Hall of Fame glibly blame Dorothy for just about everything odd that happens. Lost your stapler? It must be Dorothy. Can't find a file? It must be Dorothy. As a longtime employee of the Hockey Hall of Fame, Ron Ellis has actually witnessed Dorothy. "I've heard her, but believe me, after playing for Punch Imlach, nothing scares me anymore."

CHAPTER TWENTY-THREE

Fans

Every hockey fan has a favourite player, and the reasons behind their choices are often interesting. Some love the skilled player who leads the team in scoring, like Mats Sundin. Others love the colourful guy who hits and scraps; in Toronto, Tie Domi sweaters sell like hotcakes. Many students of the game appreciate a player like Darcy Tucker, who gives a determined effort on every shift of every game.

Such was the case during Ron Ellis's years with the Toronto Maple Leafs. Sure, some fans liked Darryl Sittler, while others favoured Tiger Williams. But Ron's diligent and determined efforts night after night drew his own followers.

At times, meeting a childhood idol can destroy the illusion you've harboured for so many years. Players can be preoccupied, or short of time. The surroundings may not be conducive to an interview. But there is not a fan yet who has walked away from meeting Ellis without commenting on how impressed they are by him.

Patrick McCarthy, a lifelong Toronto Maple Leafs fan, recalls how Ron Ellis has impacted his entire family. "Back in the '70s, my wife and I had season tickets in the greys at Maple Leaf Gardens. Ron Ellis and Tiger Williams were our favourites. The first time I met Ron was when they opened up the new location of the Hockey Hall of Fame in 1993. I was walking up the stairs, on my way to see the Stanley Cup in the Great Hall, when I saw him. I was quite excited, so I stopped Ron there at the top of the stairs and introduced myself. 'I have to tell you what a thrill it is to meet you,' I said. 'You've been my favourite player for a long time.' That was hard to do — after all, I wasn't a kid anymore. But Ron was great. He took me around for a tour of the Hall. All I could think was, 'Wow! I got to meet Ron Ellis.' I had to get up enough gumption, but I finally pulled out a Ron Ellis hockey card I had in my pocket and asked him to sign it. That moment, we became friends. I treasure that card.

"I started at the Toronto Zoo in 1979," McCarthy continues. "From time to time through the '90s, Ron would come to the Zoo to find out more about education courses and information about tourism. It was part of Ron's position at the Hockey Hall of Fame, and he wanted to learn more about tourist attractions. It was strange for me. All I could think was, 'Well, slap my face! Here's a guy I idolized, and now he's coming to me for advice.'

Their friendship grew over the years. "I was going through my own turmoils and had to take a stress leave from my job at the Zoo between July and October 2000. I was off for several months, and during that time, Ron would call me at home just to let me know he was thinking of me. We had lunch a few times. I have to tell you, it really helped me out. He gave me a lot of support when I needed it most.

"Karolina and I have two daughters — Sarah and Alexandra. My daughter Alex had to have back surgery and was in Sick Kids Hospital in November 2000. It was the Hockey Hall of Fame Induction Weekend, and Ron was very busy with work. Besides preparing to have Joey Mullen and Denis Savard enter the Hall of Fame, Ron was putting together the oldtimers' game on Sunday afternoon. He promised me he'd come by to see Alex in the hospital, and sure enough, Sunday morning at seven, in walks Ron Ellis. He brought an oldtimers jersey, signed by Bobby Hull and Guy Lafleur and a bunch of the guys. Ron and Alex had a great visit. It was almost as if he had nothing else to do and just stopped by. Yet he had to get over to the rink and had a big game that afternoon. I'll never forget that!

McCarthy has one more story that speaks of Ron's character. "I have a sister, Maryanne, who is a Sister. She has a wonderful friend, Sister Eileen, who is also with the order of St. Joseph in Toronto." Eileen was a huge hockey fan who was celebrating fifty years as a Sister. "For an extra-special surprise, I asked Ron if there was any way Eileen could meet Mats Sundin. Ron explained that players get so many requests like that, but he'd see what he could do, especially considering it was such a special occasion. I was so appreciative.

"Sure enough, Ron was able to arrange for Eileen to attend a Maple Leafs practice. We wanted to surprise her, so we didn't tell Eileen that she'd be meeting her favourite player. With the help of his daughter, Kitty, Ron also got me two tickets to the Leafs' game the night before the practice.

"As it turned out, Ron was signing autographs in the lobby of the Air Canada Centre before the game that night. When he was through, he escorted Eileen and Maryanne to their seats. During the game, Eileen said she didn't want to be selfish and wanted to share her good fortune. She had been able to go to the game, but thought one of the other Sisters should attend the practice the next day. Maryanne was in on the surprise, and had to coax her to the practice. Eileen did not want to go if there was someone else at the St. Joseph Mother House who would like to go.

"Ron met Eileen and Maryanne at the Lakeshore Arena, where the Leafs were practising. They sat and prepared themselves to watch the players go through their drills, and Ron said he had something to take care of." Leaf practices are very exclusive, so it was a rare treat for a member of the public to be allowed in. Shortly, Ron came around the corner with Mats Sundin, and introduced him to a starry-eyed Sister Eileen. After exchanging some pleasantries, Mats signed autographs for the two before he had to leave to dress for practice. Later on, Ron's daughter, Kitty, who works at Leafs TV as an associate producer, sent Eileen a tape of Mats Sundin highlights combined with footage of Mats talking with the Sisters at the arena that day.

"I've collected Leaf memorabilia my whole life. I've got books, sweaters, caps, pucks, hockey cards and photographs," smiles McCarthy. "I'll bet I've got twenty-five items signed by Ron Ellis alone. I'm a huge Ellis fan, but there are two reasons for that. One is certainly the way Ron played. It was always hard, but fair and honest. The other reason is the kind of man Ron is. He helped me so much during my depression and went the extra mile to visit my daughter when she was in the hospital and to make Sister Eileen happy. Those things mean so much more to me than photos and hockey cards."

And then there's the story of Ron Lucas, the Maple Leafs fan from Assiniboia, in south central Saskatchewan, who has been a Ron Ellis fan since birth. "In 1968, when I was born, Ron Ellis was my father's favourite Maple Leaf, so I was named Ronald Ellis Lucas," he says. It was no surprise, really, when you realize Ron's parents were the biggest Leafs fans in Esterhazy, a town of 2,600 about 200 kilometres northeast of Regina. "In 1959, when my oldest brother was born, my mother wanted the name Alan, and with Dad being such a huge Maple Leaf fan, he was named Alan Stanley Lucas. In 1966, when my next brother was born, the tradition continued. My parents named him Murray Oliver Lucas."

Ron Ellis Lucas offers a moving footnote to his own story: "On September 26, 2000, my wife Shannon gave birth to our son. His name is Curtis Joseph Lucas."

On November 10, 1979, the Leafs made their first visit to Winnipeg to play the Jets, who had just joined the National Hockey League. "Dad bought tickets for us so we could see our first-ever NHL game," Lucas recalls. "The day before the game, the Leafs held an afternoon skate. Back then, practices were open to the public. I wore the Christmas present I had received the previous winter — a Maple Leaf jersey with a big Number 6 on the back and the name ELLIS above it. While the practice was underway, I decided to find out where our seats were for the following night's game. After failing to find them in the big Winnipeg Arena, I started walking down the stairs. When I got close to the bottom, I noticed Mom and Dad talking to one of the Maple Leafs.

"Once I got down to where they were, the player started talking to me. He asked me why I had *his* number and name on the back of the jersey, and told me I should have 'Sittler' or 'McDonald' or 'Williams' on the back. Knowing exactly who the man was, I told him in the most nervous voice ever, 'I am named after you.' Mom pulled my birth certificate out of her purse as proof. It wasn't much longer before I was out on the ice in Winnipeg Arena getting my picture taken with Ron Ellis.

"Mr. Ellis took my parents and me down the corridor to the Leafs' dressing room, where I got to meet Darryl Sittler, Lanny McDonald, Tiger Williams, Rocky Saganiuk and Mike Palmateer. Needless to say, I was as excited as can be, but I do recall my father having a smile on his face that I will never forget.

"As far as the game the following night goes, I don't remember a lot about it. I know the Leafs won 8–4. The only other thing I remember was that towards the end of the game, the Jets' goaltender was totally frustrated. Ron Ellis was chasing a loose puck down the right wing into the corner when the Jets' goalie skated out and bodychecked Ron instead of playing the puck!"

Ron Lucas recalls another meeting with "the other" Ron Ellis. "A few years later, the family went to a Leafs alumni game in Brandon, Manitoba. I remember sitting behind the Leaf bench wearing the same Leaf sweater. During the national anthem, I was watching Ron Ellis the whole time instead of the Canadian flag. It was during the anthem when Ron glanced up at me and gave me a wink."

Life had continued on for both Ron Ellises. "In October of 1999, our company held a banquet in Saskatoon, and Ron MacLean from *Hockey Night in Canada* was the guest speaker. I had the opportunity to speak with Mr. MacLean, and asked him if he ever saw Ron Ellis. He let me know that Mr. Ellis works at the Hockey Hall of Fame. I got on the Internet and started searching for the Hockey Hall of Fame. After a period of time, I found Ron Ellis's name along with his e-mail address, so I wrote a note retelling my story and bringing up our encounter in Winnipeg, hoping that he might remember me. About a week later, my wife brought me a letter mailed from Ron Ellis. I was thrilled to read that he remembered meeting me and my dad, as if it was yesterday."

"Throughout my hockey life, Ron Ellis was always my favourite player," boasts Scott Russell, one of the hosts of *Hockey Night in Canada.* Scott's book, *Ice Time: A Canadian Hockey Journal,* includes two chapters on Ellis. "He just jumped out at me — his speed, streaking down that right wing, then swooping in on net.

"On the rare occasions when I got to see a hockey game at Maple Leaf Gardens, I couldn't take my eyes off Ellis. Through the years, it became apparent to me that he was a good person. I guess that was first cemented in my mind as a young boy playing in the Civitan Hockey League. At a banquet one year, Brian McFarlane was the master of ceremonies and brought out a special guest. It was Ron Ellis, who came out and played guitar and sang for the roomful of young hockey players. Ron was very quiet and quite obviously shy. McFarlane did all the talking that evening, but Ron was happy to sign autographs for every boy in the room.

"When I played street hockey with my friends, they always pretended they were Sittler or Keon," Russell continues. "They were the Leafs' big stars. But I was always Ron Ellis. He was never the big star, but he was my favourite. I found myself defending him — 'Why would you want to be Ron Ellis? He just goes down his wing and he misses the net as often as he hits it!' But Ron Ellis was always a guy you could count on. I really believe that the image you have of yourself is reflected in the player you choose as your favourite.

"I've always been afraid that childhood heroes won't live up to expectations. But when I finally met Ron Ellis, he was every bit of the image I had created of him. He continues to have that same devotion to the game of hockey that I saw when I was young.

"Ron Ellis is one of the greatest right wingers in the history of the Toronto Maple Leafs," states Scott boldly. "Much of that claim is based on Ron's longevity. The Leafs are the only team he ever played with, the only team he ever *wanted* to play with.

"When I wrote *Ice Time*, I was searching for people who were passionate about the game of hockey," says Scott. "It was a given that I had to include my hero in the game of hockey, and that could only be Ron Ellis. In my Day-Timer, I carry Ron's hockey card from 1973. I also carry an old black-and-white photo from the Leafs stamp collection.

"Ron Ellis was always shy about his ability. Yet he was a star with those Maple Leaf teams in the '60s and '70s. I always saw myself like that — not braggardly, just an honest, down-to-earth guy who did his job to the best of his ability every day."

Another media personality who cites Ron Ellis as his childhood hero is Steve Paikin, the co-host of TVOntario's *Studio 2*. "I went to my first Maple Leaf hockey game in 1966, when I was 6 years old. I watched the Boston Bruins lose to the Maple Leafs, 3–0, and Johnny Bower not only got the shutout, but was named the first star. I went with my parents and my 4-year-old brother, who I think was asleep by the third period. My brother decided that night that he was a Johnny Bower fan and he became a goalie. Even though I shot left, and should have become a Davey Keon fan, for some reason Ron Ellis grabbed my attention. You're 6 years old, who knows why these things happen? Over the course of the years, he became my favourite player and I started following his career. There was a grace and elegance and speed in which he played the game that I enjoyed.

"My brother and I were at another Leaf game when I was ten and he was eight, pressed up against the glass watching the skate before the game started. The ushers came along and shooed us away. My mother, who was watching this, didn't think that was a very nice thing to do, particularly since none of the adults were being shooed away, so she wrote to Stan Obodiac, the public relations guy for the Gardens, and complained about the treatment her poor children had suffered.

"They wrote back and said, 'We apologize — please be guests of the hockey team in the dressing room after the next game you choose to come to.' I can remember that game. It was January 17, 1970, against the Penguins; the Leafs won 4–0 and Keon got a hat trick. We went into the dressing room after the game and I got my picture taken with Ron Ellis. I still have it to this day. There's Ron Ellis — with his brushcut — with his arm around me in the dressing room. It was a phenomenal day. The irony of the story is that women weren't allowed into the dressing room back then, so my dad and my brother and I all got in but my mother did not. Having this picture further solidified my commitment to being an Ellis fan. Every hockey jersey I ever bought had a Number 6 on the back. It's still the case.

"Around 1994 or '95, *Studio 2* did a full edition on hockey," remembers Paikin. "One of the scenes we had to do was shoot a pickup hockey game in somebody's flooded backyard. They said, 'We want to get an NHLer involved in this. Who do you want?' I said, 'Let's get Ron Ellis.' We went up to Newmarket, where some family had a rink in the back, and the kids laced on the blades. We all got in the backyard and there I was, playing hockey with Ronnie Ellis. It doesn't get any better than that.

"At one point, he hipchecked me into a snowbank; I considered it an honour. We invited a bunch of kids to come for the shoot, and Ron was signing hockey cards for the kids. He looked at me and said, 'Do you want one, too?' I said, 'You bet your ass I do, but I was too ashamed to ask for one!' So he signed one and gave it to me. I kept that autographed hockey card in my wallet all the time, and the sad thing was, that wallet got stolen about a year ago. The credit cards, I replaced. The driver's licence, I replaced. The money, I replaced. But that hockey card was irreplaceable, and I'm so disappointed I lost it."

Most men would be a little hesitant to admit they continued to stand in awe of their childhood hero well into their adult life. Not Steve Paikin; he is as proud of his choice of favourite player now as he was when he was 6 years old. "I still play hockey once a week in a Tuesday night pickup game that's been going on for twenty-five years. You'll know me because I'm the guy out there in the Leaf sweater wearing Number 6."

CHAPTER TWENTY-FOUR

Jan

"My father was a pilot in the Air Force, and like most military families, we moved quite often," Ron begins. "Dad got transferred from North Bay to Toronto when I was 9 years old. He was a test pilot, flying the CF-100s that were being manufactured out at Malton Airport. I ended up going to Rexdale Public School because it was close to the airport. Jan happened to be in my Grade 4 class.

"You know how you get talking with kids in the class — 'My dad's a pilot.' Well, Jan said, 'My dad's a pilot, too.' Her dad was flying with Air Canada at the time. So she went home and said, 'There's a boy in my class who has a dad who is a pilot, too. His name is Ron Ellis.' That name rang a bell with Jan's father. 'Ask Ron if his father's name is Randy,' he told her. So she came back to class the next day and asked me, and of course, my dad's name *is* Randy.

"It turns out my father and Jan's joined the Air Force together. They were in the same class, flew together and were pretty good friends. After the war, my dad left the Air Force to pursue his hockey career, while Jan's father, Lyle Greenlaw, went from the Air Force straight into Trans-Canada Airlines, which became Air Canada."

"It was interesting being in the same class with Ronnie," giggles Jan. "You know how kids are when they're 9 years old. He teased me all the time. We rode our bikes together and took our dogs for walks. We lived two streets apart and our fathers hadn't seen each other in ten years since their Air Force days. Our parents became friends."

"We got the families together and had a little reunion. Jan and

I became pretty good friends." Ron smiles. "Then, in Grade 6, my dad got transferred to Ottawa, so away we go again."

"I thought my heart had broken," Jan admits. "As much as you can have a crush in Grades 4, 5 and 6, we had crushes on each other. He was the paper boy, and when he'd ring the doorbell, I'd go running — 'There's Ronnie!' Then he'd throw snow in my face or something. All the silly things you do when you're that age."

"Our families kept in touch through Christmas cards and notes," remembers Ron. "When it was decided that I would leave home to come to Toronto to play with the Marlies Junior B team, Jan's mom, Eveline, assured my parents that they would have me over for dinner. I was boarding with the Gurr family in Weston, and they did everything they could to make it easier for a home-sick 15-year-old. If the Greenlaws hadn't invited me over, I would have stayed with my billets and not gone anywhere."

"I thought he was really cute," beams Jan. "He just didn't seem to have time for dating because he was really into school and doing really well with his hockey. Ronnie excels at everything he does. He was giving it 100 percent. I spent a lot of time writing Ronnie's name on my schoolbooks and putting hearts around it. He finally asked me out when we were 16. We were very young. He took me to the drive-in — it's probably all we could afford. Often, we'd go to Heart Lake and walk and talk and walk and talk. We started as really good friends, but by the time we got to the latter part of high school, it was getting pretty serious."

Ron recounts the early days of the relationship. "Jan and I started to date. We went together all through my days with the Marlies, right up until my decision to turn pro. Jan never missed a Sunday-afternoon game at Maple Leaf Gardens. It's not easy try-ing to date and schedule your time together around hockey games and school."

"He didn't think he'd ever make it in the NHL, so Ronnie sug-gested we should break up. He thought he would be going to uni-versity in the States on a scholarship and it wouldn't be fair to have a long-distance romance. I thought my heart had been ripped out, but after a few weeks, he was more determined than ever to make it." Jan laughs.

Jan describes the effect of Ron's decision to turn pro on the young couple's lifestyle. "We went from such an innocent life in high school to the Toronto Maple Leafs. It was a really big transition. Ronnie may have seen more than I would have, when he played Junior A. Some of those guys were pretty wild and there was a lot of drinking. In my high school, any kids I knew who drank or smoked were bad kids. My friends had good, clean fun at pizza parties with crazy games. To go from that to a Toronto Maple Leaf party was a whole new world. My Mom and Dad had really sheltered me. I just couldn't believe the things that were going on at those parties compared to high school. They probably weren't any different than in any other business, but I hadn't been exposed to that. I would tell my Mom what I heard and saw and she'd gasp! I asked her, 'Isn't that what happens at your Air Canada parties?' And she'd say, 'Noooooo!'

"Hockey players are famous. People idolize them. Everything's given to them. They're very pampered. They're told what do every step of the way. 'Catch this plane. Go to this practice.' It was a whole different life," Jan observes.

"Nancy Bower definitely took me under her wing," she recalls. "Lori Horton was always very nice to me — I liked her a lot. A lot of the wives were that much older than I was. But remember, I was just the girlfriend. Until I became engaged, they treated me differently."

"I'd known the Greenlaw family since I was 9 years old and I became even closer to Jan's mom and dad after Jan and I had dated for a number of years," Ron continues. "Talk of marriage came up very naturally. Her mom would say something like, 'When you and Jan are married...' There was no official proposal; her father seemed to buy into the idea as well. I went along with it, too; I thought Jan was the woman I wanted to spend my life with. After my first year with the Leafs, on April 16, 1965, I gave Jan an engagement ring at the Old Mill Restaurant. She was really quite surprised to get it. She knew that it was coming — she just didn't know when. I remember Jan saying, 'You had better not forget this night!' So I pounded *April 16 — Old Mill — white dress* into my head until I could recite it every April 16 from that day on!"

"A girlfriend of mine had received an engagement ring she didn't like. So I told Ron, 'I would like to be involved in picking out the ring. After all, I have to wear it the rest of my life, so I have to like it.' So he let me pick it out, but he wouldn't let me have it," Jan states. "Punch didn't want Ron to get married. 'You have to stay focused on hockey.' It was so ridiculous. After we were married and they left home for six weeks of training camp, I had to sneak into a motel to see my husband! I felt so cheap!

"It was Good Friday when we went to the Old Mill for dinner. I was pretty sure that was going to be the night. He had gone home to see his parents in Ottawa and to show them the ring, so I was pretty sure. And the Old Mill was a pretty fancy-schmancy place. I got all dressed up. If he hadn't given me the ring that night, he probably would have had his dinner all over his head! I had waited long enough!

"After dessert, Ronnie gave me the ring. I was in seventh heaven. It was a really romantic setting. At the Old Mill, they had a beautiful dance floor and a big-band orchestra. The music was great and we were out in the middle of the dance floor and I'll never forget this: a lady came over and tapped Ronnie on the shoulder and said, 'I'm a friend of Stafford Smythe's. So what did you think of the last game?' Ronnie had just given me the ring and I was all emotional. Twenty minutes. She talked to Ron for twenty minutes! Twenty minutes in the middle of the dance floor. That should have been a clue to me that this was going to be the way it was for the rest of my life."

"After my second year, we got married. The date was May 28, 1966," Ron grins. It obviously stirs up wonderful memories. "We got married at Rexdale United Church. It was a fairly large wedding — about 175 guests — and the whole Leaf team came to the wedding. Even Punch Imlach and King Clancy. I asked Brit Selby to be my best man, but he declined. He did agree to be in my wedding party, though. We had been pretty good pals in junior and we hung out the first couple years of pro. My first cousin was my best man."

Jan takes a wedding photo of a beautiful young couple off the wall. "We had a police escort outside the church because word had spread through the neighbourhood that the whole team was in the church. You couldn't just invite one or two from the team. It was everybody or nobody. By that time, Ronnie had played two years. We were twenty and twenty-one when we got married. It was a wedding that the rest of our friends and family will never forget."

The reception was held at the Constellation Hotel on the airport strip. "We had a great time with the dancing and the whole thing," Jan recalls. "It was just what I wanted for a wedding. We didn't want it to cost my parents a fortune. Ronnie was making $9,000 a year, which is hard to believe, so it wasn't like we had a whole pile of money. I was a secretary at the head office for all the Dominion Stores in Canada. I wasn't making a huge salary, either. But we had enough to put a roof over our heads and to have a car. We managed to get through on a whole lot of love.

"We went away for a week to Freeport in the Bahamas," smiles Jan. "It was lovely, and our first chance to get away together."

"We originally lived in a three-bedroom apartment in the Martingrove and Westway area of Toronto," mentions Ron. An article in the Leaf program that fall described Jan as "a willowy blonde with fair skin, luminous eyes and a ready laugh. She still gets a kick out of their one shopping spree for furniture. It took them one hour to buy everything they needed and nothing had to be returned."

"Jan and I are still like that," Ron confirms. "We see something that catches our eye and we know it's the item we want — in spite of the efforts of the salespeople."

"I could see that, no matter where we went and no matter what we did, Ron was going to be recognized and stopped." Jan sighs, realizing it was a special but often cumbersome part of their life. "The Toronto Maple Leafs are worshipped in this city. It was always easier to leave Ron at home. I remember one time Ron had a knee injury and had a great big cast on his leg. He said, 'I'll come shopping with you.' He never had before, and he didn't know what it was like to be in a grocery store. We had R.J. with us — he would have been about three. We got stopped every step along the way — 'Oh, it's Ron Ellis!' I figured I could get my shopping done three times as fast if Ron hadn't been there. But R.J. said, 'Gee, Dad, I didn't know you had so many friends!' He had no idea that his dad was popular."

Jan remembers what it was like at Maple Leaf Gardens. "I always tried to stay anonymous. But one time, this guy was all over Ronnie from the second he stepped on the ice. He didn't have a nice word to say about Ron. He had no idea who I was, but a lot of people in the section knew because I sat in the same seats for about seven years with Mike Pelyk's wife. I was pregnant at the time. For two periods, this guy was on Ronnie's case. Maybe it was the mother in me. He didn't know my husband and he was saying these mean things about him. After two periods, I couldn't take it any more. I finally stood up and did something I've never even done to our dogs. I turned around and screamed, 'YOU! SHUT UP!!' Everybody laughed their heads off, but the guy never showed up for the third period."

"A year after the playoffs, Brian and Sue Conacher invited Jan and me to join them for a holiday in Florida," remembers Ron fondly. "Sue's mom and dad had a place down in Sarasota, and we had a great time together. Sue and Jan were seatmates back then. Each player got two tickets for every home game, so you usually paired up with another player so the two wives could sit together. This freed up a pair of tickets that would be available on alternate games for family and friends. Sue and Jan sat together for a year or two. Then Mike Pelyk's wife Diane sat with Jan for a number of years."

"Ronnie could see where I sat at the games. Once I got some seniority, I got two seats right on the aisle. That way, I could duck out when there was thirty seconds left and get ahead of the crowd. The wives' room was just the old Marlies dressing room, but there was a pot of coffee and I could catch up with the other girls. If I got caught up in conversation with one of the other wives and was late getting back to my seat, I'd hear about it after the game. 'So… I noticed you didn't get back for the third period until five minutes had gone by.' And I'd laugh and say, 'I thought you were supposed to be focusing on the hockey game!'"

Ron had a distinct routine on game days. "He'd have to go down to the Gardens for a meeting in the morning. He'd come home and have to have his steak cooked a certain way, served with a baked potato at one o'clock exactly. Then it was ice cream with chocolate sauce. Then Ronnie would go to bed for the afternoon. I would get him up at four. Every game day, I would bake fresh chocolate chip cookies and he would have those with tea. Then I would run around like crazy and get myself ready.

"Later on, when the kids came, we were living close to my mom and dad, so I got them fed and changed, ready for my mom, who babysat a lot of the time. Then we were out the door. We had to be there for six-thirty. If Ron was five minutes late, he was fined a lot of money. And we had to take the same route down to the Gardens. Talk about superstitions! Ohhh!

"We didn't adopt Kitty until I was 25. Ron and I were married when I was 20, so there were five years when we could do whatever we wanted with the other couples who didn't have children. We'd all go out as a team to one of the steak houses near the Gardens. They'd give us the whole room, so nobody would disturb the players for autographs. And Ron would have another steak dinner at midnight!"

The topic of vacations brings back a flood of wonderful memories to Jan. "Usually every April, I would tell Ronnie I had to get out of here. The last thing Ronnie wanted to do was travel and stay in a hotel, because that's what he did all season. But it was the *first* thing I wanted to do — 'Take me to Florida.' Florida was always nice in April. We often went there. We went with the Sittlers, the Glennies, the Hendersons, Garry Monahan and his wife. I really enjoyed our holidays with the other couples.

"To be honest, I was never much of a hockey fan," admits Jan. "When we were young, the rink was the only place we could date as teenagers. But the way I looked at it later was that it was Ronnie's job. I wanted to support him, and really cared if he was in a slump — I would be really, really concerned because it changed his whole personality. I'd have to walk on eggshells around him. I tried to make things easy around the house for him so he wouldn't have stress at home. There was a lot of pressure, and the whole world knows every little mistake you might make on the ice.

"I tried to be a good hockey wife, but I never really got into the games. Still, through Ron's entire career, I only missed a handful of home games. I was always afraid that if I stayed away, Ronnie might get injured. There are so many games that by the time February rolled around, we were wiped out. But then you'd get into March, and momentum would build towards the playoffs and the adrenaline would flow. I did love the playoffs and the special events, of course.

"I resented everything about hockey for a long time. They treated the wives as though we were nonexistent. For example, when Ronnie was gifted with Ace Bailey's Number 6, it was a very special time in his life. They had a great big luncheon and it was great big deal in the papers. I wasn't allowed to go. I was told I was not allowed to be there. There were aspects of hockey that I thought were so chauvinistic. The wives and families didn't count. If you were having a baby, tough; the player left his wife in labour and went on to the next game.

"Hockey wives will tell you that people treated you as if you counted for nothing. 'Who's that? His wife? Oh. Could you move out of the way so I can get your husband's autograph?' It made you feel awful — really hurt your self-esteem. I became resentful.

"And my kids had to defend themselves in the schoolyard for being the child of a Toronto Maple Leaf. Some kids would be all friendly because my kids' dad was in the NHL. Other kids were jealous and gave them a very rough time. It was an interesting life — not a glamorous life the way everybody thinks."

"Jan has been very, very important to any success I've enjoyed on or off the ice," insists Ron. "She has been a phenomenal life partner and just an incredible tower of strength to this family. Being a hockey wife is not an easy job, yet Jan was thrust into the role and did a fantastic job. She knew when to leave me alone after a game, knew just when to say the right things to keep me going and, according to her, I never played a bad game. It takes a very special woman not to jump ship during the down times of her husband's fifteen-year NHL career or a ten-year dark journey with depression. It's been thirty-six years since our wedding day on May 28, 1966, and I love Jan more now than ever. The kids have moved on and are making their own lives. After all these years, we have a chance to spend some quality time together, just the two of us and a couple of dogs. I really like the idea of growing old together. That's a thought that makes me very happy and very content."

CHAPTER TWENTY-FIVE

Kitty and R.J.

"Once Jan and I were married, we certainly wanted to have children," Ron says. "I come from a family with five children and Jan comes from a family of three children. We waited a couple of years, to get established in our marriage before deciding to start our family. Nothing happened, so we went to our family doctor, and he reassured us that a lot of couples go through a period of not being able to conceive. The man is the easier of the two to test, so they checked me out first and concluded that everything was okay. The tests they ran on Jan were more in-depth.

"The doctor came back to us and said, 'Sorry, but it's just not going to happen for you.' Janny's fallopian tubes were blocked. She was heartbroken. It made it even tougher because her girlfriends were having babies. When I realized how my wife was feeling, I knew immediately what we had to do. I said, 'Okay, fine. We'll adopt.' We wanted to raise a child in our home.

"At first, Jan was devastated that we wouldn't have a child of our own. But the decision to adopt a baby was great for the two of us, and really gave us hope. At that time, you could adopt privately," Ron explains. "It's almost impossible to do that today. Our family doctor put us in touch with another doctor, and we let him know we were interested in adopting, and it didn't matter whether it was a girl or a boy, just as long as the baby was healthy."

Ron gets noticeably excited. "It wasn't very long afterwards that we got a phone call. This doctor said, 'I have a patient. She's seventeen and will be giving birth on this particular date.' Well, we were delighted! This was only two or three months after we had made the initial phone call. All of a sudden, we were going to be parents!"

"I had the most vivid dream a few days before the lawyer called," Jan says. "I dreamed that we were having a little redheaded girl. What were the odds? And then, when I saw our baby — she was a beautiful redheaded girl! There was no way I could have known the sex or the hair colour of the baby in advance. In fact, the mother was brunette and the father was blonde."

"There's so much red hair in our families, especially on Ronnie's side of the family," giggles Jan. "My mother and my sister have red hair, too. No one could believe she was adopted when they found out. 'Oh, she's got red hair just like her uncles and her aunt.' It was very special. And she was a beautiful baby."

Ron picks up the story. "Jan was able to see our new baby when she was only four days old. The nurses let her come and watch them bathe our beautiful baby girl! The mother never saw the baby after her birth. She was only 17 and wanted to get on with her life. As soon as she had the baby, all they told her was she had a healthy girl with ten fingers and ten toes. They didn't even tell her the colour of her hair. They took the child away immediately."

As soon as the Ellises learned they were about to adopt a girl, Ron suggested a name. "I liked a character named Kitty on the TV show *Gunsmoke*. The character was the owner of the Long Branch Saloon; she had a tough exterior but a very soft heart. She liked Marshall Matt Dillon. The actress, Amanda Blake, had red hair like our baby. Although we've called her Kitty from the moment we got her, her name officially is Kathleen."

Jan laughs. "At first, she thought we had done this rotten thing to her by calling her Kitty. But now, with all these women on TV with names like Katie and Kelly, she doesn't think Kitty is so bad."

Kitty was born on October 18, 1970. "Everybody loved her," Ron proclaims. "She was a bouncing baby and just beautiful. Kitty was the first grandchild for both sides of the family, and both families accepted her immediately. Kitty was part of the family from day one. She is so special. We brought her home when she was ten days old.

"We were so happy with the way our first adoption turned out, that about three years later, we decided we'd like to adopt again," Ron continues. "We were a little more specific this time; we'd decided that we would like a boy. We were just getting the whole process started when Jan got pregnant."

"It's hard on a woman's self-esteem not to be able to have a child," Jan admits. "We really wanted children, and in fact had our names in for a little brother for Kitty. Then, on Kitty's third birthday, I found out I was pregnant. I told the doctor and he told me that it was impossible, and that I shouldn't be getting my hopes up. But I knew. A woman knows her body and I knew!"

"I just know that it's one of God's wonderful miracles," Ron says. On June 4, 1974, Jan gave birth to a son. "We call him R.J., but his given name is Ronald John," Ron points out.

Jan calls R.J. their "miracle baby." "He was never supposed to happen, but he did, and we were so happy. He looked exactly like Ron as a baby. In fact, if you looked at R.J.'s baby picture and then looked at Ronnie's, you would never tell them apart. Except," she adds with a laugh, "Ronnie's picture would be in black and white."

* * *

"As a kid, you don't really realize that your father is any different from anybody else's," states Kitty. "Hockey was part of my life, and most of the people we associated with were from the same arena. The Hendersons were dear family friends; Jilly and I played together. The same applies to the Glennies and their kids. I don't think I thought that anything was all that different, except at school I sometimes got picked on and I could never figure out why. I wasn't sure if it was because I had red hair and freckles and my name was Kitty, or because my dad had had a bad game the night before. In Grade 5, the teacher and principal called my parents and suggested that they might be wise to put me in a private school, because I was getting picked on and beaten up at school."

"We lived in a nice, upper-middle-class neighbourhood, but there were people who had pools and tennis courts — we didn't have those kinds of things. We had Sand Lake and the lodge. I never felt like I was different. I always felt like the situation was very normal.

"My dad was pretty good at protecting us," Kitty explains. "We always lived in a suburb of Toronto. After Grade 10, Dad opened up a sports store and we moved from Orangeville to Brampton. Starting Grade 11 in a new school can be difficult. On my first day at the new high school, all the popular boys would say, 'Hey, you're Kitty Ellis. Your dad is Ron Ellis.' So then, all the popular girls immediately got their backs up. The dynamics of teenagers!

The boys were always nice to me and the girls wouldn't give me the time of day. In high school, I wasn't one of the popular kids. I knew who everybody was but didn't hang around with any one group.

"My first boyfriend, whom I dated for five years from the time I was 16 until I was 21, wasn't a sports guy. His dad ended up being my dad's partner in the sports store. I dated a guy who played a little hockey in university. My husband had never heard of my dad. I met him, and when I left the table for a few minutes, one of the other guys said, 'Do you know that she is Ron Ellis's daughter? And Keith said, 'Who's Ron Ellis?' That was great," laughs Kitty.

"Once I was a teenager, I started to really understand what it meant to be the daughter of Ron Ellis. Sometimes it was a benefit, and sometimes it wasn't. I was pretty selective who I told."

Kitty reflects on Toronto Maple Leaf game nights. "I remember going to games with my mom. It was a social evening out. All the players' wives were there with the kids. We'd get all dressed up and my hair would be curled just right. I used to sit in the wives' room and we'd watch television — not the Leafs game. Hockey was different for R.J. He loved hockey and the excitement. For me as a kid, hockey was something that took my dad away.

"I had a huge crush on Laurie Boschman," Kitty admits, finding it impossible to stifle a grin. "Dad was a bit of a mentor to Laurie, and he used to come up to Teen Ranch. When he got traded, I was so upset. I even wrote a letter to Harold Ballard.

"My dad is phenomenal," reports the bubbly redhead. "He focuses on something and never deviates from that path. As a kid, I flitted from one thing to the next. I figure skated for a while, then did gymnastics for a while and then got into horseback riding for a number of years. I'd ride up at Teen Ranch. My parents bought me a horse when I was 15. I was a blessed kid. I got to do so many cool things, and hockey is the reason we got to do them.

"When I was in my early teens, I thought I might like to be an actress. I didn't do well at school. I was bored. I often wouldn't go to class, although I wasn't partying or sitting in the cafeteria playing cards — I would be in the library reading. I knew I should be getting better grades, but I had no answers when my dad asked me what was going wrong. I knew I should be doing my homework assignments, but I didn't do them. Dad would sit across the kitchen table and talk to me for two hours, and everything he would say to me was right. Dad wouldn't yell, he'd just ask me to focus and wonder why I was getting Ds in math.

"Dad is so black and white and I'm so grey. R.J. is just like my dad. He used to sit on the stairs watching when I was getting a talk from my dad, and would tell me, 'I don't want to be a teenager. I don't want to get in that kind of trouble!'"

After graduating from high school, Kitty took a year off and then worked for American Airlines. "After sailing through the exams in Texas, I came back to Toronto to work at the check-in counter, but I wasn't mature enough to work five o'clock mornings. I realized I love to read, I love to write, so I decided I wanted to get into journalism. I went to Ryerson [Polytechnic University], then was a volunteer at the New VR [CKVR-TV in Barrie] for six months before I got hired on.

"The Ron Ellis connection opened some doors for me," Kitty admits, "but when I started at Leafs TV, I used the name 'Kitty Butler,' so a lot of people didn't know I was Ron Ellis's daughter in the beginning. But I earned my way there, and when people find out, they realize I grew up around hockey my entire life, so I must know something. Women in sportscasting is a huge issue right now, with models being hired who have no sports credibility. I use Butler rather than Ellis so I can stand on my own two feet."

Kitty says Ron and Jan never hid from her the fact that she was adopted. "Mom used to call me her precious little girl, and told me that I was special because, of all the little girls in the world, she and Dad picked me." Still, there were questions that had gone unanswered. "I'm a curious person by nature. I'll do whatever comes into my mind. Sometimes I don't think things through," she admits. "When I was in high school in Brampton, around 17 years old, I went through my parents' safe and found my adoption papers and the name of the lawyer who handled the adoption. I said goodbye to my mom and dad as though I was going to school, then got on the bus and went to downtown Toronto.

"I marched into the lawyer's office and announced, 'I'm Kitty Ellis and I want to know who my birth mother is.' She was very nice to me, but said, 'You have to be 18, and I'd prefer you wait until you're at least 20, but come back and talk to me.' I left, probably grudgingly, but by the time I got home she had called my parents to let them know.

"My parents had always told me that if I wanted to find my birth mother, they would help me," Kitty says. "I know Dad would have preferred that things remain status quo, but he was supportive."

Kitty put her quest on the backburner for a few years, but couldn't get over the fact that, every time she visited a doctor, she would be asked about her medical history, and would have no choice but to say, "I don't know."

"I remember watching a television show about adoption and I started crying. 'I just need to know,' I thought to myself."

Ron remembers that, when Kitty was 21, she announced her intention to seek out her birth mother. "We supported her," he says. "In my mind, I thought it was important that Kitty get the medical information. But I have to be honest — we were anxious about it. We didn't know how it would turn out. I assumed, incorrectly, that it would take a couple of years, and that if we found the mother at all, she'd likely be living in Vancouver and there wouldn't be any big deal. Kitty would get the information she wanted and that would be it."

Kitty continues. "I went to the lawyer's office, and it turned out she was changing specialties, from family to immigration law. The Children's Aid Society was going to take all her files the next week. If I had come one week later, I would never have seen my files." There was a bit of a cloak-and-dagger flavour to the meeting. "She said, 'I'm going to leave this room for ten minutes, and when I return, you're going to have to leave.' I said, 'Okay.' She left a folder on the table.

"I looked through the folder, and it had a lot of things blacked out. I couldn't find anything. Just as I was giving up hope, I looked on the inside of the manila folder and found a name and phone number in pencil. It was the name of the birth grandparents at the time of my adoption.

Kitty took down the information, wished the lawyer luck, and went back to school. "Because I wanted to be a journalist, I thought I was going to have to go to libraries and through old phone books and old medical records and do all sorts of research. But I didn't need to: I looked in the phone book and there was the name and the phone number, exactly the same as twenty-one years earlier. I was shocked. My hand was shaking.

"I contacted an organization and met with a man about the adoption. He suggested that he act as an intermediary. He called the birth grandparents and said he was a friend of their daughter's from high school and wondered if they would pass along my birth mother's phone number. They said, 'Oh, she'll be so happy to hear from you.' Of course, he was lying.

"I called my birth mother at work," says Kitty. "She was stunned but excited. We have very similar personalities. She was married — her husband knew the story — plus two small children. She knew that everything could change from then on, so she said she needed a month to six weeks to get ready. She got some counselling to prepare herself for the meeting."

Kitty was excited, and started to speculate on the circumstances that had led to her being given up for adoption. "She was so young when she had me, so I imagined that I might be meeting somebody who maybe hadn't had the opportunity to amount to much. Life would have been very tough. But I was shocked. She told me she was a professional. She mailed me a picture with a note saying she'd meet me, but I couldn't look at the photo. I told my boyfriend at the time, 'I can't look at it. You look at it.' My heart was pounding, pounding, pounding. I had an image of my birth mother as mousy, with curly hair and glasses. My boyfriend opened the envelope and said, 'Oh, my God! She's so young. She has the exact same eyes as you. You won't believe it!'

"I looked at the picture and she was a beautiful, successful, young woman. She was completely different from what I imagined. That was really shocking. But I was really interested to discover what her personality was like.

"Two weeks later, she called and said she'd meet me at the Four Seasons Hotel in Yorkville. She said, 'I'll get you a room at the hotel. My husband and I are going to stay there for a week. I've got to relax. On the fifth day, I'll meet you.'"

Kitty could barely contain her excitement. "I was living at my boyfriend's grandmother's house at the time, and I think that helped," she says. "I didn't want to hurt my parents. I didn't want them to see my excitement. I was very excited to meet this woman, but I knew she wasn't my mother. She may have given birth to me, but she would never be my real mother.

"I went to the hotel and checked into my room. At the designated time, I took the elevator down, knocked on her door and when she opened it, we both shrieked, 'Oh my God!' We grabbed each other's arms and she led me into the room. We were so much alike, it was crazy."

Ron and Jan were concerned about where this new door Kitty was opening would lead. Ron heaps praise on his wife. "I always knew Jan was special, but it was at this point that I realized exactly how special. I was a little harder to deal with on this issue than Jan was, yet I think she had much more at stake. When Jan and I talked privately, we were frightened. 'Are Kitty and her birth mother going to re-establish a relationship?' 'Are we going to lose our daughter?' All those thoughts went through our minds. We knew these things could and would happen."

Ron takes a moment before continuing. "Kitty and her birth mother established an instant relationship. It was like long-lost friends had found each other. They started to do things together. Kitty even got a job where her birth mother worked, so they saw each other every day. This was hard — really, really hard for Jan and me. Jan did everything she could to co-operate. She gave Kitty every opportunity to re-establish this relationship. Then we had to let it go. I think our faith had a lot to do with how we coped. We had to trust that we had raised Kitty the best we knew how, that we had given her unconditional love. And we had to hope and pray that that would be enough to hold her in our family. We eventually met the birth mother and her husband and had dinner with them. That was much more difficult than my first contract experience with Punch!"

"About the time we were to meet the birth mother, Ron was in one of his depressive moods," Jan recalls. "But I prayed a lot about it and went. She was lovely, and not at all what I expected. She was very attractive and a professional with a good income, so was able to get her hair done at the best salons, buy the best clothes, go to the most expensive health clubs, which would definitely make an impression on Kitty. She bought Kitty expensive presents. I had to keep reminding myself, 'I'm not in competition.' But it was hard to see them grow so close. They really became best of friends."

"The way I describe it is like a love affair," explains Kitty. "When you first meet somebody special, you are consumed. That's all you can think about. You want to spend every waking moment with them. Because I hadn't seen a therapist or gone to anybody to help me understand, I let the relationship consume me. My birth mother and I were so much alike. We got along very well. I realized that I should have done better in high school because I come from good stock. All of a sudden I was getting straight As in school, whereas before, I had never received an A in my entire life. We started to do everything together. We went to the movies together. We worked out at the gym together. We became like very good girlfriends."

Ron suspects that Kitty's birth grandmother deduced the identity of her daughter's child, but kept the secret locked tightly away. "She had been reassured by the people at the hospital, 'Don't worry. Your daughter's baby has been adopted by a well-known personality in Toronto.' A couple of weeks later, the front page of the *Toronto Star* had a photo and article about the adoption, and talked about our 'beautiful redheaded baby.' She would have put two and two together and realized that the baby in the paper was very likely her daughter's child. She never said anything to anybody, but she started following our family in the media. Every Christmas, the newspapers and TV stations had family photos and pictures from the team Christmas party, and she'd see this little redheaded girl growing up."

Jan remembers the day that the *Star* photo appeared. "I opened the door one morning and saw this huge picture of the three of us on the front page of the newspaper. I just about croaked. It was just before Christmas, and they had come to take a little picture for the paper. Kitty was two months old.

"We had no idea, but Kitty's birth grandmother had gone down to the nursery to look at the baby. She didn't tell anyone — not even her husband. So she knew her daughter's baby was redheaded. The lawyer told her a well-known young couple in Toronto had adopted the baby. She clipped that picture out of the paper."

Years later, when Kitty's birth mother called her mother and said, "You're not going to believe it. My birth daughter found me and her name is Kitty," she replied, "No, it isn't. It's Kathleen," and produced the yellowed newspaper clipping. "The grandmother couldn't be 100 percent sure," Jan says, "but everything added up together."

"My birth was a traumatic time for my birth mother," Kitty explains. "It was like she put the episode in a box and decided never to open that box again. She had signed away all rights to the child and had no desire ever to see the child again. She couldn't deal with it. But now that the box had been opened up, all this emotion came flooding out. And that was really hard on my parents.

"Suddenly one day, I came to a realization," Kitty explains. "My parents were so loving and they were there for me. I realized that they are my real parents. They're the ones who are there day to day for me, for everything. I realized I had put my parents through a lot without thinking. My mom told me that, through the first year of my life, every time the phone rang she feared it was going to be somebody telling her, 'The adoption didn't go through. You can't have her anymore.' I didn't consider that.

"Dad had another relapse when I was in my twenties. There was a lot going on at the time, but I truly feel that meeting my birth mother contributed to it. I came to the conscious decision to say, 'Mom and Dad, you are my family.'

"My relationship with my birth mother cooled. I decided to keep in touch with a card once a year or so — find out how the kids are doing and keep her up to date on what I was doing. That's healthy. It was good for me to learn a lot of things," she concludes, "but it may have been unhealthy at the same time."

"It was pretty obvious that Kitty and her birth mother were not going to be able to continue their relationship because they were so much alike," Ron observes. "They started to clash."

The final word goes to Jan, who says, "I knew within my heart that Kitty would eventually see the light. In any relationship, after a while the rose-coloured glasses come off and reality sets in."

"In time, it all worked out for the best," sighs Ron. "Kitty realized she came from very good genes. Her mother is very bright, and the fact she was a professional gave Kitty confidence. That time Kitty spent with her birth mother was positive. When we first met her, we were astonished at the similarities. They laughed the same. They were the same size. Their movements were the same. The theory that environment dictates your personality — uh uh. Their mannerisms were exactly the same — it was amazing!

"This is just one of the things that makes my wife so special, so extraordinarily special. She took the situation with Kitty, went the extra mile and handled it beautifully." The largest smile imaginable stops Ron's conversation for a few moments.

Ron summarizes the situation. "You never know what will happen when you adopt. We've heard some horror stories from other couples, although we've heard some very positive stories, too. But all in all, Kitty was, and is, a beautiful child. There was some rebellion during the teen years, but it was worth the struggle. I'm happy to say today, Kitty and I have a solid relationship. I'm proud of her. I'm proud of her accomplishments. I'm proud of the man she's chosen to be her partner. Keith is the right guy for Kitty, for sure. And some of the things I've tried to suggest to Kitty years ago are starting to make some sense to her now, especially when they are reinforced by Keith. Kitty is quite the young lady. I'm proud to call her my daughter."

* * *

"R.J. is a gift as well," Ron beams. "They're both miracles. R.J. and Kitty couldn't be any more different in personalities, and yet they're very close and I am most thankful.

"Kitty always loved to have friends around her. She could not sit in a room by herself — no way. R.J. loved his friends, too, but he also had the ability to sit by himself for hours with a Lego set, content to put them together."

"R.J. was just the best kid," Jan agrees. "He never gave me a moment's headache. He played quietly by himself so often. That was such a change from Kitty. Kitty was very social, and needed other kids around all the time. When she was 3, we put her in nursery school, and she loved being with the other kids. So at 3, we did the same with R.J., and the first day he screamed, 'Mommy, don't leave me!' We kept him home for another full year and that suited R.J. just fine."

The contrast extended to their studies. "Kitty was not really a student," Ron says. "I'm not saying she isn't intelligent, because she is, but she just didn't apply herself. There'd be a lot of comments on Kitty's report card that told us she needed to apply herself more, or talk a little less in class. R.J. was more like me — he just worked his butt off in school. He always brought home good marks and there was never a problem with the teachers. In fact, he always had glowing comments.

"As parents, how do you balance the two kids and not show favouritism? I said to Jan, 'In a way, we didn't give R.J. as much praise as we should have because we were always worried about hurting the feelings of this little girl over here.' But through it all, we must have done a pretty good job, because the two kids have a special bond.

"R.J. was a boys' boy," Ron recalls. "We had decided that if we had a boy, we were going to name him R.J. — Ronald John, which is my name."

"Right down to the wire, we couldn't agree on a name," Jan chimes in. "We were set for a girl's name should we have a little girl, but any boy's name I liked, Ron didn't, and I didn't like any name Ron suggested. I finally said, 'Ron, if it's a boy, let's name him after you.'" Jan admits to an ulterior motive. "Secretly, I had a crush on Robert Wagner, the actor, and they used to call him R.J.

"He grew into his name very quickly," Jan adds. "He got very big very fast."

"R.J. was a going concern as a toddler," agrees a proud father. "He loved anything to do with sports, he loved his Big Wheel and his bike and would jump from one to the other. He liked to try anything and everything. But one of the traits I remember so clearly is that, as a child, R.J. could entertain himself alone for hours. He'd sit by himself and build his planes. He was good with his hands. I guess that's why he's a pilot today. Kitty's skill was talking, and she's using that skill today, too."

It only seemed fitting that R.J. would learn to skate at an early age. Jan laughs when she remembers his first day at an arena. "I signed up for 'Moms and Tots' when R.J. was 3. I wanted to learn to figure skate and I decided R.J. should learn to skate. But after our first session, I asked R.J. how he had enjoyed himself and he said, 'Mommy, I never want to skate again.' Well, thank goodness he didn't stick to that!" By the age of 5, R.J. was playing hockey. "Of course, Ron was on the road, so here I was in the dressing room with all the other fathers," Jan recalls. "I had R.J.'s pads on all wrong and I could never tie his skates tight enough. He learned to love hockey, though.

"Both Ron and I insisted we would not push him into playing," Jan points out. "In fact, I would have preferred him to take up skiing, because that's something you can do as a family more easily than hockey."

Jan talks about the roots of another passion that R.J. inherited. "My dad and R.J. were very close. Dad had a little Cessna he kept out at the Brampton Flying Club and he used to take R.J. up in it." Ron remembers a photograph taken on the day Lyle, Jan's father, retired. "When you're making your last flight, it's a special event and your entire family goes out. In the picture, Jan's dad has his uniform on, and R.J. is sitting on Grandpa's lap in the cockpit of a 747.

"Grandpa said, 'R.J., would you like to be a pilot someday?

Would you like to fly this plane?' And R.J. looked up at Jan's dad and said, 'No way, Grandpa! It's too high up here!' I framed the picture and put the little quote on the bottom and gave it to R.J. when he got his wings." Ron beams with pride.

"When R.J. was going to high school at J.A. Turner in Brampton, they offered an aviation course," Ron continues. "That's what got him interested in flying. The following summer, he went to Space Camp in Alabama. My parents took him down in their trailer and he had a wonderful time. A little further along, it was time to start thinking about careers." He might have gone to university on a hockey scholarship, but instead R.J. came up with the idea of Royal Military College in Kingston, Ontario. "When he investigated everything, that was the quickest way for him to become a pilot," Ron says.

"R.J. came back for his high school graduation wearing his red uniform from RMC," Jan says, grinning from ear to ear. "As he walked across the stage, my buttons almost burst with pride. All these girls came up to him and said, 'Oh, R.J., I had such a crush on you in high school,' but R.J. had his head buried in his books and had his own crush — on flying."

R.J. displayed his share of hockey talent, spending two seasons with the Brampton Capitals, a Tier II Junior A team. "He was one of the better players there," Ron says. "He had a couple of scholarship offers. He's still a very good player. But we both realized that he was not a player of NHL first-line calibre." R.J. was aware that, if he committed himself to a professional hockey career, there would be many ups and downs and that the odds were against anyone, even a player with R.J.'s pedigree. He might have to play some of his career in the minor leagues, and if he did crack an NHL lineup, there was the possibility he might not rise beyond playing on the third or fourth line. "Most kids would say, 'I'd be happy with that,'" Ron observes, "but R.J. wouldn't have been happy. He had other talents. When he made the decision to go to RMC, we put the word out that he wasn't going to pursue the NHL, so he didn't get drafted."

"I would like to have made hockey a career," admits R.J. "I mean, I was around hockey all my life. I started playing when I was 5." It is clear that he has fond memories of going to the rink as a boy. "Dad used to take me to a lot of practices at Maple Leaf Gardens when I was young. He always gave me a wink or a wave when he skated by. There were eight or nine kids around my age who would play together — their dads played with mine. Ryan Sittler and Anders Salming were two of the kids. We used to shoot tape balls at each other. One time, I hit Punch Imlach in the head with a ball of tape!

"Mike Palmateer used to get dressed early sometimes and let us take shots on him. I would have been 5 or 6 years old at the time. Laurie Boschman lived with us when he was a rookie, and he was real good about playing with me, too."

"When he was recruited by Royal Military College, they wanted him to play hockey, of course, but he had to pass many different levels of tests before he was accepted to the school," Ron remembers. "There were so many hard steps just to get there. Playing hockey really was a secondary thing. RMC didn't have a competitive team. They played in a division with the University of Toronto, the University of Guelph and Queen's University. It was a very competitive league, but R.J. showed he could play. He collected over 100 points in his four years at RMC."

"I considered going the U.S. college route versus going to RMC," starts R.J., "but when it came down to it, I decided to combine my love of flying with my love of hockey. I chose RMC."

In all four of his years at Royal Military College, 1993–97, R.J. Ellis played for the Redmen. Like his dad, he is a right-hand shot and he played right wing. But there is one significant difference. "I consciously stayed away from wearing Dad's Number 6," he smiles. "I wore Number 10." Coincidentally, 10 is the number his grandfather, Randy, wore in his Marlboros days.

Every year since 1923, the Redmen of Royal Military College have faced off against their counterparts at the U.S. Military Academy at West Point, New York. The series, first proposed by the legendary general Douglas MacArthur, is one of hockey's most enduring rivalries. "One year, it was agreed before the game that whoever was selected as RMC's most valuable player would have their sweater donated to the Hockey Hall of Fame and put on display. Well, R.J. was picked as MVP. I couldn't have been prouder.

"But they didn't just display the sweater by itself. In the Family Zone of the Hall of Fame, they set up an exhibit with the three generations of Ellis hockey players. There was R.J.'s white RMC sweater, the Team Canada sweater I wore at the World

Championships in '77, and my dad's Marlies sweater from 1941. I get emotional just thinking about it.

"Someday, R.J. will look back and appreciate that hockey took him where he wanted to go," Ellis says. "He'll be a lot further ahead than a lot of hockey players who can't thank the game. R.J. couldn't be happier doing what he's doing. He has found his niche. And he still has options. He can stay in the armed forces or work for an airline. The more options you have, the more control you have. With hockey, there aren't many options and you're not in control," Ron concludes.

On March 2, 2002, R.J. and his wife Norma had a baby boy, whom they named Zachary. It's the first grandchild for Ron and Jan. R.J. and Norma, who live in Belleville, Ontario, met at RMC. Like R.J., Norma is also in the military.

"We look at both children as being special," Ron says. "There is no difference between them. They're both ours, and we love them both the same. We were blessed to have a chosen child and a birth child."

CHAPTER TWENTY-SIX

Sunset

"It's been quite a ride," smiles Ron. "A couple of bumps along the way, but the bumps make you appreciate the rest of the ride. And I really believe I've learned a great deal from the bumps. They can be valuable if you don't blame them for your current situation. But they can also destroy you if you let them. You have to take the positives that you learn from the rough times and apply them to your life. They'll make you a better person, a stronger person and a more effective person.

"I think Jan always hoped that when I retired from the Leafs, that would be it for hockey. Hockey does have its drawbacks where the family is concerned. Jan had to raise the kids while I was away. Even when you're home, you're thinking about the next game — especially if you're in a slump. Sometimes, players aren't the nicest guys to be around if they haven't scored for three weeks. Jan weathered all of that and hoped that I'd have a normal life after I retired. This is an area we've had to work on in our marriage.

"When I made the Leafs, my goal was to play ten years. At the time, they told us that if you got ten years, you would have a good pension. Well, that turned out to be a bit of a joke," laughs Ron. "But my goal was ten years and then I'd move on. We all knew we'd have to move on one day. We made good money while we were playing, but it would only last ten years, unless you were fortunate enough to have made some good investments or played the stock market properly. We all knew we'd have to take on a second career.

Ron gets emotional as he continues. "Jan has been solid through so many areas. She took the wedding vows with absolute seriousness. Just now, we're at the stage in our life where we can enjoy the blessings. We've been together for thirty-six years and we're realizing that whatever years the good Lord blesses us with will be the best years of our lives. Grandchildren are coming and our time is freed up to do more of the things that we've always wanted to do.

"I'm always going to have something to puddle away at. Travel may be part of that, but just spending time with Jan — that's what's important to me," admits Ron. "Everything I've ever done has been about starting fresh. But every time you start something new, it requires time — some time apart. We deserve some time together, and that's what we're looking forward to.

"Jan is quite the lady. She's loved by a lot of people.

"I'm not saying the rest of my life is going to be all roses. There are going to be challenges. There will be health challenges with Jan's mom and my father. I just feel that at this stage in my life, I'm very blessed. I've finally found peace and contentment.

"I'm prepared for more challenges, but I know Jan and I can handle anything that comes down the road. We've handled tough things before. When you go through trials, you can come out the other side a better person. You learn to appreciate things more. You learn to be content with what you have. It's a process. It can be a very tough process, too. As the Bible says in Isaiah 43:2, 'When you pass through the waters, I will be with you; and through the rivers, they shall not overwhelm you; when you walk through fire with me you shall not be burned, and the flame shall not consume you.'

"I'll always cherish the quality of relationships I've made through hockey. It really struck me when I was standing on the ice at the final game at Maple Leaf Gardens. I realized it was the only home rink I had ever had. I played four years with the Marlboros and fifteen with the Leafs, all based in the Gardens. And while I was standing there, I drifted a little, recalling the important goals, the key plays, Punch's practices, the great fans, winking at Jan and the kids from the ice surface. But as I looked around me, I realized that it was the friends I made that really were important. And I looked around and saw the smiling faces of some of my dearest friends — Paul Henderson, Brian Glennie, Darryl Sittler, Mike Pelyk, Dave Burrows, Brian Conacher, Johnny Bower.

"I could go on and on, but that's what I took away from the game. That's exactly what I took away from the game. It was those friendships, those lifelong friendships. That's what I'll cherish when the pucks and sticks have lost much of their meaning.

"Yes, in spite of the challenges, I have to admit I've been blessed," Ron Ellis concludes. "Life is good."

He laughs, then adds, "I guess I've made it over the boards."

CHAPTER TWENTY-SEVEN

Quotes about Ron Ellis

Andy Bathgate

"I can't say enough about what a quality guy Ronnie was, on and off the ice. You meet so many people in the hockey industry, but Ronnie stands out. He has a kind word for everyone. He's always a gentleman. Ronnie Ellis is one of the class acts in the hockey business."

Dave Burrows

"Ron was the elder statesman when I went to Toronto, and he was very well respected by everybody on the team, not only because he had played with the Leafs for so long, but because of the person that he was."

Wayne Carleton

"With Ronnie, 'still waters run deep.' Ron's gone through a lot of things. Life hasn't been as easy as a lot of people think. But he battled through them."

Brian Conacher

"Ronnie is a person in the hockey business who is respected by his peers. And that is a word you do not hear a lot in hockey any more. He was respected on the ice and off the ice by the people he played with and by those he played against."

Yvan Cournoyer

"Ron Ellis was a very honest player. He was a very, very good skater. I think Ronnie was better than all the credit he got."

Marcel Dionne
"I was only going into my second season when I played for Team Canada in 1972. But while I was there, I got to know Ron Ellis as a committed player, respected by his peers and a very good two-way player."

Alan Eagleson
"Anybody who has ever asked Ronnie to do anything knows that it gets done properly. He's a gentle, caring, decent man."

Mike Gartner
"I look up to Ron Ellis as a man of integrity. He has conducted his life as a player, as a former player and as a Christian in a manner I can look up to — and have, through the course of my life. There are certain people who can be considered mentors in your life. I've been fortunate to have had several of these quality people, like Ron Ellis, in my life. I've never really sat down and talked at length with Ron, but by watching the manner in which he conducts his life, I've received encouragement and am pleased to count Ron Ellis as a role model."

Brian Glennie
"Ronnie was my roommate on the road for six years. He always got to use the bathroom first. I had to let him — he had seniority. Ron is the godfather to both my children. I have tremendous respect for Ron. I think he was an incredible hockey player. I'd be proud to have him on my team at any time. Ron and I will always have a special bond. He's a very good friend."

Jim Gregory
"You'd be hard pressed to find anybody who didn't have good things to say about Ron Ellis. And the things that are said about him are deserved."

Paul Henderson
"Ronnie has always done more for other people than he ever does for himself. He's got such a tender heart for people. He's one of the finest individuals you'll ever meet in your life. We will remain friends until the day we die."

Red Kelly

"Ron came up as a rookie and played on my wing. He had a great high shot and was a terrific two-way player. He was an industrious player — a real hard worker. He never caused a ripple of problems at any time. He just went out and did his job. Ronnie was a pleasure to play with — a great teammate and a great asset to our club."

David Keon

"Ronnie was a very good player. He worked real hard and he really cared about winning and he cared about his own play. He was a professional and that's how he approached it."

Lanny McDonald

"Ellis was a hero of mine when I was growing up. I still looked at Ellis that way when I played for the Maple Leafs. There are times in life when you expect too much from people, but Ellis was the type who gave and never stopped giving. I wanted to be just like him, and I still think of Ronnie as a hero."

Roger Neilson

"In his quiet way, Ron Ellis was one of the top right wingers in Leafs' history. He was a solid winger with good speed, an excellent scoring touch, superlative defensive instincts and a strong work ethic. Ron epitomizes the type of character player that every coach wants on his team. Along with his hockey skills, Ron always demonstrated a strong Christian faith. He was highly respected by his teammates, his opponents, his coaches and the entire hockey community."

Mark Osborne

"I have a lot of respect for Ron Ellis. I admire the fact he has made himself transparent as a human being, letting everyone know about his self-admitted struggles. With Ron, actions speak louder than words. He may be quiet in many respects, but he's a quality guy, a friend and someone who has given me great encouragement through the years."

Jean-Paul Parise

"Ron Ellis was a class act to play against. He was a right winger and

I played left wing, so we lined up against each other. He was a great skater, he played hard, he played tough — never dirty. I didn't realize how good he was until I played with him for Team Canada. Ever since, all my associations with Ron Ellis have shown me he's a class act — a class person."

Mike Pelyk
"Ronnie had lots of skills, but was very demanding of himself. He was very cognizant of his role on the team. He worked as hard on his role preventing the other team from scoring as he did on his offence. As a result, it took away from his statistics, no question. Game in and game out, Ron gave his utmost as a player. As a friend, Ron is very loyal. If Ronnie asked me for a favour, I'd do it for him in a second because I know he'd do the same for me. Ron Ellis values relationships, and that's something you don't see a lot these days."

Rod Seiling
"Ronnie had been, was and always will be salt of the earth. He's just an all-around outstanding person. A good friend, a great hockey player. From a defenceman's standpoint, Ron was a dream come true in terms of a winger being where he needed to be when he needed to be and helping you out doing all those good things. Ron was a team player, a quality player and a quality person."

Darryl Sittler
"Through all the crazy times, Ron was a man of honour and integrity. Ronnie always knew what his role was, and did whatever it took to do it to the best of his ability. He was a real team player. And he tried to fulfill his role the best he could both on and off the ice."

Dale Tallon
"Ron Ellis is the perfect gentleman. Every shift of every game he ever played, he gave it his all. Just a class act on and off the ice."

Acknowledgements

The following gave their time and memories for the content of *Over the Boards*. To each of them, involved intrinsically in some aspect of Ron's life, the co-authors would like to extend heartfelt thanks.

Ross Andrew taught at W.E. Gowling Public School in Ottawa between 1955 and 1963, and inspired a young Grade 7 student by the name of Ron Ellis. During his teaching career, which extended from 1949 to 1986, Mr. Andrew was a principal at four different elementary schools in Ottawa. He was later president of the Ontario Public Schools Teachers' Federation. Between 1980 and 1986, Ross Andrew was general secretary of the Ontario Public Schools Teachers' Federation, retiring to Portland, Ontario, in 1987.

"Ross Andrew was the teacher I remember that had the greatest impact on my life by helping me believe in myself as a person."

Andy Bathgate played the better part of twelve seasons as a New York Ranger, winning the Hart Trophy as Most Valuable Player in 1959 and earning First and Second All-Star honours twice each. During the playoff run of 1964, Bathgate and Don McKenney were traded to Toronto for Dick Duff, Bob Nevin, Rod Seiling, Arnie Brown and Bill Collins. Andy played with the Leafs until May 1965, when he was traded to Detroit. Today, Andy Bathgate is the owner of Bathgate Golf Centre at Highway 403 and Eglinton Avenue in Mississauga.

"Andy was, and still is, a first-class act. He was my first centre and roommate with the Leafs. I learned a great deal observing this wise veteran and am happy to say, after our playing days, we have continued a friendship."

Laurie Boschman joined the Toronto Maple Leafs in 1979 as a 19-year-old first-round draft choice. During his third season as a Leaf, Laurie was traded to the Edmonton Oilers. His finest professional seasons came as a Winnipeg Jet, where he enjoyed four seasons with 20 or more goals. Boschman also played with the New Jersey Devils and Ottawa Senators before he retired. Today, Laurie Boschman is the Ottawa and Eastern Ontario Director of Hockey Ministries International, and conducts summer hockey clinics across Canada, the United States and Europe. The clinics combine quality hockey instruction with Bible-based principles. Hockey Ministries International also conducts non-denominational chapel programs for several players and teams in the National Hockey League.

"Laurie was a young man who impressed me from the first day I met him when he became a Leaf. I knew he had the potential to be a solid NHLer, but I also knew he was a good human being with a lot to offer others. He proved me right in both cases."

Dave Burrows entered the NHL in 1971 as a member of the Pittsburgh Penguins. In 1978, the Maple Leafs brought Dave to Toronto in exchange for Randy Carlyle and George Ferguson to Pittsburgh. Burrows was a Maple Leaf for two seasons before he was traded back to the Penguins, with whom he finished his career. After being involved with Teen Ranch for a number of years, Dave Burrows is now retired. He and his wife Carol are very involved with their church near their home in Parry Sound, Ontario. The couple provide marriage and relationship counselling, using the Bible as their source of information.

"Dave Burrows was the defenceman on our team that no one wanted to take on in one-on-one drills. What a gifted skater! We have laughed and cried together, and it is a privilege to have Dave and Carol as friends."

Kitty Butler, the bubbly daughter of Ron and Jan Ellis, was welcomed to the world on the front page of the Toronto Star under the headline, 'Christmas Comes Early for Ellis.' Married to Keith Butler, Kitty is an associate producer with the new digital channels, Leafs TV and Raptors TV.

"Kitty will always be a little redhead. She has overcome some of life's challenges and is making a life of her own and a life with her husband Keith. We are family."

Wayne Carleton played parts of five seasons as a Toronto Maple

Leaf after coming up though their system. Joining the Boston Bruins via a December 1969 trade, Wayne played for a Stanley Cup winner. After a season with the California Golden Seals, Carleton spent four seasons in the WHA. Today, Wayne Carleton owns and operates KWC Financial, a mutual fund business in Collingwood, Ontario.

"Wayne and I go back to the early days with the Marlies. He was a gifted player who has taken his skills into a successful business career. We both reside in Collingwood, and it is always a pleasure to be in Wayne's company."

Brian Conacher is a member of one of hockey's most highly regarded families. His uncles Charlie and Roy are both Honoured Members of the Hockey Hall of Fame, while his father, Lionel, is not only in the Hall of Fame, but was also chosen the Canadian Athlete of the Half-Century (1900 to 1950). Brian had his own fine hockey career, winning the Stanley Cup with the 1966–67 Toronto Maple Leafs before playing with the Detroit Red Wings and the WHA's Ottawa Nationals. He was also a proud member of Canada's National Team for five seasons. Today, Brian Conacher is a founder and the Chief Operating Officer of the Recreational Hockey Network, the largest network of independently run hockey leagues in Canada.

"Brian and I shared some time with the Marlies and experienced a Stanley Cup win together playing on the same line in the finals. Our post-hockey careers have separated us occasionally, however, a mutual respect remains."

Yvan Cournoyer broke into the NHL during the same season as Ron Ellis — 1964-65. Both were known for their lightning quickness, and played on Team Canada together in 1972. During his fifteen season Hockey Hall of Fame career, Cournoyer played on an astounding ten Stanley Cup championship teams.

"I have total respect for this man, and am honoured to call him a friend. We competed against each other in junior, turned pro the same year and ended our careers about the same time. His play was outstanding in the Summit Series in 1972. It was this experience that brought us close."

Jeff Denomme, who has worked closely with Ron Ellis for over ten years, is the President, Chief Operating Officer, and Treasurer of the Hockey Hall of Fame.

"I report to Jeff at the Hockey Hall of Fame. We have an excellent working relationship. His willingness to support a flexible schedule has given me the opportunity to be productive in my roles at the Hall, and also stay involved with the Leaf Alumni and Team Canada '72."

Marcel Dionne had just completed his rookie season with the Detroit Red Wings in 1971-72 when he was named to Team Canada. Marcel went on to enjoy an outstanding NHL career, scoring 1,771 points over the course of eight seasons and earned membership to the Hockey Hall of Fame.

"Marcel is a very gifted athlete whose NHL stats speak for themselves. He would have had the status of Guy Lafleur if he had played in Montreal, however, he took his skills to Los Angeles and solidified that franchise."

Alan Eagleson was Ron Ellis's agent during most of his career with the Toronto Maple Leafs. Eagleson was also the driving force behind the two international competitions in which Ron Ellis played — the 1972 Summit Series and the 1977 World Championships. Alan later hired Ron to assist in the organization of the 1991 Canada Cup. Alan Eagleson and his wife Nancy split their year between London, England, and a home near Collingwood, Ontario.

"Alan provided critical advice and support through many crises in my hockey and private life. I know he had some influence on my being invited to the Team Canada '72 training camp. I am so grateful I did not let him down."

Jan (Greenlaw) Ellis met a shy little boy named Ron in her Grade 4 class after he moved to Toronto from Ottawa. On May 28, 2002, Jan and Ron celebrated their 36th wedding anniversary. The couple have two grown children, Kitty and R.J., and enjoy life in Collingwood, Ontario.

"Another book could be written about my special lady. I only hope Kevin and I have been successful in giving readers the proper picture of my life partner."

Randy Ellis brought the Ellis name to hockey prominence long before his son, Ron. After starring with local teams in and around Lindsay, Ontario, Randy played for the Toronto Marlboros for two seasons in the early 1940s. After serving as a pilot during World War II, Randy stayed overseas, tearing up the Scottish League with his incredible goal-scoring prowess. Returning to North America, Randy Ellis enjoyed a career in the Chicago Blackhawks system until a knee injury ended his NHL dream. Today, Randy continues to travel playing oldtimers hockey, and is a member of both the Canadian Oldtimers Hockey Hall of Fame and the Lindsay and District Sports Hall of Fame. Randy and his wife Florence live in Huntsville, Ontario.

"My father was a student of the game and I could never pull the wool over his eyes. He was a hard man to please, but I think that was one reason I kept working so hard in all areas of my life looking for his approval. Dad was part of a generation of men who found it difficult to express their love. I know now that it was always there."

R.J. Ellis claims that the best coach he ever had was his Dad, Ron Ellis. After graduating from Royal Military College in Kingston, Ontario, where he was a high-scoring right winger, R.J. is now a pilot in the Royal Canadian Air Force. In March 2002, R.J. and wife Norma welcomed Zachary to the world, a first grandchild for Ron and Jan Ellis.

"R.J. is the son to die for. And I would."

Mike Gartner, in a manner not dissimilar to Ron Ellis, was the model of consistency during his spectacular nineteen-season NHL career. Mike scored 30 or more goals seventeen times in his career, finishing with 1,432 games played, 708 goals, 627 assists and 1,335 regular-season points while entertaining fans in Washington, Minnesota, New York, Toronto and Phoenix. Mike Gartner currently works for the National Hockey League Players' Association, and in 2001 was selected as an Honoured Member of the Hockey Hall of Fame.

"Mike Gartner was the class act of the NHL in the late '80s and early '90s. My son has a hockey hero and his name is Mike Gartner. I couldn't be more pleased with his choice."

Brian Glennie joined the Toronto Maple Leafs in 1969, and was a mainstay of their defence for nine years. In 1972, Brian was asked to join Team Canada for the Summit Series — a testament to his worth as a blue liner. Glennie completed his career with one season as a Los Angeles King. After being involved in the restaurant business for a number of years, Brian Glennie encountered health problems, and today is retired and living in the Muskoka area.

"Brian and I became very close friends during the difficult 1970s at Maple Leaf Gardens. We were roommates for many years. I am proud to be the godfather of his children."

Jim Gregory coached Ron Ellis with the Toronto Marlboros junior team that won the Memorial Cup in 1964. When Punch Imlach was fired after the 1969 playoffs, Gregory was hired as general manager of the Toronto Maple Leafs, a position he held until May 1979. Ironically, it was Imlach who replaced Gregory as GM at that time. Jim Gregory is currently the senior vice president of hockey operations for the National Hockey League.

"I am one of many players who have benefited from knowing Jim Gregory. He became a mentor, encourager and confidant."

George Gross started covering sports for the *Toronto Telegram* in 1957, taking over the hockey beat in 1962. As a writer who travelled with the team, Gross watched the Toronto Maple Leafs win their last four Stanley Cups, and witnessed the introduction of a young Ron Ellis to the Leafs lineup. The *Telegram* folded in October 1971, but was immediately reborn as the *Toronto Sun*, where Gross was named sports editor. Today, George Gross is the corporate sports editor of the *Toronto Sun*. He is also the president of Sports Media Canada. George Gross earned a spot in the Hockey Hall of Fame as winner of the Elmer Ferguson Memorial Award for distinguished service to the newspaper profession.

"George Gross is still a very respected sportswriter. He is a man of integrity and a man you could trust with confidential information. That is why I am so grateful he accepted my calls when I wanted him to handle my retirements."

Bob Haggert joined the Toronto Maple Leafs organization in 1949–50 as a clubhouse boy for the Toronto Marlboros senior team. A year later, Bob was named trainer of the junior Marlboros. In the spring of 1955, Hap Day asked Haggert to join the Toronto Maple Leafs. After the death of Tim Daly, Haggert took over as the head trainer in 1959–60, becoming the youngest trainer in the history of the NHL. After retiring from the Maple Leafs in the spring of 1968, Bob started his pioneering Sports Representatives Limited, managing the commercial activities of NHL players including Bobby Orr, Darryl Sittler, Lanny McDonald, Paul Henderson and Ron Ellis. The company consults parties interested in buying or selling sports and entertainment rights. Through the years, Sports Representatives Limited has represented the NHL, the NHLPA, Hockey Canada and Major League Baseball.

"Bobby Haggert gave me a lot of advice as a young player with the Leafs in his role as head trainer. He later took me on as a client in his sports marketing business. Bob is always only a phone call away."

Paul Henderson began his career in the Detroit Red Wings organization, breaking into the NHL in 1963. During his fifth season in Detroit, Paul was sent to Toronto with Norm Ullman, Floyd Smith and Doug Barrie while Frank Mahovlich, Peter Stemkowski, Garry Unger and Carl Brewer went to the Red Wings. Henderson played six seasons in Toronto, mostly paired at left wing, with Ron Ellis on the right side. In 1974, Paul Henderson jumped to the WHA, but finished his major-league career with the NHL's Atlanta Flames. Still best friends with Ron today, Paul is in the Canadian Sports Hall of Fame and is a popular guest speaker. Paul Henderson is also president of The Leadership Group, a forum that provides the business community with the opportunity to share ideas on their business, personal and spiritual lives.

"If we are fortunate enough to have four or five true friends in a lifetime, Paul Henderson would be at the top of my list. His encouraging phone calls provide a great start to a day. We have an unbreakable bond."

Leonard "Red" Kelly spent an All-Star career as a defenceman with the Detroit Red Wings between 1947 and 1960. Then, after being traded to Toronto for Marc Reaume in February 1960, Red was moved to forward. In 1964–65, Red Kelly centred a line that featured a rookie right winger named Ron Ellis. Through 1,316 NHL games, Kelly earned 823 points, four Lady Byng Trophies as most gentlemanly player, one Norris Trophy as the NHL's best defenceman, and a total of eight selections to either the First or Second All-Star Team. Red Kelly won four Stanley Cups in Detroit and another four in Toronto during his twenty-year career as an NHL player before retiring in 1967 to coach. He is an Honoured Member of the Hockey Hall of Fame.

"Red has been a teammate, a coach and more importantly, a friend. I have a lot of time for this man and his family."

David Keon came through the Maple Leafs system, joining Toronto straight from junior in 1960–61. During fifteen illustrious seasons in Toronto, David won four Stanley Cups, the Calder Trophy as the league's rookie of the year in 1961, back-to-back Lady Byng Trophies as the most gentlemanly player in 1962 and '63, and the Conn Smythe Trophy as the NHL's most valuable playoff performer in 1967. Keon captained the Leafs from 1969 to

1975. He played four seasons in the WHA, and then was welcomed back to the NHL as a Hartford Whaler when that franchise joined the league. Keon scored 986 points in 1,296 NHL games as well as 291 in 301 WHA contests. Keon was selected as an Honoured Member of the Hockey Hall of Fame in 1985. Today, David Keon is retired, and enjoys travelling and playing golf near his Florida home.

"I admire David Keon for his talents as a hockey player and his on-ice leadership. He is a man of few words and a man of principle. I respect his decision regarding the Maple Leafs, but I do miss the opportunities to be in his presence."

Marty King attended Downsview Collegiate Institute in Toronto with Ron Ellis in 1963. A retired secondary school teacher, Marty is now a supply teacher for the Durham Board of Education.

"Marty is a true Leaf fan and loves Frank Mahovlich, as I do. Marty was a good school friend and we have continued the friendship to this day."

Ron Ellis Lucas, named after the Leafs' Number 6, lives in Assiniboia, Saskatchewan with his wife Shannon and their son, Curtis Joseph Lucas. Ron is the Meat Manager for Southland Co-Operatives Limited.

"It is indeed an honour to have someone named after you, and also a little intimidating to try to live up to it. Hopefully, for the most part, I have."

Patrick McCarthy has been a fan of Ron Ellis's for over thirty years. A friend of the Leafs' star right winger, Patrick McCarthy is supervisor of public relations and marketing at the Toronto Zoo.

"My ten-year friendship with Pat has been beneficial to both of us. We are good checkpoints for each other."

Roger Neilson was inducted into the Hockey Hall of Fame as a builder in November 2002. His career coaching Toronto, Buffalo, Vancouver, Los Angeles, the Rangers, Florida, Philadelphia and Ottawa has proven that Roger's studious approach to the game is much sought after in the NHL. At the end of the 2001-2002 season, the Senators gave their assistant coach the opportunity to step behind the bench for two games, giving Neilson an even 1,000 games as an NHL head coach.

"Roger was a major reason I made my comeback in 1977. I admired his professionalism and the way he lives his life. It was a pleasure playing for Roger, as he has a wonderful knack of making everyone on the team feel like they are contributing to the team goals. His game preparation was second to none and he was a players' coach. Roger is a special man."

Mark Osborne enjoyed a fourteen-year NHL career, playing with the Detroit Red Wings, New York Rangers, Toronto Maple Leafs and Winnipeg Jets between 1981 and 1995. The popular Osborne is assistant general manager of the Mississauga Ice Dogs of the Ontario Hockey League, and in involved on an ongoing basis with Hockey Ministries International.

"Mark is another of the NHL's quality individuals. We have grown to know each other better through the Christian community. When I was president of the Leafs Alumni, I knew Mark was the man I wanted added to the board of directors."

Steve Paikin, a longtime Ron Ellis fan, is the co-host of *Studio 2* on TVOntario.

"When Steve shared his story with me about having my hockey card in his wallet, all I could do was say thank you. We never know whom we might be influencing. Thanks for reminding me, Steve."

Jean-Paul Parise was a tough left winger who lined up opposite Ron Ellis many times during his career. J.P. and Ron were teammates on Team Canada in the Summit Series versus the Soviet Union in 1972.

"You cannot win the game of hockey without a Jean-Paul Parise-type player on your team. This man came to play every night, did his job in both ends of the rink and provided leadership in the locker room. He made valuable contributions to Team Canada '72."

Mike Pelyk is a Toronto native who, like Ron Ellis, played his junior hockey with the Marlboros and his entire NHL career with the Toronto Maple Leafs. Joining the Leafs in 1967–68, Pelyk played defence in Toronto until 1974, when he joined the WHA for two seasons. He returned to the Leafs in 1976–77 for two seasons. Today, Mike Pelyk is vice president of retail leasing with Oxford Development Group, the largest commercial management company in Canada.

"Mike and I played together with the Leafs on a couple of occasions. He could play the game, but I always knew he was a very intelligent person. I appreciate his friendship and helpful conversations."

Dr. Edgardo Perez is the CEO and chief of medical staff at the Homewood Health Centre in Guelph, Ontario, where Ron was hospitalized during the depths of his depression. Dr. Perez is also a professor of psychiatry at the Universities of Toronto, Ottawa and McMaster in Hamilton.

"Dr. Perez in the only person on this list who isn't a hockey fan. You know there is more to life than hockey. I am honoured to say that Dr. Perez is my friend. He is widely acclaimed around the world for his work in the mental health field. How fortunate I was to have him come into my life. I think he knows who the Leafs are now!"

Philip Pritchard, known to many as the "keeper of Lord Stanley's Cup" from the MasterCard TV commercials, is the Director of Hockey Operations and Curator at the Hockey Hall of Fame, where he has worked since 1988.

"I sit with Phil Pritchard on the senior management team at the Hockey Hall of Fame. Phil brings numerous skills and knowledge to his role as curator. I thoroughly enjoy being a business associate of this talented young man."

Joel Quenneville was Toronto's first draft pick in 1978, and played a season and a half in blue and white before being traded with Lanny McDonald to Colorado. After 13 NHL seasons, Joel returned to the Maple Leafs organization as a playing assistant coach with Toronto's AHL affiliate in St. John's. Today, as head coach of the St. Louis Blues, Quenneville is acknowledged as one of the best coaches in the National Hockey League, and was awarded the Jack Adams Award as the league's top coach in 2000.

"Joel and I played together on the Leafs during the years of turmoil in the '70s. He was a young defenceman who listened well and studied the game from all angles. It's not surprising that he is a successful head coach today."

Bob Ruffo, Ron's longtime friend and one-time trainer, is retired, but continues to train friends as a hobby.

"I met Bob through a chance meeting in a gym. We clicked and remain good friends today."

Scott Russell has been a host on Hockey Night in Canada since 1989. He writes of his admiration for Ron Ellis in his book, *Ice Time: A Canadian Hockey Journey.*

"Scott honoured me in his book as his favourite Leaf. We had some great talks when he interviewed me for his book. Our discussion was one of the factors that led me to believe that there might possibly be some merit in my own story."

Rod Seiling began his career in the Toronto Maple Leaf

organization. His NHL career includes ten seasons with the New York Rangers followed by a return to the Toronto Maple Leafs, two seasons in St. Louis and a final season with Atlanta. Besides being teammates with Ron Ellis on the Toronto Marlboros and Maple Leafs, Rod also played alongside him with Team Canada in 1972. Today, Rod Seiling is president of the Greater Toronto Hotel Association.

"Rod and I have one thing in common – we both married the girls we were dating in junior. Although we have been friends for a long time, the Team Canada '72 bond holds us close."

Brit Selby made quite an impact in his first full season as a Toronto Maple Leaf, when he won the Calder Trophy as rookie of the year in 1966. After playing with the expansion Philadelphia Flyers, Brit returned to the Leafs for parts of three seasons. After two seasons in St. Louis, Selby joined the WHA, and returned to Toronto as a Toro between 1973 and 1975. Today, Brit Selby teaches history at North Toronto Collegiate.

"Brit and I are a lot alike and we spent a lot of time together in our early years with the Leafs. Brit could play the game of hockey, but found his true self in his teaching career and his family life."

Darryl Sittler, the Toronto Maple Leafs' captain between 1975 and 1981, played eleven and a half seasons with Toronto before becoming a Philadelphia Flyer and then closing out his career as a Detroit Red Wing. During his extraordinary career, Darryl scored 1,121 points in 1,096 NHL games and has been selected as an Honoured Member of the Hockey Hall of Fame. Today, Darryl is community representative for the Maple Leafs, representing the team at many community and alumni functions.

"I admire this man for many reasons. As a Leafs veteran, I watched Darryl Sittler take his skills to new levels through an unmatched work ethic and with a big heart. His induction into the Hockey Hall of Fame was well deserved and earned."

Peter Stemkowski played his first NHL game in January 1964 as a member of the Toronto Maple Leafs. During his fourth season in blue and white, Stemkowski was part of the trade that sent Frank Mahovlich, Garry Unger and Carl Brewer to the Red Wings. Detroit was home to Peter until October 1970, when he was traded to the New York Rangers. Stemkowski played seven seasons in New York, then finished his NHL career with a season in Los Angeles. Today, Peter Stemkowski is part owner of a travel agency on Long Island, New York, and during hockey season is the colour commentator on San Jose Sharks radio broadcasts.

"Peter and I have different personalities, but when we were on the ice together, we made things happen. He is one of hockey's truly wonderful characters."

Mel Stevens is the founder and director of Teen Ranch, a charitable Christian ranch near Orangeville, Ontario. It was through Mel Stevens that a number of athletes, including Ron Ellis, were introduced to the teachings of Jesus Christ.

"Mel is a man who lives his faith every day. He inspired me to investigate the claims of Christianity. He has been my spiritual mentor and friend for many years."

Dale Tallon was the first-ever draft choice of the Vancouver Canucks. Dale was selected to participate in the Summit Series in 1972, where he was a teammate of Ron's on Team Canada.

"Dale came into the NHL with the pressures that surround a top draft pick. I was impressed by his level of maturity in handling the pressure and also his willingness to learn from others. I believe the '72 series was very valuable in his development as a pro as he observed and learned from his peers. And you should see the guy hit a golf ball!"

Norm Ullman is an Honoured Member of the Hockey Hall of Fame, after playing 1,410 games split between the Detroit Red Wings and the Toronto Maple Leafs. Ullman scored 490 goals, 739 assists and 1,229 points during his twenty-year NHL career, adding 47 more goals and 130 additional points in two seasons with Edmonton of the WHA. Norm Ullman is retired and living in Unionville, Ontario.

"What a consummate professional. By playing on a line with Normie in the seventies, I got through some very difficult years for the Maple Leafs. He was one of the reasons I went to the rink every day."

Our appreciation goes to several others who made valuable contributions to *Over the Boards*.

To H.B. Fenn and Company, our thanks for believing in *Over the Boards*. Publisher Jordan Fenn saw merit in this project and allowed us to realize a dream. Our thanks, too, to Heidi Winter, who is not only a wonderful publicist but has assisted in every aspect of the creation and marketing of this book. And we would also like to congratulate Harold and Sylvia Fenn and their entire team on the twenty-fifth anniversary of H.B. Fenn and Company. Happy Birthday!

Special thanks to our many friends at the Hockey Hall of Fame for their encouragement through the creation of *Over the Boards*. Specific thanks to Philip Pritchard, Craig Campbell and Tyler Wolosewich for allowing open access to resource materials and in securing the photographs for the book. We'd also like to thank president Jeff Denomme for his continual support.

Our sincere appreciation to Lloyd Davis for his outstanding work editing *Over the Boards*

Thanks to Nancy Gilks and Maple Leaf Sports and Entertainment for their assistance.

Lyn Watkin-Merek, a manager at the Centre for Addiction and Mental Health, is a volunteer at the Courage to Come Back Awards Dinner held in Toronto.

Our gratitude to IMG Canada for encouragement.

A note of appreciation to Jefferson Davis.

Kevin Shea would like to acknowledge special family and friends who supported the creation of *Over the Boards*. Much love to my mother and stepfather, Margaret and Gerry England, and to my brother Dale, who watched Ron Ellis on Hockey Night in Canada with me every Saturday night through all those seasons. And sincere thanks must also go to friends who supported with their encouragement — Maureen and Tim Burgess, Ian Marchant, Andrea Orlick, Steve Waxman, Kim Cooke, Cam Gardiner, Bruce Barker and Susan Eansor.

* * *

Finally, to hockey fans everywhere, we hope you find enjoyment and inspiration in *Over the Boards*.

.